Freshwater Politics in Canada

Freshwater Politics in Canada

PETER CLANCY

UNIVERSITY OF TORONTO PRESS

LIBRARY AND ARCHIVES CANADA CATALOGUING IN PUBLICATION

Clancy, Peter, 1949–, author
Freshwater politics in Canada / Peter Clancy.

Includes bibliographical references and index.

Issued in print and electronic formats.

ISBN 978-1-4426-0927-3 (bound).—ISBN 978-1-4426-0926-6 (pbk.).—
ISBN 978-1-4426-0928-0 (pdf).—ISBN 978-1-4426-0929-7 (epub)

   1. Watershed management—Political aspects—Canada—Case studies. 2. Fresh water—Political aspects—Canada—Case studies. 3. Integrated water development—Government policy—Canada—Case studies. 4. Water use—Government policy—Canada—Case studies. I. Title.

TC426.C63 2014   333.730971   C2013-908644-7
                                  C2013-908645-5

We welcome comments and suggestions regarding any aspect of our publications—please feel free to contact us at news@utphighereducation.com or visit our Internet site at www.utppublishing.com.

North America
5201 Dufferin Street
North York, Ontario, Canada, M3H 5T8

2250 Military Road
Tonawanda, New York, USA, 14150

ORDERS PHONE: 1–800–565–9523
ORDERS FAX: 1–800–221–9985
ORDERS E-MAIL: utpbooks@utpress.utoronto.ca

UK, Ireland, and continental Europe
NBN International
Estover Road, Plymouth, PL6 7PY, UK
ORDERS PHONE: 44 (0) 1752 202301
ORDERS FAX: 44 (0) 1752 202333
ORDERS E-MAIL: enquiries@nbninternational.com

Every effort has been made to contact copyright holders; in the event of an error or omission, please notify the publisher.

The University of Toronto Press acknowledges the financial support for its publishing activities of the Government of Canada through the Canada Book Fund.

To the ISAR community that spurred the idea

Contents

Illustrations

Figures

Maps

Tables

Introduction

THIS IS A BOOK FOR STUDENTS of freshwater politics, defined in the broadest sense. I hope that it speaks to the concerns of citizens, students, policy makers, and administrators. In addition, I hope that it offers some new perspectives and some practical tools that can be applied to the understanding of local settings across Canada. First and foremost, the book poses questions about water politics. Where should we search for the political dimensions of this resource and what can we learn from past practice? What issues, problems, and trends point the way to our water future?

There are excellent studies available on water politics in Canada. Two fine edited collections offer valuable thematic surveys (Bakker 2007; Sproule Jones et al. 2008). The list of river histories is also mounting (e.g., Armstrong et al. 2009; Evenden 2004; Wood 2013). Another thread of study is group politics, where monographs on Aboriginal peoples (Harris 2001), irrigated farms (Glenn 1999), and big hydro-power (Salisbury 1986; Waldram 1988) point the way. In this book I plan to add another perspective by building a framework for understanding the practice of water politics, a framework that can be applied to a range of policy subsectors and illustrated in particular watersheds. The fit between watersheds and politics is a central theme in the chapters below.

Until recently, freshwater was often portrayed as a neglected natural resource—taken for granted in social terms, treated as an open-access product in economic terms, and (partly as a result of the previous factors) languishing on almost everyone's political agenda. By this account, water is assumed to be in inexhaustible supply in Canada and it has been treated as a virtually free good in pricing terms. Little wonder then that governments pay less attention to freshwater than they do to farmland, minerals, oil and gas, and forests.

Of course there are episodes to the contrary. Acute flood events remind Canadians of the extraordinary physical force and destruction that can be visited on riverside communities. Regional water shortages remind us that there are physical limits on supply and that withdrawals need to be managed as social demand grows. Anglers are keenly aware of the fragility of freshwater fish stocks in the face of habitat degradations ranging from factory effluent to acid rain. Anxieties about drinking-water safety have spread similarly across the country since the Walkerton fiasco in 2000, and the particular crisis of First Nations communities is increasingly evident in this regard. In short, the freshwater resource plays a part in many contemporary policy fields.

Even there, however, the issues are often framed to highlight an absence of political attention and a condition of governmental laxity. Many of these very real failures in water resource management are attributed to political neglect—to a vacuum of authority. This accords with the premise that the water resource remains marginal and underattended, relative to other natural resources and in an absolute political sense.

The thrust of this book is different. It argues that water, far from being neglected, has been the object of extended political attention in Canada. Such concern is driven by a variety of interests and is evident in a multitude of spatial and temporal settings. Cumulatively, these forces have resulted in a highly regulated resource, though not necessarily regulated in the directions and for the purposes that serve it, or the public interest, best. This is a political attribute worth pondering. If "organized water" is the domain of lawyers, technocrats, and consultants more than of voters, consumers, and the public at large, what does this say about the texture of public life in the freshwater sector?

My argument is not that freshwater is too little organized but that its organization is more often than not uneven and dysfunctional, with a discernible tilt toward partial and vested interests. Policy and management failures are less a result of "absence of mind" than a result of fixed commitments, prior interventions, and deliberate choices whose imperfect functioning exacerbates our problems. Consequently there is an urgent need to acknowledge and correct these tendencies.

Several concepts will play important roles in the interpretation that follows. Central to the discussion is the notion of power, or the capacity to realize defined interests in the face of rival claimants. In its raw physical form, freshwater is the target of multiple interest holders, and the conflicts that this engenders go a long way toward determining how water is regulated in Canada. It is important to recognize different faces of power. Another key concept is group politics—an essential link between identifying an interest and advancing that interest through collective organization or group action. In the water field, groups come in many shapes and sizes, and it is important to be able to identify them and assess their performances. A third concept is the state, the political authority that takes key decisions under the force of law, setting the rules of water use and management and making key allocative choices among contending interests. States are complex structures that must be charted and appraised in terms of their key decisions. Here we will build a model of the "freshwater state" in Canada.

An important insight in modern policy studies is that organized groups and state authorities tend to coalesce according to specialized subjects of concern. So while we can speak of public policy at large, the arenas in which decisions are taken are usually more restricted policy fields. For this reason we talk about mineral policy or foreign policy or health policy, each with its own constellation of organized interests, state actors, ways of thinking, and central issues. Policy fields can be highly structured and display high levels of continuity in the ways that groups and state actors interact. This can be captured in the notion of policy networks that link groups and state actors in particular ways. The notion of governance centres on the study of such interactive relationships.

Freshwater politics is one policy field that can be profitably approached from a governance perspective. It can be grasped as a whole and it can also be disaggregated into a series of subsectors with distinctive group/state patterns. The recognition of policy subsectors within the freshwater domain is an important tool in advancing our understanding. First, it fits with the reality that the water resource has been viewed and treated in different ways according to prime concern. A set of group and state interests may coalesce for purposes of fishing. Another may take form for purposes of irrigated farming or flood control or hydro-power generation or drinking water supply.

The sequence in which water policy subsectors appear can be a key influence on the shape of freshwater politics. Early actions can set a template for policy thinking that infiltrates subsectors formed later. Alternatively, each subsector may be framed according to its own core interests and problems, displaying a distinct policy logic and power structure. Many of the inconsistencies and contradictions that emerge in a policy sector can be rooted in the relative autonomy enjoyed by subsectors. First there are issues of spill-over, when actions in one subsector generate problems that surface in another. Then there are problems of high-level coordination, since any effort to frame an overall strategy or an integrated approach bumps into existing power structures at the intermediate level. There are further questions worth posing about the freshwater sector. Among the various functioning subsectors, does one hold a place of priority or dominance over others? If so, can a dominant subsector imprint its template on the freshwater field as a whole? Even if subsectors are largely autonomous within their own boundaries, which ones prevail when cross-sectoral issues must be addressed? These questions are especially intriguing in the present context, since it can be argued that the freshwater field has been relatively decentralized in structure in the past. Today, when cross-sector problems are increasingly being exposed, solutions are elusive and new governing patterns are urgently being sought. This involves grappling with the legacy of freshwater power structures forged in the twentieth century. Prior political and policy choices constrain today's options but never entirely dictate them. It is more accurate to say that water politics today is shaped jointly, by inherited power structures on the one hand and new water values and policy problems on the other. Ongoing commitments to established ways of operating reflect the weight of past choices. Contemporary controversies, crises, and newly emerging perspectives pose challenges to the water establishment. As a result, ongoing political relationships and policy arrangements can either facilitate or block the evolution of new water politics.

In this book we will draw upon diverse materials. Any successful encounter with the politics of natural resources or environments must be willing to cross boundaries, and an encounter with freshwater politics is no exception. Its study is enhanced immeasurably by the extensive knowledge that has been generated in the natural and applied sciences, particularly in the fields of hydrology, aquatic ecology, and hydraulic engineering. It is not by accident that these specialties figure prominently among researchers, consultants, and advocates. Indeed, to the extent that a science establishment shapes freshwater policy choices, it tends to be based in these fields. However, at the same time our central subject involves communities, societies, and governments and the way in which collective choices are organized. This is the domain of anthropology, history, economics, and political science. Here too we encounter a rich field of prior study that can be repointed for freshwater insights. How, then, to proceed? Students of water politics need to grasp each of these two major constitutive domains—the biophysical and the socioeconomic—and, equally important, to grasp their interplay.

Often this involves pushing against familiar tendencies. The challenge arises, in large part, from the conventional organization of academic knowledge and in particular the longstanding division between natural and social sciences. This was not always the case. In the early nineteenth century, natural history and moral philosophy were broad synthetic endeavours in which aspiring scholars were versed. The subsequent rise of specialist disciplines doubtlessly advanced the power of our understanding but often at the cost of fragmentation. The incentives for cross-disciplinary dialogue gave way to parallel solitudes, sometimes fuelled by mutual doubts as to method and relevance. Physical and biological researchers asked whether social study could ever truly attain the rigour of science, and social researchers complained about the natural disciplines being tone-deaf to societal needs.

One answer to the problem of such knowledge divides is to build new bridges between them. This offers a way to broaden and deepen explanatory reach and is captured in the call for interdisciplinary effort. The growing complexity of central problems in modern life, along with the urgency for generating responses, has accelerated this process in recent decades. It is reflected in the diversified composition of research teams, the sanctioning of new fields of cross-specialty training, and the concentration on applied problems as an organizational fulcrum.

At this point some of the exciting new themes can be previewed. Not only is it important to appreciate the significance of the hydrologic cycle, but that cycle must also be fitted with a social and political framework. Not only can we recognize the renewed importance of the values of nature, but we must develop appropriate tools to deal with the aquatic part of nature's estate. Not only is there growing acceptance of the need for structured environmental appraisals and reviews, but the participative and deliberative scales of such processes must broaden beyond the professional and technical classes. Integral to this is the proliferation of civil society interests as a critical third pillar of freshwater politics, alongside corporate and state institutions. Finally, there are complicated jurisdictional challenges to effective water management in Canada, including the need to tackle cross-jurisdictional water systems.

As indicated above, the purpose of this book is to highlight a dimension of freshwater systems that is sometimes neglected in Canada. To this extent it is a study in *social* science that harbours interdisciplinary ambitions. One of the most effective ways to achieve this is through a focus on examples of freshwater issues as they are manifest in concrete settings. Fortunately we have available an organizing concept that respects complexity, particularity, and variability. This involves a *watershed* focus. A watershed is a territory in which water drains into a connected set of streams, rivers, and lakes. It combines spatial, water flow, and social occupancy dimensions. The challenge is to explore the connections between these several dimensions.

One of the most powerful expressions of conservation and ecological ethics is Aldo Leopold's essay "Thinking Like a Mountain" (1970). Leopold was a forester and biologist in the first half of twentieth-century America. He worked for the US Forest Service at the field level in its southwest region. This is a mountain and desert ecology where Leopold's understanding led him to differ with many accepted government policies. "Thinking Like a Mountain" is a powerful piece that calls on us to view the natural and physical world from a nonhuman perspective. The first necessary change is in time frame, since the mountain has been in place for millennia. It is solid and stationary and changes happen slowly. Only the mountain can see the full picture, for as people we concentrate on the selective parts that we need and value.

The howl of the wolf is a signature sound on a mountain, where that species is a key to the mountain ecosystem. In the culture of ranchers, hunters, and government game officers, however, wolves were seen as destructive predators that threatened deer or cattle populations. In effect, wolves competed with human hunters and, should deer numbers decline or more humans arrive, wolves were treated as an expendable variable that could be reduced or eliminated by cash bounty or poison bait schemes. The outlook here was an instrumental one that seized on the wolf/deer relationship and accepted the equation that fewer wolves equalled more deer.

Leopold contends that the mountain, home to a complete natural system unfolding over centuries, would disagree and see things differently. Deer are not simply a stock of wild animals in forests and meadows that offer a challenge to hunters. Deer browse on mountain vegetation like bush and tree leaves. Similarly wolves are not just fierce predators that deplete grazing herds. Rather, wolf predation shapes deer populations by culling weak or old or excess animals from the range. They are both, in short, elements of an interdependent system. The removal of wolves serves to intensify the grazing pressure on natural vegetation, Leopold says. "While a buck pulled down by wolves can be replaced in two to three years, a range pulled down by too many deer may fail of replacement in as many decades" (Leopold 1970, 140). In sum, the exclusive focus on one species aims to make safe that species (deer) but in so doing it can threaten the wider web of life. Only the mountain appreciates when the web is skewed too sharply.

Like a mountain, a watershed is both a space and an ecosystem. It links and sustains many elements of land, air, and water, both above and below ground. A watershed is not static, but persists within certain limits by adapting to change and rebalancing internally. At the same time, there is danger in elevating any single element or relationship. To focus on one species or use, in isolation from habitat or ecology, is as deeply flawed in the watershed as it is on the mountain.

Leopold remarked that the impulse behind many resource management projects is increased resource security. Paradoxically, this can be counterproductive, as "too much safety yields only danger in the long run" (Leopold 1970, 141). For example, building a levy to protect low-lying lands against flood can also prevent the nutrient replenishment that comes with floods. Constructing a dam to impound water for irrigation or electricity will in the process block or alter downstream flows and aquatic conditions. A landowner who chooses to cut trees right down to the stream's edge can maximize his or her harvest of timber but destabilize riparian banks and alter water conditions and fisheries. Such practices are the watershed equivalents of the war on wolves. In sum, before we can think like a watershed (or a river) we have to look at what the river sees. It is a unique perspective and far more comprehensive than that of single-purpose users or managers (Worster 1993).

This kind of thinking is not just a diagnostic tool but an important part of politics and decision-making. In a social context, who will speak for a watershed and ensure that watershed needs are not neglected? Certain interests—individuals, groups, and institutions—tend to be well represented. But biophysical systems need representation as well, and this is where the watershed offers a distinct scale for politics. Watershed politics is far from new but it remains a work in progress. Watersheds can be visible or invisible, organized or unorganized, powerful or powerless.

To this end I illustrate each chapter with a brief watershed case study. These are intended to ground the political relationships under discussion while also offering a unifying thread within the book. Overall, my approach is to follow the freshwater politics in whatever form they take, remaining faithful to disciplinary fundamentals while pushing their implications further than is normally done within the familiar and traditional paradigms. The watershed case study sites are illustrated in Map 0.1.

The book is organized in the following way. It begins with an exploration of how political activity arises in Canada's freshwater sector. Part One raises questions about the nature of politics, the role of power, and the significance of group organization. Here we introduce the key concepts that can advance the analysis. Freshwater politics is shown to be rooted in the diversity of interests that characterize communities and societies. Power is linked to the capacity to realize preferred interests, particularly in the face of rival or contrary interests. Group politics offers a means for defining, and mobilizing support for, such interests. Another essential framework involves the state structures that impinge on freshwater decision-making. Modern states take a variety of forms, but they share the quality of institutional complexity (i.e., they are made up of many parts). In Canada, the freshwater state involves several jurisdictional levels—national, provincial, regional, and local. In the chapters below we inquire into the roles of

Map 0.1 Drainage Basins and Watershed Case Study Sites

each actor: the centrality of provincial powers for water administration; the rise and fall of federal freshwater initiatives in the decades since 1950; the roles of regional authorities in dealing with conservation management; and the potential for municipal governments to exert greater prominence.

Part Two addresses five leading policy issues affecting freshwater politics—fisheries and pollution, irrigation agriculture, flood control, hydro-electric development, and groundwater management. Each policy subsector has a revealing historical past and each one remains pressing today. The subsectors will illustrate how political power is manifest in public policy and how political issues shape water use patterns. Here we see compelling evidence that Canadian freshwater policy has been driven more by purpose than by neglect, even if the traditional purposes are under intensifying dispute today. Also evident is the challenge of dealing, simultaneously, with multiple water uses. In fact, the limits of traditional administrative tools have propelled a creative new discussion of water politics, drawing increasingly on ecology, governance, and sustainability. Part Two closes with a discussion of emerging trends in freshwater politics.

A final ambition of this book is to encourage the study and practice of freshwater politics at the local and regional levels. The concepts and propositions advanced in the chapters that follow can offer tools for political action. The watersheds and sub-watersheds where readers live can be the settings for observation, exploration, and intervention. The discussions in this volume can stimulate parallel investigations and applications in the thousands of sub-watersheds and local drainages where people live across Canada. I hope that this book helps readers to think differently about the freshwater resource and what we do with it.

Freshwater Politics

1
Water Politics as Diversity

THIS CHAPTER INTRODUCES FRESHWATER AND WATERSHEDS as political phenomena. It begins with some comments on politics as an activity. Next, the watershed is introduced as a unit that can demarcate water constituencies and highlight water interests. Watersheds range from the very large to the very small and are often nested within one another. Here we consider a range of watershed scales, from the continental drainage to the major river basin to the tributary basin and the sub-watershed. For the purposes of this chapter, four types of watershed relationships deserve particular attention—in-stream interests, riparian (shoreline) interests, surface to subsurface interests, and changing historical interests through time. To illustrate the shape of watershed politics, this chapter's case study is based on the James and West River drainage in Nova Scotia.

Politics is about shared social concerns and can arise anywhere beyond the private world of the individual. In groups, people must deal with both personal and collective matters. This generates complicated challenges, and when ideas, interests, or behaviours collide, the question is how to deal with them.

One answer is to impose a unilateral solution that is enforced on all parties. This is the standard response for dictators and authoritarians: in the face of social diversity, they opt to ignore, deny, or suppress it. An alternative is to acknowledge differences as legitimate and seek ways to bridge or reconcile them. In liberal democracy, for example, the classic method is to follow the majority principle while at the same time protecting the interests or rights of minorities. This generally involves open discussion, persuasion, bargaining, and compromise—all classic "political" activities. Problems may not be settled for all time, but they can be resolved for a while. Sometimes this works well and one fault line recedes to be replaced by another. Other times the process fails and conflicts can recur and deepen.

Many of these preferences and differences are rooted in our backgrounds. The American political scientist E.E. Schattschneider remarked that much of the raw material of politics can be found in the content of the census rolls. He meant that every nation's census recorded a series of social distinctions with the potential to fuel political difference in modern life: religion, language, ethnicity, locale, class, gender, and age to name a few (Schattschneider 1967). This is precisely what makes society complex—the myriad affiliations that unite and divide peoples. At any given time and on any given issue, the political battle assumes a particular shape. Water politics is no exception.

So we might say that politics arises out of conditions of social diversity and the need to meet challenges of different ideas, interests, and behaviours. In addition, politics involves the activity of managing this complexity and the conflicts it generates. Notice that, by this account, conflict is natural, inevitable, and possibly even creative. There are a variety of techniques and practices available to meet this challenge and many of them will be explored in future chapters.

How might we approach the role of politics in the freshwater resource? No one denies that water is one of the vital elements supporting life on earth—animal, vegetable, and human. There is an impressive global supply of freshwater, but it is very unevenly distributed. Many nations and societies are water-rich while others are water-poor. Nor is there any necessary correlation between areas of ample or surplus supply and areas of intense human habitation. Indeed the struggles to survive in circumstances of water shortage, or to secure adequate water access, drives politics on many scales. Looking beyond humans to the wider natural world, ecosystems are closely framed by water regimes that can determine their range of viable species, habitats, and environmental adaptive patterns. Even in the immediate absence of humans, water catchments and water flows directly influence the conditions of life. So it is not surprising that the interests of nonhuman life can occupy a significant place in water politics. Modern concerns with protecting biodiversity and habitat health are cases in point.

The Watershed Unit

Such factors underline the need to look beyond the individual constituents to highlight water systems. In the 1300s the Germans fashioned the term *wasserschiede*, which translates into English as "water partition." It underlines the fact that when water falls to the earth's surface as precipitation, it flows according to gravity within topographic landforms. Part of this flow is absorbed at the earth's surface and may enter a subterranean groundwater complex. Another part flows across surface land, feeding streams and rivers that follow contours of declining elevation. Thus *wasserschiede* and its English derivation *watershed* are defined spatially to encompass an inclusive territory between heights of land.

A watershed is of primary importance in both a physical and a political sense. Physically, it delineates a landscape connected by a shared water system. Given the centrality of flow, it makes sense to think of the drainage area as an interdependent unit. Politically, a watershed defines a community of residents with a shared social experience. Part of this experience involves activities that impact the watershed. As Schattschneider might say, the census data in a watershed offer clues to the shape of the water constituency. This is not to say that a community always consciously defines itself this way, or that the watershed is the overriding scale of community. Nevertheless, the shared circumstance of life in the watershed is an underlying physical and social reality.

As an example, take the major social and economic consumptive uses of Canadian freshwater. In 2005 the largest use-category nationally was for thermal-electric power generation (Statistics Canada 2009). Here fossil fuel and nuclear plants use two-thirds of all water withdrawals, for steam production and cooling. The next largest category is manufacturing with 14 per cent of all withdrawals. Pulp and paper is the leading sector, followed by primary metals and chemical production. Residential water consumption comes next and accounts for 9 per cent.

The final 10 per cent is shared between agriculture, commercial, public water distribution systems, mining, and oil and gas. It should be noted that these aggregate uses only begin to chart the shape of the water constituency. Most flowing water in Canada is not directly consumed each year, and a far wider set of interests have stakes in its nonconsumptive uses.

Looking at them more closely, most watersheds are not just single linear systems so much as networks of nested systems. The most elementary are the small streams that first collect flowing water. These feed, in turn, into ever larger rivers as the system unfolds. River ecologists capture these relations in the notion of "stream ordering." When several primary or originating streams converge, they create a stream of a second order. Similarly several secondary streams join to create one of a third order. Any river system can be mapped in this way, with complex watersheds involving up to a dozen or more orders. Within this sequence, physical conditions can be expected to range along a continuum, so that the river not only means different things to different persons but is objectively different from place to place (Vannote, Minshall, Cummins, Sedell, and Cushing 1980). There is also a social dimension of stream ordering that has not received as much attention. Where and how people live within a watershed—on the main stem, on a tributary, in a catchment basin but away from the stream flow—matters in shaping political interests and alignments.

A watershed, then, is a geopolitical drainage unit that figures at several levels. In Canada the largest scale involves the five great continental drainage areas that empty into oceans. In order of size of area drained, these are the Hudson Bay, the Arctic, the Great Lakes–St. Lawrence, the Pacific, and the Gulf of Mexico drainages (whose headwaters include modest stretches of river in southern Alberta and Saskatchewan).

In an effort to remind us about our cultural as well as physical aquatic heritage, Hugh MacLennan wrote a book about seven great Canadian rivers—the Fraser, Mackenzie, Saskatchewan, Red, St. Lawrence, Ottawa, and Saint John (McLennan 1961). While these figure prominently in the great historical sweep of the nation, they are not alone. In total, Statistics Canada (2009) identifies 25 major river basins or drainage regions. Some of these, particularly in the Arctic and Hudson Bay drainage areas, remain in their wild form today. Most others, however, have been heavily modified by the combined forces of habitation and engineering. There was once a time when river basins provided a basis for social organization—for Aboriginal peoples, commercial fur traders, and colonial timber merchants. This declined sharply, however, with the rise of state sovereignty and industrial capitalism. Furthermore, drainage geography does not coincide with units of government. Three-quarters of the 25 major river basins straddle either provincial or international boundaries. This asymmetry adds yet another layer of political complication that is taken up in chapters below.

A third scale of watershed function is the tributary basin or subdrainage that is enclosed within one of the major river basins. Here Statistics Canada lists 164 separate units. In southern Alberta, for example, the Bow, Red Deer, and

Oldman Rivers are all significant tributaries to the South Saskatchewan River system. In Manitoba, the Assiniboine and the Souris have a similar relation to the Red River. Often it is the tributary basin that delimits the scope of a regional water community most accurately, since it is here that people share a regional and local awareness of basin interdependence. Accordingly, an important challenge in watershed analysis is to clarify the modes of linkage between tributary and main river systems. The Athabasca watershed that is explored in chapter 3 hosts 11 tributary basins. Such tributaries also tend to be the base units for the studies of river stress and river health that figure prominently in "state of the watershed" reporting.

A fourth scale, numbering in the thousands across the country, is the sub-watershed. It is difficult to specify exact proportions here. In Alberta, the Milk River might be considered a sub-watershed in the vast Missouri River system, which is itself a tributary of the Mississippi. Yet the Milk River drainage encompasses 61,000 km^2 (in Alberta and Montana) with 30 tributaries of its own. This is an area larger than the entire province of Nova Scotia where, incidentally, there are no unifying river basins on a larger scale. Instead, Nova Scotia contains 44 primary watersheds, of which the Mersey River is the largest at a modest area of 2,800 km^2. Parts of Atlantic Canada are sometimes characterized as "maritime coastal" to capture a distinct pattern of small sub-watersheds and micro-catchments that represent genuinely "local" river flows. One of these, the West River of Antigonish County, Nova Scotia, is described in greater detail below.

A Watershed in Four Dimensions

While the physical watershed is a necessary starting point, it is human habitation that fuels freshwater politics. This is a world of extraordinary variation, raising questions of culture, economy, and society. For this study, however, we begin with a simple premise. People's underlying interests in water tend to be activity-centred and site-specific. It is the surprising range of these commitments that drive the politics. So, recalling Schattschneider's observation, we need to start by asking who makes up a watershed community or population.

Earlier in the discussion we surveyed the territorial dimension of water systems. While a focus on water does not necessarily require an awareness of watersheds, it tends eventually to lead back to them. It is the fixed character of the water supply variable that initially dictates the spatial focus. But it is the social activity that dictates the nature of an interest or claim. Indigenous fishers know the prime pools and river reaches to exploit and the prime times of year in which to do so. Cattle drovers followed "trails" that were devised to ensure their herds had periodic access to watering holes and rivers. Fur merchants built their trade posts at the confluence of river systems that maximized canoe traffic flows. Farmers prize lands that are adjacent to waterways, as do commercial towns and industrial mills. Hydro-electric businesses seek out sites where large volumes of water can be impounded behind dams, creating substantial hydraulic heads to drive turbines.

While each may be fashioned in terms of its specific rationale, such activities eventually interact with one another. Consider a simple example. We know that people rely upon freshwater for a variety of purposes, the most basic of which might include personal consumption, support for vegetative cover (forests to fields), support for animals on land (wild and domestic), support for aquatic wildlife, transportation, and kinetic energy (mill wheels and turbines). These are diverse and potentially incompatible claims. Given the finite and uneven supply of water, rules of access are required to guide the consumption, production, and distribution of this resource. Clearly water access has a value. It can be captured, possessed, used, stored, sold, and licensed. In short, its finite quantity and uneven availability makes water socially and politically contestable.

Many diverse and innately political questions arise from the collision of uses and interests. Is there sufficient drinking and sanitary water, in quantity and quality, and should this assume priority status? This is a distributive question that turns on a single use. Should that water be treated as a basic entitlement or a scarce commodity? What, then, about in-stream water uses for fishing or transportation? Each can entail modifications in the streamflow, in the form of weirs and fish nets or channel dredging or straightening. Who can capture aquatic animals and in what measure? Then there is the question of water diversion away from its natural flow, to irrigate fields for crop cultivation or to water livestock. Are there limits as to the manner of appropriating and diverting flows away from the stream? Similarly, what regulates the impoundment of water to harness hydraulic energy to power machinery?

It is clear that many if not most of these water-centred interests have the capacity to facilitate or detract from other interests. Many of the complications arise from the characteristics of "flow," which links interests at different sites along the watercourse. Upstream residents are in a position to alter the prospects of downstream users, both in quantitative (water withdrawal) and qualitative (water pollution) terms. Downstream residents can reverse the effect, by damming a river and flooding upstream lands. Finally, we must factor in the variable of time. Do early entrants enjoy a superior claim to late arrivals? What about the shifting historical profiles of water demand? Do new ways of thinking (science studies or technological applications, for example) modify the uses, practices, and regulations of earlier eras? How will changing philosophies on the role of the state and the market affect freshwater regimes?

Taking all of this into account it is evident that, regardless of size, any watershed can be usefully approached through a four-dimensional framework, set out in Figure 1.1. As Stanford and Ward put it, "rivers are four-dimensional environments that involve processes that connect upstream-downstream, channel-hyporheic (groundwater) and channel-floodplain (riparian) zones or patches, and these differ temporally" (Stanford and Ward 1992, 91). This can be applied for social as well as ecological purposes. The sections that follow will address each in turn.

The Water Channel: Upstream/Downstream Relations

For most people, the most readily recognizable aspect of a watershed system is flow. A river rises at a source, proceeds downstream, may be joined by tributaries

Figure 1.1 A Watershed in Four Dimensions

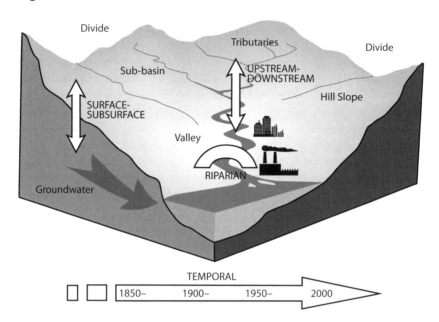

or interrupted by lakes and waterfalls, and eventually reaches its end. It travels in what hydrologists describe as the water channel, the area between banks where the stream normally runs. Water channels are dynamic, with speed and temperature varying within the stream. The channel footprint can also be altered by natural forces over longer time frames, carving out new directions, depths, and borders.

In various phases of culture, humans can make differing imprints on the channel. Hunters and gatherers step lightly, taking fish, riding the current, and adapting to seasonal change. This is not to suggest that their water technologies were crude—in fact quite the opposite. A stone weir constructed across a stream holds up migrating fish long enough for spearing or basket dipping, while the weir can be repaired or rebuilt in each new season. Equally, the bark canoe that was perfected by Amerindians proved to be the most effective mode of travel for centuries and was a critical underpinning of the European fur trade (Morse 1969).

As the colonial economy shifted from fish and fur to timber, however, the water needs changed. The eastern Canadian forests offered potentially valuable commodities if the logs could be transported from stump to mill. Since this distance could be dozens or hundreds of kilometres, however, the timber trade looked to rivers as the only available transport medium. Trees were felled in the bush and the logs hauled to a river bank. When streamflow surged with the spring melt, the logs were dumped in to float downstream where they would eventually be recaptured by the producer (Lower 1938).

The orderly conduct of a log-drive, however, required that the river be engineered for the purpose. Part of this involved the construction of splash dams on feeder streams, to hold back spring waters until a timed release that augmented the flow and extended the drive period. Another part involved the elimination of chronic bottlenecks to the timber flow. Nothing was more disruptive than a log jam at a tight meander in the channel or a set of rock outcrops or rapids. A common response was to straighten the river by digging an alternate channel that cut out the meanders to make a less obstructed run. In the face of more dramatic physical obstacles such as falls and canyons, an artificial flow route could be constructed by building an elevated flume or canal to bypass the problem or even to switch the log flow between rivers. None of this could eliminate all difficulties, though, and the skills of the river driving crews that rode the logs downstream to release the jams were critical to delivering an entire year's log harvest (MacKay 1978).

It is interesting to note that on major driving rivers such as the Ottawa, where logs flowed from dozens of tributaries toward a common stem stream, rival companies often recognized the need for collective action. In effect, they negotiated formal understandings to coordinate their driving efforts and reduce the mutually destructive rush for primacy. This could involve the joint financing and operation of river works among the crews sharing a watercourse, the pooling of (marked) logs in common drives, and the eventual sorting of the product at the lower end (Lower 1938). In effect, the timber barons fashioned an early governing structure for single-use river management. None of this was without costs to the natural functioning of the river ecology. Log drives were notorious for scarring the beds, and the various engineering works could alter the natural services of the channel.

But this was just the beginning. The industrial era depended on the ability to tap reliable energy sources to drive machines. Flowing water was an early candidate, as kinetic energy could be captured by water wheels and could be geared to power machines in a factory. While run-of-the-river mills had modest effects upon stream conditions, mill-pond water storage was the first step toward the dams and reservoirs that would dramatically transform river flows. Industrial manufacturing also treated freshwater as a plumbing system by discharging wastes that the current would sweep away. From sawdust and wood chips to toxic chemicals and mine tailings, the industrial economy exploited streamflow for private profit. As the old slogan put it, "the solution to pollution is dilution." By the 1960s, such sentiments came under increasing challenge.

The Riparian Transect: Stream/Bank Relations

The second dimension highlights the complicated interactions between streamflow and the land-based features that confine it. This is often described as "riparian" and captures the interplay between shore activity and water. As a result, ecologists speak of a riparian zone as the transitional space along a bank, and lawyers deal with riparian law as the rules governing shore-based access to water flow. In this section we consider how designs on water trigger complications among shore-based political interests.

A distinct pattern of instream transformations attended the new industrial towns of nineteenth-century New England and eastern Canada. For the early factory manufacturer, one of the greatest challenges was a source of motive power to drive machines. A flowing river offered a potential answer if it could be brought under control. This was far from straightforward, however. In particular, the law of the time guaranteed many rights of use in the rural economy that ran along the streamflows and prevented any single "owner" from seizing control.

In a now classic study, Steinberg describes the political transformation of the 186-km Merrimack River that rises in New Hampshire and flows first south then east, emptying into the Atlantic north of Boston. Between 1825 and 1850 four significant factory towns grew up along its lower reaches. In Lowell, Mass., for example, a series of textile mills became the backbone to the town and water energy was commodified and sold. This required the town to change its approach and treat water power as an overriding priority, to help finance the major dams required to impound water and in so doing to block the river at multiple points. Once business interests were licensed and in possession of water power, they could sell it to energy consumers. At Lowell, a series of canals delivered water through the town where mills bought it on a flow-through basis. Here power was denominated in the new economic unit of "mill power," that measured the energy needed to drive a quantum of spindles and looms (Steinberg 1991).

Of course these measures had echo effects on other riparian interests along the length of the Merrimack valley. In addition to the many dams that were built to impound water for the industrial towns, the power developers faced another challenge. Precipitation and waterflow varied seasonally while factory operations were constant, and as a result the demand for water tended to outpace the river supply, especially during the summer. This led power developers to acquire land and water rights at points upstream where water could be held back to supplement flows during the low season (an amplification of the timber cutters' splash dam system).

By the 1850s the dams had reached the headwaters of the river in a lake system in New Hampshire that fed the Merrimack River. The Lake Company acquired the necessary rights and closed the flow with a new dam at Lake Village in 1851. The lake waters then rose above the shoreline, inundating farm and pasture lands and disrupting the businesses of ferries and log rafters. The growing political conflict exploded in September 1859 when a group of 50 men attacked the dam and sought to destroy it (Steinberg 1991). Here we see an example of a common syndrome, in which political grievances between community and outside interests accumulate until they reach a trigger point when local resistance breaks out. In this case we see how the social watershed defines both the protagonists (farmers, loggers, pastoralists, power generators, mill owners, and town leaders, among others) and the political fault lines (agrarian alliance and industrial alliance) between new and prior users.

An aggravating feature in riparian politics is that the property and tenure rules for streams, stream beds, and adjacent lands seldom coincide. It is possible to have private property along stream banks, and crown or public property in the water channel, while stream beds may be private or public, as specified in law. A further complication comes from residents and potential water users not immediately adjacent to waterflows. This brings in questions of right-of-way and easements for public works that serve communities set back from the waterfront.

The Groundwater Resource: Surface/Subsurface Relations

Water stored below ground is the hidden face of the hydrologic cycle. Even today, many people find it impossible to conceive the scale or the structure of this resource. Indeed, for much of human history it was mysterious—bubbling to the surface as springs or pooling at the bottom of dug wells that seemed to go dry as often as not.

Many early cultures developed a sophisticated approach to groundwater. Despite the severity of desert landscapes, people maintained wells along their travel routes. This was possible because of ancient water deposited in former river strata from glacial times. In parts of the Middle East and North Africa, quite elaborate systems of groundwater supply known as *qanats* were constructed as early as 1000 BC. Each consisted of a central supply (or "mother") well dug, if possible, in foothills that were amply endowed with groundwater. Then an underground tunnel ran out from this point to villages at lower elevations, with periodic access shafts along the way. Qanat tunnels could run for 40–45 km (Cech 2003).

A modern understanding of groundwater emerged in the geological science of the nineteenth century. Scientists showed that water seeped into the ground where it lodged in the porous spaces of sedimentary deposits. A water table marked the boundary between saturated sediments and aerated ones, a dynamic frontier that rose and fell according to precipitation and absorptive capacities (and was reflected in those shifting well water levels). Along with this came a new understanding that surface to subsurface flows went both ways. Surface water can infiltrate the substrate to enter the groundwater. Equally, groundwater can re-enter surface streams, particularly on sloped surfaces where the water table rises above the channel level.

In North America, the agricultural frontier expanded along waterways wherever possible. Eventually, however, a rush of western settlement was set loose by the US *Homestead Act* of 1862 and the *Dominion Lands Act* of 1872 in Canada. In time, river valley lands were fully taken and late arrivals had to contend with prairie drylands. Here the rural well became the first necessity for a viable livelihood, and by the 1870s windmills dotted the prairie horizon, lifting well water for surface use. While the farm windmills are now largely gone, groundwater dependence is still a defining feature of country life and distinguishes it from urban culture. When rural neighbours ask one another "How's your water?" they are acknowledging the pivotal role of residential wells in supporting habitation.

The law also has been challenged to arbitrate groundwater titles, rights, and obligations. One doctrine known as the rule of capture gave landowners the right to extract groundwater without limit from beneath owned lands. In nineteenth-century England, judges conceded their ignorance of how groundwater worked while endorsing a "capture" doctrine for groundwater appropriation, usually with some rules of priority. When competition for groundwater intensified, other rules such as reasonable use (by neighbouring users) were factored into some laws while in others, sharing criteria were defined to achieve minimum levels of entitlement.

The Temporal Dimension: Cumulative and Successive Development

The factor of time belongs, in some ways, to historians whether they study natural or social life. Some of the most insightful contributions to water politics have come through histories of particular rivers or basins. In recent years the Fraser and the Bow in Canada, and the Colorado and the Columbia in the United States, have all been presented in this way (Evenden 2004; Armstrong et al. 2009; Fradkin 1996; White 1995). An essential element in the understanding of water politics involves the structural "layering" of physical and social changes from past to present. Geographers and political economists sometimes speak of the phenomenon of "uneven and combined development." This highlights the fact that spatial areas evolve at different paces, and their profile at a particular point in time is a product of successive changes. In this sense, the watershed unit involves a complicated dialectic of time, place, and activity.

There is one more preliminary point to be made about watershed politics. In sociopolitical terms, watersheds are never completely self-contained. While the resident population demarcates a political constituency, there are higher order systems that inevitable impinge. Two of these are the nation state and global capitalism. Ever since the age of European empire, outside forces have treated lands and waters as sources of potential wealth. The fur merchants of the 1700s and the timber barons of the 1800s did not hesitate to transform the Canadian hinterland into engines of commercial profit. Neither did the immigrant settlers arriving on the prairies in the early 1900s or the electricity magnates who drove the hydro-power revolution in the twentieth century. It is important to realize that the political polarities of watershed politics often involve forces and interests "external" to the watershed itself. Even if such interests have a local presence, a full understanding of their behaviour requires that wider horizons be factored in.

CASE STUDY: THE JAMES-WEST RIVER, NOVA SCOTIA

Local rivers and streams are the most familiar manifestation of watersheds. Consider a small but representative Canadian example of a local watershed that still awaits the writing of its history. In rural Nova Scotia, the West River and its tributaries flow through the western half of Antigonish County. The river drains an area of approximately 900 km², an intermediate size among the province's 44 small watersheds. The system begins in the highlands where three main tributaries are sourced: the James, Beaver, and Ohio Rivers. Each flows easterly as it descends and they converge near the midpoint of the basin to become the West River, which continues for 12 km before emptying into the sea at Antigonish Harbour. Map 1.1 illustrates the West River, its tributaries, and the adjacent local watersheds. Overall the territory offers striking variations, from the forested uplands where the source waters rise, to the alluvial floodplains of the lower river and the broad estuary at the river's mouth at Antigonish town.

The area was extensively traversed by Aboriginal Mi'kmaq people for millennia before the arrival of European immigrants in the late eighteenth century. Scots settlers took up coastal lands from the 1780s, and a group of decommissioned colonial soldiers received land grants around the river estuary in 1784.

Map 1.1 James–West River Watershed, Nova Scotia

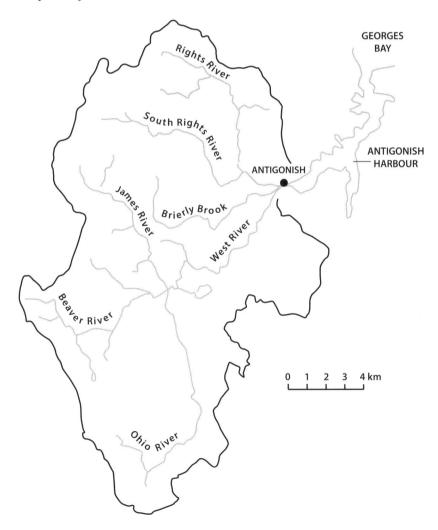

A town emerged to service the commercial needs of this frontier society. As settlement accelerated over the next half century, pioneer farms and villages dotted the land, first as subsistence producers and later as mixed domestic and commercial farming operations. The earliest land titles were taken out along the coast and on river banks along the lower reaches of the West River. By the 1870s and 1880s, even the more remote interior was intensively occupied. In fact, this was the time when the county population peaked. Thereafter, small farms were increasingly abandoned, beginning with the marginal upland properties where the soils were poorer, the growing season was shorter, and the yields were lower. Typically such cleared farmland grew back into forest over a period of 30–40 years, leaving little evidence, beyond the crumbling stone foundations, of the extent of frontier agriculture.

In the 1800s pioneer logging was an important seasonal activity as well, with small sawmills located along numerous waterways. As elsewhere in the country, the channels of the upper tributaries were in some cases straightened for timber driving, by cutting off the meanders to facilitate more direct water flow. In the lower reaches of the watershed, the county town was incorporated in 1889 at the mouth of the West River. In fact, three small watersheds converged at this point to empty into Antigonish Harbour.

The townsite proved to be highly functional as an entrepôt, linking up-land farms to commercial marine traffic and trade in the Gulf of St. Lawrence. However, the convergence of local drainages meant that the town was highly vulnerable to seasonal floods, both during the spring melt and as a result of sudden summer storms. Indeed, the history of Antigonish town can be written in part through the 27 major flood events that were recorded over the century before 1982 (MacLaren Plansearch 1983).

In Antigonish County, as elsewhere in Nova Scotia, the rural land base was predominantly privately owned by 1900. This was a result of a century of land grants and sales of rural property that left the provincial crown with less than 15 per cent of the total. It did, however, facilitate a farm, village, and small town social structure in the West River watershed and few legal rules on water use. In the early twentieth century the social access to the watershed was extremely decentralized. In addition to farm properties, clusters of houses sprang up along stream paths adjacent to mills or local stores, and dozens of local communities dotted the landscape. Grist- and sawmills required permits, but otherwise water politics, to the extent that it arose, was either settled by private arrangements or by the courts and common law. The 1919 *Water Act* vested streams in provincial crown title to facilitate hydro-electric development and curtail rural resistance to such projects. But in Antigonish County, the first major dam and reservoir project was probably the town water supply scheme built on the Rights River at Clydesdale.

Not until the 1970s and 1980s did state authority begin to impinge on the watershed in significant ways. When this happened, it took a revealing form. A variety of federal and provincial administrative agencies drew on separate pieces of legislation to make their marks. As a result, watershed regulation tended to be segmented by function, institution, and spatial focus. In some sections the predominant concern was flood control, in others fish habitat protection, and in still others farm practices, timber harvesting, drinking water supply, or wilderness protection.

One of the first emerging policy concerns was flood control. Under the terms of the new Canada-Nova Scotia Flood Damage Reduction Program of 1975, Antigonish town was one of five designated sites within the province. A dam was built on the Brierley Brook in 1976 to slow the flood surge from this very "flashy" river before it reached the town. Flood mapping was also done in conjunction with municipal zoning, and funds were provided to modify bridges that aggravated ice flow build-up in spring.

In the 1980s the federal Department of Fisheries and Oceans announced a major turn toward fish habitat protection. This broke new ground with the mandate to regulate "harmful alteration, damage or destruction" of fish habitat. It gave federal officials leverage to monitor river flow rates and establish base flow rates when dams and reservoirs were involved.

When Antigonish town demand for drinking water exceeded the storage capacity of the Clydesdale reservoir located on the Rights River, a new location was chosen in the middle reaches of the James River. This represented the most significant historical alteration of a tributary basin to date. It altered the flow characteristics by impounding approximately 9 million gallons (50 million litres) behind an earth-filled concrete dam. A water treatment facility was installed below the new dam and the water moved by gravity pipe to the town storage towers. A decade later, in the face of further shortfalls and the need for dam upgrades, the dam height was raised by more than 2 metres and the reservoir storage enlarged to 22 million gallons. This included a maintenance flow passage for downstream fish habitat (CBCL Ltd. 2003). Almost immediately the supply situation tightened again, and the prospect of further impoundments, perhaps by way of a second dam further upstream, has been considered. In 1988 the Nova Scotia Department of Environment designated the James River drainage above the dam as a protected source area. As a result, land use was curtailed within this former timbershed, to minimize the likelihood of contamination.

In the 1990s, the provincial Department of Agriculture began to promote environmental farm practices that included excluding livestock from river access and limiting fertilizer applications in riparian zones to protect against manure and chemical runoffs. This applied particularly to the West River between the confluence of tributaries and the river mouth.

Forestry science has long recognized the links between rainfall, vegetative cover, and erosion. However, in a private land culture such as Nova Scotia's, where farm and woodlot owners have long harboured suspicions about government intent, the provincial government has been reluctant to exercise its water title powers. Best practice management "guidelines" have been far more frequent than legal rules when it came to timber harvesting in riparian zones. In 2002, however, the province enacted Watercourse Forest Protection regulations that defined a protected corridor along stream flows. While this applies throughout watersheds, its particular impact on the West River system is in the upper tributaries.

Late in the 1990s the Eigg Mountain area, including parts of the upper James River watershed, was nominated as a candidate wilderness area under the Nova Scotia protected areas scheme. It was sponsored by several environmental NGOs (nongovernmental organizations) campaigning for a highland wilderness to be set aside in eastern Nova Scotia. The fact that the area was one of the few crown-owned areas in Antigonish County eased the land tenure sensitivities, though it also contributed to the irregular (patchwork) shape of the Eigg Mountain wilderness. The result is that commercial activity is significantly curtailed in the designated areas.

A final phase of basin regulation involves the mouth of the West River where it empties into the estuary at Antigonish Harbour. Here the freshwater from the river mixes with saltwater from the ocean to create a distinct ecosystem. Estuaries tend to be rich in species and highly productive. They also tend to be vulnerable to upstream pollution, whether it involves wood chip wastes, soil deposition, fertilizer leaching, dam and reservoir constraints, or urban pollution. Traditionally it was assumed that tidal flushing could remedy many of these problems. More recently, however, water monitoring programs have been imposed by federal and provincial authorities, often unevenly and in response to particular concerns. One agency might sample shellfish beds while another might sample water chemistry.

In sum, at least seven distinct government regulatory regimes now impinge on the West River watershed. It is hard to argue that instruments for watershed management are lacking. Indeed, their accumulation marks a qualitative shift in public sector involvement. Equally striking, however, is the pattern of administrative overlay. This is extremely segmented, with multiple agencies exercising distinct tools for separate policy purposes. There is little formal coordination or integration among them, though local officials do tend to talk to one another and certain enforcement powers can be delegated among different services. It is best described as an unplanned accumulation of programs that arose in response to different problems. From mouth to source, this includes federal water monitoring in the estuary (Environment Canada), federal-provincial-municipal flood planning in the town and provincial farm activity rules (Department of Agriculture), provincial watercourse timber rules (Department of Natural Resources), federal fish habitat protection (Fisheries and Oceans), provincial drinking water supply regulations (Department of Environment), and provincial wilderness protected areas (Department of Environment). The interests of municipal government have already been addressed. The West River regulatory profile is not unusual in Canada and it helps explain today's calls for more integrated watershed management.

Conclusion

We have seen above that freshwater politics is driven by ideas and interests that are diverse and complex. Each community has a particular pattern of social and political interests and this pattern evolves over time. Watersheds provide a promising framework for the study of freshwater politics, by delineating social geographies with a shared interest in the water resource. Among the watershed dimensions that can structure water politics, it is useful to consider stream flows, riparian relations, surface to groundwater, and the temporal dimension. However, freshwater politics also extend well beyond the watershed scale. The centralized state and the globalized market are two cases in point. Here key decisions are made externally even though the impacts will eventually register locally. Indeed, it may be that the interplay of these different scales—regional, national, and global—drives the course of freshwater politics.

The West River history helps to illustrate the cumulative and connected nature of human activities, with the potential to affect any or all levels of the watershed. The nineteenth century saw the first significant social transformation, as Euro-Canadian immigrants occupied small rural properties for farming and timber cutting. This socially decentralized economy, which peaked in the 1880s, was closely aligned with watercourses. The turn of the century saw a decline of the rural economy. Not only was land abandoned but new rail and highway modes of transport made watercourses less central to rural life. In the late twentieth century state authorities began to grasp the importance of watersheds in a multidimensional way, with separate agencies extending their mandates to different aspects of the West River system. By the turn of this century at least seven distinct programs played a role. The James River tributary was the most dramatically affected when the town of Antigonish established its new drinking water supply system. The potential for overlaps, contradictions, and complications is substantial and capable of triggering differing degrees of state intervention. We see the growth of a mosaic of social habitation, water use constituencies, and water regulatory programs, though it often occurs with little appreciation of the watershed as an integrated system. As in most of Canada, holistic watershed planning remains a challenge for the future.

There is probably no such thing as a "typical" watershed in Canada. The rural and small-town character of the West River system seems a long way from the Credit River watershed of the city of Toronto or the Wascana River watershed in Regina. However, each corresponds to a representative type. Of the 164 drainage sub-basins identified in a recent study, over half are classified as "highly rural." (It should be noted that over half of the highly rural sub-basins are in the three northern Territories.) However, only one-fifth of the rural population lives in watersheds where rural residents form a majority. In other words, the social and political interaction of rural and urban elements is an animating factor in Canadian watersheds (Rothwell 2006).

2
Power and Freshwater

THIS CHAPTER EXPLORES THE CONCEPT OF political power and its place in water politics. We begin with a discussion of power and a breakdown of its various dimensions. There are several types of power relations that are usefully distinguished from one another. To make this more concrete, the concept is linked with the history of the Mi'kmaq Aboriginal peoples of Maritime Canada, from precontact times to the present. After this, a case study is presented in the watershed surrounding Boat Harbour, Nova Scotia. This is a little-known but very important story of industrial pollution, imposed on a small Aboriginal community on questionable terms and perpetuated for more than half a century by an alliance of corporate and governmental interests. The power relations underlying this case are particularly revealing.

Faces of Power

Politics is rooted in the diversity of interests that is found in social situations. Should diversity give rise to conflict, clearly not all can win. Political "power" can be described as the capacity to prevail in situations of conflict. The concept is useful in understanding the potential pathways to reconcile differences. Power, then, is a relational concept. In one classic formulation, Steven Lukes describes it as the capacity to achieve preferred goals in a contested setting, that is the capacity to prevail over rival claimants. A has power over B and C if A's preferred goals are achieved while B's and C's are not (Lukes 1974).

It is not difficult to see the relevance of this perspective to freshwater resources. Indeed, it should be clear that conflicting claims to water use arise continually. Upstream residents may impound, divert, or degrade the flows of water to downstream residents. Riparian landowners may block or restrict access to stream flows by residents who are set back from the banks. High-volume commercial extractions of groundwater can lower the water table and thereby deprive residents who depend on rural wells. What about the natural flow needs of a river to support aquatic life and riparian landscapes? How best to protect the interests of future generations that have no ready advocates when yesterday's and today's water users lock up preferential access?

The natural flow structure of a drainage system cannot be assumed constant, either. With modern hydrological engineering it is possible to physically transform watersheds in the most fundamental ways. Dam and reservoir systems block natural flow patterns and turn rivers into segmented systems. Also, by means of canals and pipelines it is possible to divert waterflows between adjacent basins, creating permanent discrepancies. Physical alterations, large or small, have the potential to reorder the terms of advantage and disadvantage among interests. All of these tensions drive the water policy agendas of public life.

The powerful, then, are those that can realize their goals. The powerless are those who cannot prevail, those who try and fail or who never get the chance to engage at all. The last comment alludes to more subtle variants of power that go beyond visible decision-making. For example, Peter Bachrach and Morton Baratz advanced the concept of the "non-decision." This refers to the capacity to block or suppress an issue before it can become part of the public debate. Thus a question or concern that might reasonably be expected to arise in light of the alignment of interests fails to register in political discussion (Bachrach and Baratz 1962, 1970). Non-decision-making involves keeping an issue off the public agenda. It implies that there are gatekeepers and veto-agents in the policy process who can, either on their own account or on behalf of others, exercise a subtle form of control in the early stages of a power sequence. Such absences are politically telling, as they can reflect a capacity by dominating interests to control the policy agenda to the point of preventing certain issues from even being raised. For example, when the government of British Columbia decided to control the headwaters of the Peace River by means of a massive hydro-electric dam and reservoir installation, it carried major consequences for communities downstream in the province of Alberta. By law, the federal government of Canada holds responsibilities for regulating navigable waters such as the Peace, and could have intervened to influence the project at the design stage. Yet Ottawa opted not to step in. This is an example of a non-decision, in which the federal government deliberately chose not to raise an issue after weighing the balance of rival interests.

John Gaventa pushes beyond the circumstances of observable situational conflict to explore other nuanced dimensions of power. In particular he questions the significance of missing political interests—those that would be expected by virtue of their social circumstances to be active in politics but are not. There are several possibilities here. It may be that after repeated but unsuccessful attempts to shape issue outcomes, powerless interests conclude that the deck is stacked against them, accept their fate, and simply withdraw. This retreat from politics, it could be argued, is a rational response based on experiential outcomes. It does, however, leave a gap in the universe of organized interests. Another variation is a cultural or subcultural bias that tilts the social awareness of the powerless in directions compatible with the status quo and away from directions that entail challenge (Gaventa 1980). For example, in a patriarchal society, women are unlikely to be recognized as legitimate actors and their issues are unlikely to find voice. In a devoutly Catholic country with an extensive church hierarchy, issues of socialism, poverty, and modernity may be similarly repressed. In a culture where private property and profit-seeking are predominant, claims for community or public interest priorities will get short shrift.

Within the general notion of power, several significant variations are commonly observed. For Lukes (1974), one of these is *force*, defined as the imposition of a desired outcome by physical domination, including violence. The colonist driving Indigenous peoples off traditional lands, the industrial capitalist hiring thugs to eliminate union organizers, and the dictator murdering or imprisoning political rivals are all cases in point. It is one of the most common forms of power in human history, within and between families, tribes, kingdoms, or nations.

Related but distinct from force is *coercion*. Here the anticipation of the threat of physical force is sufficient to induce compliance. This may be a function of past experience or awareness, where the memory of physical repression lingers on. Amerindian peoples may retreat from their traditional lands rather than face the ruthless suppression that they have seen already from the army, workers may opt not to organize unions in the workplace after witnessing the brutality of the Pinkerton agents or police, and reformers may abandon public protest in the face of abductions of the "disappeared." Some agents of power understand the crucial significance of the bloody, violent deed in establishing a context of credible threat.

Authority is another variant of power that is distinguished by securing compliance by consent. Here rivals are willing to accept political choices, even when they run against preferred outcomes, by virtue of the processes that have been followed. "Legitimacy" refers to an acceptance of a state of affairs as appropriate or necessary. This contrasts sharply with the earlier variants. Now B and C are willing to tolerate their relative subservience to A on an issue because, rather than simply being imposed by force, it has been decided in an acceptable way. It often turns on the institutional channels by which decisions are made. If such procedures are accepted as appropriate and reasonable, then the ensuing outputs can be treated the same way. If the Indigenous group has access to the courts but cannot convince a judge despite an opportunity to argue its case, if union organizers fail to sign up most workers in a secret workplace ballot mandated under labour laws, or if the authoritarian leader wins power by means of a relatively fair and open election—the outcomes reflect relations of authority.

Finally, there is a relationship of *influence*. This can be described as a capacity to affect the flow of decision without fully controlling it. Here political interventions make a difference but do not render the desired results. The ensuing outcome is different than it would be without that agent's involvement, but not so different that the agent in question fully succeeds. In this case, the Indigenous group succeeds in achieving limited land rights over only a part of traditional territories, the factory owner chooses to raise wages or improve shop conditions to head off union certification, and the dictator is obliged to concede an electoral voice to the people while continuing to exercise full executive powers. Because power relations are not necessarily "zero-sum" transactions where one party's gain must be another party's loss, it is quite possible to observe mixed results that point to influence as well as power.

It can be useful to distinguish between these variants of power, as they point to specific mechanisms that can resolve conflicts. This can enhance our understanding of social and political control. The next section offers a more sustained example.

Mi'kmaq and Colonists: Dimensions of Power

The Mi'kmaq peoples have considered the Atlantic region their homeland for millennia. In traditional life (i.e., before contact with Europeans), people followed a seasonal cycle of movements between coastal and inland settings, drawing upon a variety of material resources based on hunting, fishing, and gathering. A large part of this involved freshwater resources on rivers, lakes, and estuaries. People congregated at such sites, often working together to capture and process fish during prime seasons. This could involve building a weir across a stream to slow the fish passage for spearing, or use of a net or basket, or fishing from a boat on the water (sometimes with torches) at night. These were significant social occasions where families or bands came together, staging a feast and curing and storing fish for later consumption.

When European explorers such as Cartier and Champlain came ashore in the 1500s and planted the flags of French kings, the Mi'kmaq paid these visitors little initial attention. Latent in European claims, however, was a powerful transformative force. Beginning in the 1600s European immigrants began to arrive. Some were soldiers who opted to stay on after their military obligations were fulfilled while others were missionaries or traders or pioneer settlers. At first they had little impact on the Mi'kmaq. The Europeans were ignorant about how to survive and they relied heavily on the Indians for local knowledge and exchange. In fact they often sought "alliances" with Mi'kmaq as warriors or producers. The extended rivalries of English and French colonies, each with their own frontiers of influence, exacerbated this (Upton 1979).

During this early phase, the advantage of force lay as much with the Mi'kmaq as with the immigrants. The Indians were an armed presence and often defeated Europeans, putting soldiers and settlers alike on the run. Put another way, territory was hotly contested. The mere threat of Mi'kmaq resistance (i.e., coercion) posed great problems to English colonial authorities. A common response after periods of open warfare was the negotiation of a treaty of peace and friendship. Equally frequent was the collapse of a treaty in response to subsequent provocations. Such volatile relationships suggest that power was far from stable in eighteenth-century Maritime Canada.

However, the resort to treaties indicates a new stage of politics and power, where a negotiation between separate parties yielded a mutual agreement geared to regulating future relations. Certainly this is reflected in the language of the treaties with their undertakings and guarantees. Indians pledged to be amicable with settlers while the crown guaranteed Indian lands against encroachment and established truckhouses for regulated trade. For example, the Mascarene Treaty of 1725 assured the signatories continued rights to "hunting, fishing, gathering and all other their lawful occasions" (Mascarene Treaty 1725).

In the 1700s the social balance began to shift again, as European numbers mounted and their interests changed. The Acadian farmers, who tended to ally with Indians, were expelled from the colony in 1756. English immigration quickened after the French withdrawal with the Treaty of Paris in 1763. Following their defeat in the American War of Independence, tens of thousands of British "loyalists" fled to the colony of Nova Scotia. The newcomers sought to locate in the same areas occupied traditionally by Mi'kmaq: in the coastal margins, at river mouths and estuaries, and in the lower valleys where soils were best. To settlers ignorant of Aboriginal culture, the land might seem to be empty, a state of nature that begged for occupation and improvement. Colonial authorities encouraged this point of view, and confrontations over land proliferated. In the eyes of newly arrived deed holders, Mi'kmaq camping parties were unwanted "trespassers."

This was exacerbated as English colonial authorities expanded the offer of private land titles to immigrants. The prospect of free 100-acre plots lured massive immigration from the British Isles in the early 1800s. Forty thousand Scots alone arrived in Nova Scotia between 1815 and 1838 and a similar number of Irish entered New Brunswick between 1840 and 1860. As the alluvial river plains were exhausted, late arrivals took up land in less favourable river uplands, where soil was poorer, growing seasons shorter, and trips to market longer. Subject to neglect and hostility, the Mi'kmaq population declined to only a fraction of its precontact numbers.

By the 1830s, colonial governments were bent on the pursuit of material exports and local commerce. Treaties were ignored and traditional Aboriginal land use was dismissed, at both the official and the popular levels. As Harald Prins puts it, "Outnumbered by hordes of poor immigrants running from cruel exploitation and squalor in Europe, Mi'kmaqs found themselves pressured into misery. Ranging through their former domains they saw gangs of white loggers destroying the woods and felt the pain of hunger when the game was gone. Great was their anger when aggressive newcomers refused them access to their ancient fishing sites or chased them from their favourite camping grounds. Even firewood was denied them" (Prins 1996, 165).

By the end of the 1800s, Indians were confined to small tracts of federal "reserved" lands. For many, fishing was one of the few remaining lifelines. Then even access to the fishery was challenged by white society. Bill Parenteau has captured the complex processes by which Mi'kmaq fishing came under assault, in the Miramichi and other Atlantic salmon watersheds, in the closing decades of the nineteenth century (Parenteau 1998). This arose in part from white recreational fishers whose sense of "sport" and "chase" was offended by Mi'kmaq techniques including river nettings and torch fishing by night. It was as much a distributional conflict as a cultural one, since the anglers and tourist operators aimed to secure long-term stocks by excluding a rival harvest. They found willing allies in the federal fisheries department and, over time, statutory measures were comprehensively framed to curb or even outlaw the Aboriginal fishery. Whether by land court or fisheries act enforcement, the prevailing patterns of authority were arraigned against the interests of the Aboriginal minority.

In the face of this combined displacement from terrestrial and aquatic resources, Mi'kmaq were not passive. Chiefs made representations to government officials and appealed for respect of treaty provisions. Some Indian agents also sought to soften the rough treatment by settler governments, and church figures sometimes intervened with government on the Indians' behalf. While none of these forces was able to blunt the predominant political vectors, they could at times dampen the local impacts. In short, these mediating elements could exercise occasional influence without altering the entrenched power relations.

In 1919 the government of Nova Scotia extended its jurisdiction dramatically with the passage of the *Water Act*. Inland water was declared a crown resource. Previous riparian rights were expropriated and authority to license water use, diversion, and appropriation was vested in the province. This was a response to mounting disputes around the construction of power dams and the success of nonindustrial landowners in winning compensation claims. In the face of common law judgments that put private property rights (and compensation) first, the province legislated to win control of water licensing for productive uses, principally water power (Nedelsky 1990). Given the government's predilection for commercial hydro projects, the new provincial crown water jurisdiction served to further separate Mi'kmaq peoples from the freshwater resource. It is important to note that, despite the treaty guarantees mentioned earlier, the law provided no support for an Aboriginal right of water use at that time. Bartlett (1988) argues, however, that for reserves established before 1919 water rights should be legally retained, and Phare (2009) argues that the time is ripe for a judicial clarification in Canada.

Knowledge as Power

Another perspective that offers significant insights to freshwater politics examines the power of organized knowledge. The sociologist Michel Foucault makes key contributions to this field by asking penetrating questions about how knowledge is organized, who defines what is important in a knowledge domain, and how knowledge is codified and transmitted in modern life. Foucault published case studies about prisons, medicine, psychiatry, and sexuality as institutional embodiments of knowledge (Foucault 1980). Central to each domain is a form of discourse—a way of arranging ideas to make sense of the world. While rival discourses may compete for influence in a field, a particular discourse that permeates social institutions can be dominant.

Here we will ask similar questions about the way knowledge is organized in relation to freshwater. There is a long tradition here, stretching back to the Greek, Roman, and Islamic empires. Highly sophisticated works were devised to store, transport, and distribute water. However, it could be argued that hydraulic engineering began to emerge as a master domain in Europe in the 1600s. The Dutch were early leaders in this field, and their skills were sought across the continent and in Britain. Through personal contacts, training, and field experience, the knowledge was diffused. At its base lay a vision and a confidence about the purposive control of riverine nature. Frederick the Great was a patron of rural reclamation throughout his reign, and over the eighteenth century many marsh clearance and river valley defence schemes were launched across Prussia.

Although far from the first, the towering figure in German hydraulic engineering is probably Johann Gottfried Tulla in the German state of Baden. Tulla is most famously described as "the man who tamed the wild Rhine" (Blackbourn 2006). In the 1700s much of the North German plain was marsh and fenland, unsuitable for either cultivation or grazing. The rivers had multiple channels, the tributary structures were complex, seasonal pulses of water were intense, and flooding and waterlogging were endemic. The challenge was to drain the marshes, channelize the rivers, reduce the meanders, and reinforce the banks against flooding. In the terminology of engineering, the goal was to "regulate" or "rectify" what were hitherto wild rivers. Having studied engineering, surveying, and hydraulics and put them to work in a variety of practical projects, Johann Tulla submitted to Baden a proposal in 1812 to redesign the upper Rhine watershed.

It is significant that no political decision was possible on this matter without the consent of the German principalities as well as the French state that held sway on the west bank of the river. The territorial expansion of some of the more "progressive" German states, such as Baden and Bavaria, advanced the prospect as well. Following a year of intense flooding, a treaty was signed in 1817 and Tulla was appointed director of the military command of water and road construction that same year. In this way he presided over both the planning and the initial decade of work to regulate the upper Rhine. The scope of the project was extraordinary. It called for carefully planned cuts, excavations, removal of islands, consolidation of channels, and construction of dikes along riverbanks. Overall, the goal was for the Rhine to be "directed into a single bed with gentle curves adapted to nature or … where it is practicable, a straight line" (Blackbourn 2006, 85). The result was dramatic. In the stretch of the upper river from Basle to Worms, the length was reduced from 355 km to 275 km. Overall, the Rhine project was so extensive that it continued for 45 years after Tulla died in 1828. It put German engineers in the forefront of hydraulic research, training, and practice, in Europe and beyond. It also reflected a new confidence by state authorities that nature could be conquered.

In his study of Tulla and the Rhine, historian David Blackbourn poses some penetrating analytic questions that go to the heart of understanding political power: "why were these measures taken, who decided on them, and what were their consequences" (Blackbourn 2006, 3). The political authorities of the German states that negotiated a complex agreement for "Rhine rectification" saw river regulation as a necessary step in the economic development of the region. In setting this project in motion, they took explicitly political choices. The fact is that every hydraulic change to a river sets interests against one another. Forces in favour are weighed with forces against. The fishers and hunters who thrived in marshlands and fenlands were set against the prospective estate owners and farmers of newly drained lands. The interests of agriculture could clash with those of industry. River transporters regarded the rivers differently from water power operators. Local interests were often arrayed against regional or national priorities when it came to the timing, design, and finance of river works. But the process of river regulation, once formalized in treaty and funded by sponsoring states, acquired a superior standing as a power mandate. As a result, decision outcomes and nondecision patterns were structurally shaped.

In the spirit of Foucault, we might say that hydraulic engineering posits rivers as natural flow systems, subject to scientific principles, that can be planned and modified for increased social and economic efficiency. Among his achievements, Tulla founded an engineering school at Karlsruhe, where advanced techniques were taught to generations of aspiring watershed architects. Tulla also helped make the uniformed engineers a force for nation-building.

The role of a militarized engineering service in hydraulic design was not unique to Germany. It had a surprising parallel in the New World. In the United States, the Army Corps of Engineers was established in the early 1800s. Initially charged with the design of military installations and frontier surveys to chart rail and wagon routes through unknown terrain, the Corps's mandate was repointed toward river works in 1824 when it was assigned responsibility for river surveys and improvements on the Ohio and Mississippi Rivers. As it consolidated and expanded in scale, the Corps adopted institutional philosophies and mandate preferences (Shallat 1994). For example, when the Corps accepted the 1861 Humphreys-Abbott survey, with its "levees only" strategy for flood control on the Mississippi, a new organizational philosophy took hold that would last for 60 years. Politically, the Corps solidified its place in the Washington hierarchy by cultivating intricate clientele relations with key Congressmen and with business sectors that were sensitive to river improvements (Reuss 1985).

The particular discourse embedded in the Corps is highlighted more clearly when new government agencies appear. By 1920 these included the Bureau of Reclamation, the Inland Waterways Commission (IWC), and the Soil Conservation Service. The BurRec was charged with rehabilitating degraded resources, often by means of watering arid regions. The IWC was charged with multiple-use water management that went beyond the conventional single-use approach. The Soil Conservation Service sought to improve dryland farming, particularly through irrigation works. Each of these was founded in a character-istic worldview, and conflicts among them, as well as between them and outside social orders, were common (Clarke and McCool 1996; Reisner 1986).

Once again, Foucault can point the way. By linking ideas and institutions through the concept of discourse, he offers some compelling insights into the power equation. While power can be exercised through the mobilization and clash of interests, it can also be reflected in formal organizations. Discourse can help explain the origins of institutions, the discipline and continuity that institu-tions display, the underlying interests that are embedded within them, and the means by which challenges and displacements occur. This includes a toolbox of watershed techniques that favour certain solutions and discourage others.

The combined insights of decision-making frameworks, power and author-ity relationships, and discourse analysis provide a range of analytic tools for the study of freshwater politics. In the section below, we consider a little-known yet highly expressive case study of power relationships, to which all three models are relevant.

CASE STUDY: POWER RELATIONS AT BOAT HARBOUR, NOVA SCOTIA

The themes of the previous two sections converge in the politics of pulp mill pollution at Boat Harbour. For the Pictou Landing First Nation (PLFN), the encounter with corporate forestry can be seen as the most recent example of colonization, this time by a partnership of government and industrial interests. Over more than half a century, this small Nova Scotia Aboriginal community has been repeatedly exploited by institutions invoking expertise to legitimate what were highly contentious choices.

In the early 1960s, a small sub-watershed in eastern Nova Scotia was destroyed as part of a deliberate scheme for industrial development. Virtually overnight, the aquatic life of a vibrant local basin disappeared, with profound effects on the adjacent human communities. Just how this was allowed to occur is an important story that speaks not only to local power relations but, with variations, to the hundreds of watersheds where pulp and paper or mining companies predominated in the time before modern plant effluent regulations arrived in the 1970s. Equally revealing is the series of political responses from regional community interests. This too anticipates the more complex and contentious politics that swept across the country when industrial "pollution" became recognized as a generic threat to the integrity of freshwater systems. While the story of Boat Harbour is not entirely unknown, it deserves closer attention and wider circulation as a contribution to the study of power in the water domain.

In Pictou County, the largest watershed involves the East, Middle, and West Rivers that drain into different arms of Pictou Harbour and that empty, in turn, into the sea at the Northumberland Strait. The combined drainage area is almost 1,200 km². Prior to European settlement, the area was occupied by Mi'kmaq people who pursued migratory livelihoods based on wildlife and fisheries. This included a tidal estuary known to the Mi'kmaq as A'Se'K or "the other room" (i.e., an extension of the house, outdoors). Mi'kmaq had signed a treaty in 1760 and their descendants also remembered Governor Belcher's Proclamation of the following year, which held that "the laws will be like a great Hedge about your rights and properties" (Pictou Landing First Nation 2010). The Boat Harbour locale is illustrated in Map 2.1.

Scottish settlement began in this rich natural environment in the 1770s, when immigrants from the Highland clearances arrived by boat, with a promise of free farm land. The colonial government issued grants to settlers of these Indian lands, and although the Mi'kmaq continued to live along the coast, they were viewed as trespassers in the eyes of the law and the settlers. Not until 1864 did the colony of Nova Scotia procure 20 hectares for the band between the Strait and the A'Se'K. Several other small parcels totalling about 500 hectares (5 km²) were later added. At Confederation, responsibility for "Indian lands" passed to the government of Canada. In 1960, Ottawa formally designated the Pictou Landing

Map 2.1 Boat Harbour and Pictou Watersheds, Nova Scotia

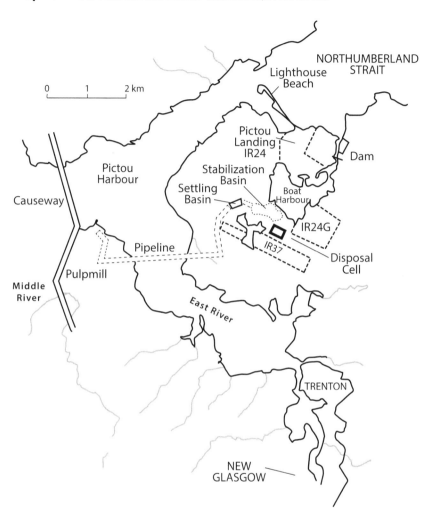

Indian Band as a band under the *Indian Act*. Today the band numbers about 560 members, three-quarters of whom live on the reserve.

Boat Harbour is a particular form of sub-watershed. It is fed by several fresh-water streams, and drains a surface area that is heavily forested with second- or third-growth spruce (the Pictou Landing First Nation have certified their lands as a sustainably managed forest by the terms of the Forest Stewardship Council). Until 1967 a defining geophysical feature was the connection of Boat Harbour to the ocean as a tidal pool. In assessing the subsequent impacts, it is important to keep this baseline in mind.

As with many Mik'maq communities, members pursued a variety of jobs in the urban and rural area. The Pictou Landing site had definite advantages. There was a clear spring for freshwater. Lighthouse Beach was a prime recreational area with its sheltered sandspit and a significant economic development opportunity for the band (a canteen was already in place). Jobs were also available at a nearby coal loading dock, and several band families maintained vessels in Boat Harbour and fished in the waters of Northumberland Strait. In the early 1960s this was about to change. The new power dynamics are explored in four stages below.

Part 1: Watershed Degradation at Boat Harbour—1965 to 1977

The provincial government led by Robert Stanfield was committed to attracting pulp and paper mills as tools of regional development. One of these was a sulphite pulp mill built on Cape Breton Island by the Swedish firm Stora Kopparberg and opened in 1962. It was followed five years later by the Scott Paper Company of Philadelphia, which opened a sulphate kraft pulp mill at Abercrombie Point, on the opposite bank of the East River from Pictou Landing. In both cases the government of Nova Scotia was prepared to offer major incentives to lure new international capital. This included concessionary stumpage rates for cutting crown timber as well as public infrastructure in support of mill operations (Sandberg and Clancy 2001). In the Scott case, the Stanfield government was prepared to virtually re-engineer Pictou Harbour to accommodate the mill at the desired site. To provide the necessary freshwater supply, it constructed a causeway across the harbour to contain the flows of the Middle and West Rivers. Furthermore, to relieve Scott of any effluent disposal costs or liabilities, the government agreed to take ownership of the effluent at the plant gate and to assume all downstream treatment and disposal obligations. These were sweeping government concessions; a fascinating series of original documents in this case can now be accessed and examined online (King's College n.d.).

The government of Nova Scotia then faced the problem of how to handle these new water use responsibilities. Of the two transactions (freshwater supply and effluent disposal), the 100 million litres (22 million gallons) per day effluent load was by far the more difficult. The Stora approach in Cape Breton, which initially relied on Atlantic ocean tidal flushing to disperse mill wastes, was not feasible in the shallower and marine-rich waters of Pictou Harbour and Northumberland Strait. Statutory authority for the water intake and outflow components of the Scott "package" fell to the Nova Scotia Water Commission as the licensing authority. Here, provincial officials identified Boat Harbour as the preferred site for a natural effluent settling pond. In an effort to secure their consent, the Band chief and a councillor were taken on a visit to Saint John, NB, and shown a sewage treatment plant with two open aeration tanks. Despite the stark differences between the Saint John facility and the proposed pulp effluent treatment set-up, this was presented to the Band leaders as an example of what could be expected at Boat Harbour. The Mi'kmaq were sufficiently convinced to

initial a handwritten consent with senior provincial officials over coffee, immediately following the site visit. As part of the deal, the province agreed to pay the
Band the sum of $65,000 as compensation for lost fishing opportunities and for
future use of the Harbour (Land and Sea 1988). There was also a commitment
to build a skidding ramp to move boats around the soon to be dammed outlet
of Boat Harbour.

When the Scott Maritime mill commenced production in 1967, a gravity flow pipe carried the chemical effluent across the bed of the East River to
Indian Cross Point. There it was released into an open ditch that fed into Boat
Harbour proper. On the first day, a ribbon of dark brown odiferous water laced
with sludge and foam arrived at the harbour, which instantly became a septic
lagoon by the blocking of its mouth at the outlet to Northumberland Strait. The
chemical inflow killed all aquatic life, and dead fish littered the shoreline while
the water level rose 2-3 metres to encroach on shore lands. The water entered
the lagoon at 33°C (91°F), which was too warm to allow outboard motors but
warm enough to prevent freezing in winter. In a short time the paint on some
of the community houses turned black. It was hardly surprising that local people
stopped visiting Lighthouse Beach the day after the effluent began to flow.

In the context of the power relations outlined earlier in this chapter, several
comments can be made. Note first the stark contrasts in allocating benefits and
costs. Hundreds of high-wage mill jobs, an enhanced rural timber supply economy, and an expanded municipal tax base benefited the dominant Euro-Canadian
society at the cost of the physical destruction of an Aboriginal band territory
and a gross defilement of its living environment. Second and equally striking is
the default by the government of Canada of its fiduciary obligation to the Band
under the *Indian Act*, given that reserve lands are held "in trust" by the federal
crown. The nondecision entailed in Ottawa's abandonment of the Pictou Landing
chief and council, in the face of the evidently compromised intent of the provincial water engineers, was a key step in facilitating the outcome. Furthermore, the
virtually fraudulent representations made by provincial officials in their presentation of the scheme in Saint John was a further abuse of public trust.

In 1971 several "upgrades" to the sewage scheme were launched. Two settling ponds were constructed where the ditch ended, and beyond that point an
aerated stabilization basin was built with a controlled outlet to the larger Boat
Harbour stabilization lagoon. The effluent would spend 12 hours in the first
phase, 8 days in the second, and 20–30 days in the lagoon before flowing into
Northumberland Strait. At this final point it was required to comply with new
federal pulp and paper effluent regulations. In 1974 a pipeline was built to replace
the open ditch flow of effluent as far as the settlement ponds, thereby removing
the crown liability for persons harmed while crossing Indian lands.

During this first phase, the mill operating system was embedded in the
Pictou Harbour watershed, with the plant on one peninsula and the treatment
facilities on another. In addition, a politically negotiated bargain dictated the legal

responsibilities of company and provincial government, with little reference to third-party interests. Key allocative choices often occur early in a decision process and become impossible to challenge thereafter. Mi'kmaq and non-native residents of Pictou Landing were marginalized and left disorganized and without allies for decades.

Part 2: The Band Challenges for Damage Done—1977 to 1995

After years of living with the bleak effects of the Boat Harbour chemical lagoon, the Pictou Landing Band began to review its legal options. Despite the extraordinary despoliation, the situation was far from straightforward. Should the challenge be directed at the federal crown (heavily compromised in the initial arrangement and in possible breach of its fiduciary responsibilities), the provincial crown (the agent of the Boat Harbour lagoon initiative and legal owner of the waste as well as potential perpetrator of fraud), or the Scott Paper Corporation? When the band approached the Scott mill, it was told that the effluent was provincial property. When it turned to the provincial government of Gerald Regan, departmental officials suggested a "political" approach. After two meetings with Attorney-General Harry How, the Band was told that any action would have to come from the federal crown and that the minister would not be meeting with them again.

Perhaps it is not surprising, given the initial alignments, that the Band felt its greatest affinity with the federal department of Indian Affairs and Northern Development (DIAND). The department, in turn, advised the Band to take action against the province and the company. After some delay in gaining the attention of federal lawyers, the Band convinced DIAND to enter a "partnership" to engage outside legal counsel. Although Indian Affairs was the client of record, the terms of the action called for the Band to be copied on all correspondence related to the case. In 1983, however, some inadvertent disclosures of federal correspondence (advising the law firm to hold back certain sensitive documents from the Band, and to exercise "discretion" in characterizing the federal position) led to a rupture. The Band engaged its own lawyer, E.A. Tony Ross, whose advice was to tackle the federal government first. An action was filed against Ottawa in Federal Court in 1986. Mi'kmaq prospects were strengthened by the Supreme Court of Canada's 1984 decision in *Guerin v. Queen*. The case confirmed the federal fiduciary responsibility to status Indians and awarded damages to British Columbia's Musqueam Band for breach of the federal trust responsibility in a valuable real estate deal.

After years of preliminaries and postponements, Ottawa opted for an out-of-court settlement in 1993, and agreed to pay $35 million. The proceeds were partly distributed to Band members as monthly back-compensation fees and partly paid into a trust fund, against the possibility that the Band would ever have to relocate its community. A section of the agreement covered joint health and environmental monitoring in the future. This resulted in a groundwater monitoring system with piezometer installations around the community and ongoing testing since 1993. It has been suggested that the Boat Harbour aquifer may be the most intensively studied formation in all of Canada. In any event, this became increasingly essential as the Band community grew in size and water needs.

The Pictou Landing Band's settlement with Ottawa marked a series of political turning points. For the first time, it altered the terms of legal and political advantage in favour of the Indians. Note that this was achieved by shifting the point of pressure from the bureaucracy to the courtroom. Not only did the settlement put significant new financial resources into the Band's control, it also enabled the Band to orchestrate positive and necessary resource management measures to begin containing the damage that had accumulated over almost a generation. Finally, it pointed the way toward continued political action.

Part 3: A New Vision for Boat Harbour Restoration—1995 to 2003

The government of Nova Scotia was not involved in the 1993 settlement, but as time progressed it became increasingly concerned for its potential liability. The province was, after all, the agent of both aquatic and terrestrial damage in the Boat Harbour drainage (solid waste from the settling facility had been deposited in volume on Band land adjacent to the aeration tanks). In addition, the province's effluent treatment contract with Scott was nearing expiry after 30 years, an uncertainty that might threaten the future of the mill. Finally, there were suggestions that Ottawa was considering a suit against the province to recover its $35 million outlay. The Band attempted to discourage Ottawa in this course and offered its good offices to seek a negotiated solution.

The shift in political leverage was confirmed in 1995 when the Pictou Landing Band reached an agreement with the province. With the Band's consent, the government of Nova Scotia renewed its treatment contract with Scott for an additional decade, to 2005. In turn, the province transferred the balance of the crown land around Boat Harbour to the Band (except for the polluted footprint of the treatment facility). Furthermore, the province agreed to stop the flow of any effluent into the harbour in 2005 and to remediate the harbour bed with the intent of restoring it to a tidal estuary accessible to boats. This commitment opened the prospect for wholesale habitat change. In the interim, the province agreed to construct an on-site landfill for solid wastes and to improve aeration in the harbour, while also lowering the water level to the mean high tide mark. Land thus recovered would also be cleaned up. With this agreement the Band opted for landscape remediation rather than continued litigation. It skillfully used the political leverage that became available, as the original pollution "bargain" evolved, to enlist the province in this aim.

This also opened the way for an accommodation with the third main protagonist, Scott Paper (acquired by Kimberly Clark Inc. in 1997). Looking beyond the 2005 deadline, the company faced options ranging from a new effluent facility, at an estimated $60–80 million capital cost, to mill sale, or closure and withdrawal. When approached by Kimberly Clark about possible terms of continuance, the Band once again moved to the bargaining table. The resulting 2003 agreement, the third major negotiated settlement, set out the terms for extended treatment operations following 2005. The company offered the Band a series of cash payments for 25 years as well as 1,600 hectares (4,000 acres) of timberland in Cumberland County. The legal point of discharge was shifted from the mouth of Boat Harbour to the aerated settling basin, with water effluent volumes reduced from 118 million litres to 72 million litres (26 million to 16 million gallons) per day. Finally, a pipeline would be constructed to carry the treated effluent (which already met federal standards) from the settling basin under Boat Harbour to the shoreline of Northumberland Strait, for release on the receding tide. All of this was compatible with the Band's goal, agreed on a best-efforts basis with Nova Scotia, to restore Boat Harbour to a tidal state (Nova Scotia 2003; Pictou Landing First Nation 2002). Over the course of four decades, the power status of the First Nation had changed dramatically—from unwilling victims of pulp mill construction to independent actors with extensive political leverage. However, bargaining is a fluid process and the terms of advantage and disadvantage can shift rapidly.

Part 4: The Bargain Unravels—2003 to Present

The context for political negotiation can change quickly if any of the major parties alters course. In the period following the 2003 deal, only the First Nation adhered to a consistent line. At the mill there were successive shifts of ownership as Neenah Paper bought out Kimberly Clark late in 2004 and was supplanted in turn by Northern Pulp in 2008. The new owners inherited the bargain described above and showed little commitment to its terms, resisting major capital outlays on treatment facilities at a time of weak pulp markets. On the government side, concerns arose when the direct pipeline/restoration plan was being prepared for federal and provincial environmental reviews. The federal Department of Fisheries and Oceans voiced reservations about the effects of removing settled toxic sediments from the Harbour and concerns about future eutrophication in Boat Harbour. In 2005 the province and Neenah Paper advised the First Nation that the pipeline installation was not a feasible option (Pictou Landing First Nation 2010).

This left open the question of what would happen after 2008 when the licence to discharge pollutants expired. Not coincidentally, Neenah had put the mill up for sale and the pollution treatment terms would figure large to any prospective buyer. In May 2008 the province decided, in confidence, that it would extend the discharge licence on a month-by-month basis. The following month the mill was purchased by a private equity firm based in New England and renamed Northern Pulp. Caught by surprise, the PLFN informed the province that it had a duty to consult on any discharge licence extensions. In December 2008, three provincial ministers met the Pictou Landing Chief and made a written pledge to close the Boat Harbour facility and build a replacement facility. Negotiations began in the spring of 2009 but ended abruptly after the New Democratic Party defeated the Conservatives in the June election. While the NDP minister of transport seemed to endorse the replacement strategy, no formal meetings were held for the balance of the year, as monthly licence extensions continued. Another NDP minister suggested that his government was not bound by their predecessor's commitment.

Events came to a head in March 2010 when the province announced more than $90 million in financial assistance to Northern Pulp, to purchase timberlands and upgrade air treatment systems. The First Nation considered this to be a double repudiation: the funds for alternate water treatment facilities, apparently deemed too great a burden for public support, could nevertheless be granted to the pulp mill to enhance its continued operations. In addition, the 1995 and 2003 deals were effectively nullified. The First Nation requested the province to terminate the pollution discharge licence by the end of June. When this did not occur, a court action was filed in September. In it, the Pictou Landing First Nation sought a declaration on continuing Aboriginal and treaty rights to traditional lands, riparian and littoral rights, the binding nature of the wastewater agreements, and the failure of the province to meet its constitutional duty to consult with and accommodate Pictou Landing (Pictou Landing First Nation 2010). This action is still ongoing at time of writing.

Power Relations at Boat Harbour: Yesterday and Today

Capturing the multiple dimensions of power relations is always a challenge. Here we approach it by contrasting the situation in the formative stages of the Boat Harbour degradation after 1967 and the situation in the more recent phases when designs for improvement and restoration were both offered and rescinded. It is useful to think of the power equation at any point in time as a multisided geometric shape whose complexity varies by the number of core interests and the substance of their ties. Each "side" connects a pair of these. In the 1960s, for example, one side involved the government of Nova Scotia deal with Scott Paper that made possible the original capital investment. This was a solidly entrenched relationship, rooted in the province's development agenda. Another side highlights the connection between the government of Canada and the Pictou Landing Band as a statutory trust relationship. Despite its constitutional foundation, this relationship was never championed by Ottawa. A third side links the government of Nova Scotia with the Band, in the form of the contractual release and compensation letter that were signed in the Saint John coffee shop. As seen above, some serious questions can be asked about the legitimacy of this deal. Notably, there was no formal instrument connecting the company and the Band. The final side links the two governments, provincial and federal. Once again there was no formal understanding, though the absence of federal advocacy on the Band's behalf underlines how a decision not to act can facilitate a power relationship as much as positive action can.

Because power is relational, it must be reinforced to be perpetuated and it can be modified in the face of new developments. The modern period takes shape in a series of steps beginning with the Band's legal challenge and the Government of Canada compensation agreement in 1993. This set in train a sequence of moves leading to the Government of Nova Scotia (GNS) agreement of 1995 and the commitment to restore the Boat Harbour tidal system. It continued with the Kimberly Clark agreement of 2003 on the terms of continued effluent treatment operations at Boat Harbour. Here the First Nation significantly enhanced its status by resort to the courts and the pollution discourse was redefined, with Mi'kmaq interests in restoration at the very centre. The province and the company were both obliged to make major concessions to maintain the mill. Here the decision instruments were negotiated agreements whose terms reflect the evolving power structure.

However, this new political bargain began to erode almost as soon as the terms were set. Declining pulp market conditions and shifting ownership gave leverage to the mill in its relations with the province. Evidence on the engineering and environmental options for alternative effluent disposal raised questions about negative impacts and raised questions of whether environmental impact licences could be secured. This led first to delays and, after the election of a new Nova Scotia NDP government, the abandonment of the 1995 and 2003 agreements by both government and company. This repudiation, coupled with the 2010 financial deal between the GNS and Northern Pulp, confirmed the extent of the power shift. The First Nation sought a new judicial remedy, grounded for the first time in Aboriginal and treaty right violations and failures of governments in their duties to consult.

Conclusion

In this chapter the concept of power has been elucidated and applied to several freshwater settings. Power is relational and social. It can be exercised in a variety of ways ranging from physical force to legitimate authority. In some cases it emerges from open contests among competing interests seeking to resolve an issue in their favour, in other cases it is manifest in nondecisions. In Canada, Aboriginal interests have suffered particular failures in the political system, evident in several centuries of continued disempowerment.

The Boat Harbour story is one example of a far wider set of aquatic pollution incidents in the pulp and paper and mining sectors. These cases began to accumulate in the nineteenth century and continue into the twenty-first. There seems to be a generic politics here, involving industrialists whose plants generate chemical effluents, federal and provincial crown authorities with legal jurisdiction over land and water use, and host communities. Key policy decisions reflect the power relationships among the key interests. Allocative decisions confer both benefits and costs on stakeholders. In any case, decisions may be visible or invisible, and interests may be organized or unorganized. Consistent patterns of policy decision imply structured power while mixed patterns of decision-making suggest shifting power. In this way, decision analysis offers a prism through which aquatic politics can be interpreted.

At Boat Harbour, we can see a range of power mechanisms at work. These are reflected in the occupancy and ownership of basin lands and waters. They are also evident in the relations between resident interests and outside interests. No watershed is politically self-contained, and the impacts of wider forces, both market-driven and governmental, can create profound impacts on local conditions. Political resources are unequally distributed. Contrast the capital possessed by Scott Paper, and the legal authority held by provincial and federal authorities, with the limited capacities of the Pictou Landing Band in the formative phase. Note also the impacts of changing judicial doctrine and emerging environmental science in reversing the initial bias and empowering the Band to a degree. Viewed politically, Boat Harbour demonstrates that power relations are integral to watersheds, large and small. These lessons carry over to future chapters.

3
Group Politics and Water

THIS CHAPTER EXPLORES THE ROLE OF organized interests in water politics. It begins by introducing some influential perspectives on group interests. This helps to clarify what we should be looking for to understand conflicts and policy choice, what is involved in getting organized, and what shapes and sizes collective interests can assume. Then the chapter turns to the case of Alberta's Athabasca River watershed. It is undoubtedly one of the most intensely contested waterways in Canada today (and it will reappear in chapter 10). The concepts presented here can be applied, in principle, to any freshwater issue or watershed. It is the mix of actors, the shape of issues, and the resulting power relations that will vary.

Group Interests and Policy Networks

The power of the individual should never be underestimated in politics. But neither should the power of the group. In political science, the 1960s was a decade when organized groups were rediscovered. At Yale University, researchers led by Robert Dahl asked the question "Who governs?" A series of case studies suggested that, in the city of New Haven at least, power was dispersed among a "plurality" of interests and that the particular cluster of engaged interests varied by policy or issue area (Dahl 1961). Viewed in this way, America seems a nation of organized groups. Not only did groups enhance democracy, by voicing public concerns and holding government accountable between elections, but, according to Dahl, the diversity of group voices and the crosscutting nature of group membership also served to moderate the intensity of political demands and to keep political agendas open to public debate. A theory of "pluralist democracy," bearing markedly optimistic expectations for democratic accountability, was extrapolated from this and subsequent work.

At the same time as the Yale studies took place, an experiment in watershed citizenship was unfolding in the Hudson River valley. This is a massive watershed in eastern New York state, with headwaters in the Allegheny Mountains and an industrialized lower section between Albany and New York City. At the time, the lower Hudson River was little more than an open sewer, with very little state regulation or private party responsibility. A focal event was the 1962 proposal by Consolidated Edison to build a massive power plant at Storm King, about 65 km upstream from Manhattan. The Scenic Hudson Preservation Council challenged the project's environmental impacts (including mass releases of thermal waters) and won. In 1966, fisherman and journalist Robert Boyle was instrumental in founding the Hudson River Fishermen's Association (HRFA) as a continuing voice for river defence. The group was able to take advantage of provisions in two longstanding federal statutes, the *Rivers and Harbours Act* of 1883 and the *Refuse Act* of 1899, that allowed private citizens to act as enforcement agents, collecting evidence and filing lawsuits against polluters (Boyle 1969).

Seventeen years later, the HRFA hired its first full-time river patroller. John Cronin was a former fisherman with political experience in Washington as a congressional aide. Organizationally, the concept of Riverkeeper was born—a privately funded watershed stewardship group with its own field presence on the river. Alongside this came an in-house legal capability through a link with the Pace University Environmental Litigation Clinic, where a dozen students and professors were engaged full time. Among the early actors here was Robert F. Kennedy Jr., who later became the chief prosecuting attorney for Riverkeeper. A third element in this advocacy model was the development of a popular network—of watershed residents, fishers, outdoorspeople, and community environmental groups—to serve as Riverkeeper's eyes and ears throughout the vast watershed. This network greatly enhanced the monitoring activity and triggered a rapid response capability (Cronin 1999).

Underlying the Riverkeeper philosophy of watershed defence was the understanding that polluters were enabled by the complexities of the legal process. This includes the near-prohibitive costs of legal challenges when mounted by individual citizens and the duration of commitment, measured in years rather than months, required to see a case from trial to appeal. However, an interest group with the expertise and capacity to stay the course could overcome these engrained disadvantages.

Beyond the courtroom, Riverkeeper outlined a powerful political program for watershed improvement: end fish kills and pollution to restore a damaged ecosystem, protect the key source of New York City drinking water, and broaden public access to the Hudson River through riparian improvements and public amenities. This remains an influential model of freshwater activism and pluralist politics. Today there are more than 120 Riverkeeper or Waterkeeper Alliance groups in the US and another 10 in Canada, along with a growing presence in the developing world (Waterkeeper Alliance n.d.).

By the 1970s, however, the theory of group politics was in flux and a revisionist critique was challenging the pluralist orthodoxy. Critics questioned many of the optimistic overtones of earlier studies. For example, how significant were the organizational barriers to group formation? Initially it seemed that the threshold costs were low: interest holders would come together, gather informational and financial resources, and join the policy debates that mattered most. Yet how, the critics asked, might the model change if interests were differentially endowed? Are capitalized business interests such as construction companies, power generators, and irrigation farmers better able to mobilize for politics than recreational users, neighbourhood residents, and naturalists? On another point, how prevalent were the diverse constituencies of rivalrous groups forecast by pluralism? Might it also be possible that more restricted sets of organized interests were engaged in lopsided contests that yielded consistently biased patterns of winners and losers? As E.E. Schattschneider famously remarked, "the flaw in the pluralist heaven is that the heavenly chorus sings with a strong upper class accent" (Schattschneider 1960, 35). Despite the innovative features of the Riverkeeper model on the Hudson, how many thousands of hinterland watersheds still await their conservationist champion?

Furthermore, might there be alternative channels of power-holding that bypass the interest group universe to deal with fundamental questions too significant for public airing? One particularly intriguing insight emerges from the notion of the "nondecision." Recall that the pluralist model stresses the importance of measuring power in terms of decision processes and their outcomes. Because every political decision is a sequence with a history, a set of participants, and a result, we can focus on the analysis of observable conflict on an issue-by-issue basis. In a hypothetical watershed, decisions might be taken on a variety of questions. These include whether to license the construction of a water supply reservoir; whether upstream commerce in logging or farming requires riparian regulation; whether fish habitat demands restorative measures; and whether factory effluent requires treatment before release. The pluralist approach will examine each such issue and establish patterns of power by mapping group preferences against decision results.

As mentioned in the previous chapter, Bachrach and Baratz argue that the observable interest group universe represents only one dimension of power. In the world of the nondecision, power is exercised by controlling what is admitted and what is excluded from the policy agenda. If threatening issues can be suppressed in advance, then the outcomes that pluralists highlight on the visible agenda tell only part of the story. Moreover, the capacity for issue suppression enables dominant interests to shape the political group landscape as well. Embryonic interests can be nipped in the bud if the issues around which they might mobilize do not see the light of day.

Another premise of pluralist theory that became increasingly shaky over time was that of the neutral or disinterested state authority. In the original models, groups initiated and governments responded. Moreover, the nature of the response was largely a function of the pressure vectors asserted by groups, as political leaders sought consensus by fashioning a path of least resistance among the most organized blocks. State officials, it was said, functioned like umpires or even weather vanes, measuring and then reacting to aggregate group claims.

The plausibility of this assumption came under challenge as decision-making case studies accumulated. Just as the size and shape of the interest group community varied according to issue-area, so too did the state institutions with which they engaged. The recognition of "interests of state"—forged and pursued by departments and agencies as part of their organizational mandates—forced a profound conceptual change. If a minister, a department, or an agency came to an issue arena with prior vested interests, then the game was entirely different. State decision-makers were no longer simply reactive umpires but rather active players with agendas of their own. If so, group interventions would be screened in a different fashion, through the filter of agency interests. Analytically, allowance needed to be made for group-state solidarities expressed not simply as advocacy but as clientelism or reciprocity or state dominance as well.

In US water politics studies this was recognized at a relatively early date. Arthur Maass (1951) highlighted the importance of the Army Corps of Engineers as the core administrative agency for river and harbour improvements. Helen Ingram (1969, 1990) established the central role of the US Congress in both legislating and budgeting for river flow activities. Daniel McCool (1994) explored the concept of "iron triangle" clientelism to western water issues, where the alignments among legislative, administrative, and corporate interests are assessed. Despite these seminal studies, much remains to be done to establish the patterns and variations of politics in the freshwater domain. While Canada lacks a water agency with the sweep of the Corps of Engineers, there is evidence of iron triangle-type dependencies in the irrigation and hydro-power sectors.

More generally, a wider generation of post-pluralist thinking absorbed these many insights, providing in the process more realistic political accounts. Interest groups and state authorities were conceptualized as joined together in "policy networks" (Pross 1992). The search for patterned relationships yielded new typologies of such networks. For example, a configuration of diverse and rivalrous groups, seeking to shape state decisions by means of policy advocacy, was described as "pressure pluralism." This recalled the classic formulation of multiple groups voicing their preferences from an orbit around the ultimate state decision-makers. Alternatively, in situations where the agendas of select groups converged with the agendas of decision-makers, a closer form of working relationship could be discerned as a type of "clientele pluralism." Here certain interest groups earn trust and confidence (put another way, privileged access) to the councils of state. Information can be exchanged, closed consultations made, and nondecisions executed. In some cases, state actors can even promote the establishment of new interest groups to champion desired interests. Yet another possibility involves issue areas where group organization is anemic and there is far less societal restraint on decision-makers. In such cases of "state autonomy" there is greater likelihood that the inner interests of institutions will define policy outcomes.

This suggests that a more accurate mapping of water policy networks rests on several propositions. First, we should recognize the possibility that interest groups are arrayed around state institutions in layered "orbits" of inner, middle, and outer proximity. The client groups are close partners while advocacy groups operate at greater distance. Some potential interests are not present at all, and their absence may be regarded as phantom interests with a political significance of their own. It may be that authority, as defined in the previous chapter, is exercised principally in the inner layers. Influence, on the other hand, may emanate from the outer orbits.

Second, the vectors of power and influence flow not just from groups to state but also from state to groups. In the United States, the Army Corps of Engineers has anchored policy networks for river public works for more than a century—dredging waterways, installing flood levees, and building lock and dam structures. In Canada, provincial departments of agriculture anchor policy networks for irrigated farming, departments of environment anchor networks for groundwater use, and state-owned electricity corporations anchor hydro-power networks. In sum, public authorities can sometimes choose which (if any) interests to recognize and to collaborate with. Governments can enhance the status of favoured groups while marginalizing others through ignorance or neglect. It is also possible to promote new groups and new group alignments to alter the political dynamics in an issue area.

Life Histories of Freshwater Interest Groups

Another insight into group politics follows from the recognition that not all groups are created equal. In seeking to explain variations in influence, we should also consider "institutional" differences. Paul Pross remarks that "institutionalization has the effect of linking a group's capacity to hear and respond to the demands of its members with its ability to carry those demands to the state" (Pross 1992, 95). It is useful to envisage a scale or continuum of organizational types. At one end are single-issue groups that spring up in response to a newly discovered concern. Sometime described as "embryonic" or "nascent" groups, these are often locally grounded and begin when concerned citizens gather to discuss an issue of mutual interest. In Sackville, Nova Scotia, in 1988, some members of a residential neighbourhood grew frustrated with the dumping of abandoned autos into the Sackville River. Their first group action was to enlist a tow truck and haul 50 submerged cars away to the wrecking yard!

If a satisfactory response is readily forthcoming, an issue may fade away and the group disperses. If, however, the struggle proves more difficult, then an interest group will find its commitment tested, as many prominent adversaries know that inertia can be a valued political tool in the face of unexpected challenge. Alternatively a single-issue group may, through its initial experience, redefine the objects of concern. Organizations that make this transition and show signs of longevity are sometime described as "fledgling" groups. Once the streambed was cleared of refuse, the Sackville Rivers Association (SRA) discovered that the federal Department of Fisheries and Oceans had declared it a legally dead waterway. Refusing to accept this outcome, the next challenge was to tackle the river's deeply degraded condition. The SRA moved forward with initiatives to promote habitat restoration, tree planting, and fish ladders. Twenty years later it is recognized as one of the leading citizen action groups in Atlantic Canada, and the Sackville River has made a significant recovery (Sackville Rivers Association n.d.).

Yet another organizational stage is marked by the arrival of a paid staff person and possibly also a permanent office establishment. This implies a quantum leap in the level of financial resources and functional capabilities and is sometimes denoted by the term "mature." Deployed effectively, even a single staff member can energize a dedicated network of volunteers. For the Hudson Riverkeepers, this moment came in the early 1980s when they recruited the first river patroller. For many advocacy-oriented NGOs, the move to a full-time presence is a challenging step. The single-staff office is a complicated operation—demanding a variety of skills ranging from fund-raising to publicity to planning to operations. It requires networking and lobbying and mobilizing members, spending more time in the field than at the desk. A basic level of "core funding" may be gained through government outreach programs or private sector or foundation sponsorship.

For example, in 1991 Environment Canada decided to promote a network of local watershed public interest groups, throughout the four Atlantic provinces, which became known as the Atlantic Coastal Action Program (ACAP n.d.). There are presently 15 such groups along with three "ecosystem initiatives." While continued affiliation is to some extent performance-based, the initial conferral of ACAP support serves to elevate the chosen groups to new operational levels. It finances a full-time director and provides project funding. At the same time, the ACAP guidelines require that an affiliate function as a stakeholder forum with ties to a variety of regional water groups. In many cases, ACAP was a vehicle to raise local groups from fledgling to institutional status, and the Sackville Rivers Association was one of these.

Sometimes the transition from a purely voluntary structure to a more formal one is accomplished when several local or community groups come together to form an umbrella association. Consider the case of the Nova Scotia Salmon Association (NSSA). It was established in 1963 by a group of avid anglers who were concerned about the damage that a proposed hydro dam would inflict on Gold River salmon stocks. Further local (river-based) affiliates gradually joined, for a total of 25 today. In 1985 the NSSA became a regional council of the Atlantic Salmon Federation, whose membership stretches across New England and Atlantic Canada. Over time several programs have emerged. First and foremost is salmon conservation work, which can occur at all levels. In addition, the NSSA engages in policy advocacy. There are also field programs ranging from Adopt-a-Stream restoration efforts to remedial work in acidified habitats to River Watch monitoring and the Fish Friends school education efforts. While the NSSA is still largely driven by its volunteer board and activists and raises funds internally, government agencies also play a critical role. Adopt-a-Stream, for example, is underwritten by a $200,000 annual allotment from the provincial government's Inland Fisheries Branch, based on a portion of the provincial licensing fee (Nova Scotia Salmon Association, n.d.).

From an organizational point of view, the "fully institutionalized" interest group represents the most fully elaborated category. It combines independently generated financial resources with significant pools of technical and policy expert staff. Business interest groups are classic examples here, in the shape of large corporations or the trade associations that speak for groups of firms in particular industries. For example, the Canadian Dam Association speaks for operators of large dams and promotes responsible practices and management as well as representing the "dam community" in policy circles (Canadian Dam Association n.d.). The Canadian Bottled Water Association was established in

1992 to advance the collective interests of bottlers, equipment suppliers, and distributors in the field. Members account for 85 per cent of the product sold in Canada today.

Institutionalized groups need not be "for profit" corporations. The Canadian Water Resources Association is a professional and public lobby for conservation and sound management. However, it originated, in a very different context, as the Western Canada Irrigation Association that was established in the 1890s to promote farm water supply in southern Alberta. Part and parcel of this was the application of engineering science to irrigation systems. In the post–World War II period, the group recognized the limits of the original mandate and opened itself to public and professional membership committed to conservation of freshwater in general (Mitchell and de Loe 1997).

The "types" of interest groups described above can be arranged on a continuum of organizational development. Table 3.1 suggests some defining features for each type, together with examples. It includes some of the actors described above, as well as references to how one organization, the Hudson Riverkeepers, evolved through time. Finally, the table identifies some of the groups that will appear in the Athabasca watershed case study below.

Despite the underlying theme of organizational advancement, I do not mean to suggest that all groups follow a linear pathway from nascent to fully institutional. Many groups find a level that "fits" with their situation and remain there. Other groups flame out and disappear. Pross (1992, 99) cautions that "groups may develop along the continuum but it is quite possible that they could regress as group characteristics change, policy capacity diminishes or even institutionalization dissipates." As seen in the examples above, the road to institutional maturity is neither inevitable nor desirable for all interest groups.

The Stakeholder Conundrum

In the 1980s, the perceived problems of a flawed water pluralism collided with the emerging social sustainability debate and delivered a new discourse of interest-based participation in terms of stakeholder democracy. There were several causes for this. First, new currents of environmental policy called for disciplined impact assessments of major commercial projects ranging from mines and mills to dams and pipelines. Explicit in this was the need to address not simply the project design but also its external impacts on third-party actors, a community that had been largely ignored in the past. The formal processes of impact assessment became, in effect, political subsystems that combined technical fact finding and adversarial representation, a volatile new combination.

Second, the rise to prominence of integrated watershed management (IWM) practices placed a premium on enabling the full range of drainage interests to participate. In effect, IWM grapples with multiple uses and involves prioritizing needs and apportioning shares. Here, too, it was an article of faith that broad stakeholder involvement (as the new terminology put it) was a prerequisite. Accordingly, the new sites of political adjudication were the planning processes, advisory forums,

Table 3.1 Continuum of Interest Groups

	Nascent	Fledgling	Mature	Fully Institutionalized
Defining features	Triggered by issue or controversy No prior organizational framework for politics Charismatic leadership and dedicated volunteers	Recognizes need to coordinate policies on multiple issues Addresses need for organizational continuity Still short-term and issue-based focus	Achieves ongoing capacity for policy interventions Greater organizational complexity including expanding professional staff role	Highly differentiated organization and hierarchy Creates a "normative order" with values inscribed in organizational structure Greatest potential to secure access, exert expert influence, and acquire administrative roles
Examples	Antigonish Harbour Watershed Association	Sackville Rivers Association Ottawa Riverkeeper	Nova Scotia Salmon Association Ecology Action Centre	Canadian Water Resources Association Canadian Dam Association Atlantic Salmon Federation
Group: Riverkeeper	Scenic Hudson Preservation Council, 1962–	Hudson River Fishermen's Association, 1966–	Riverkeeper, 1980s–	Riverkeeper, 1990s– Waterkeeper Alliance
Watershed: Athabasca	NE Wild Alberta Coalition Athabasca River Basin Coalition 16 local groups	Oil Sands Environmental Coalition Keepers of the Waters	Pembina Institute	Cumulative Environmental Management Association Suncor, Syncrude, Al-Pac

Source: Adapted from A. Paul Pross, *Group Politics and Public Policy*, 2nd ed. Toronto: Oxford University Press, 1992.

and regulatory deliberations. During the 1970s, as water basins emerged as candidates for integrated resource management in Canada, some government agencies explored an "interest-based approach" to public participation and watersheds (Mitchell 1975). Out on the radical edge, discussions involved the prospects for stakeholder "co-management" of resources alongside state administrative agencies.

Third, the United Nations social and environmental agencies strongly promoted an expanded role for nongovernmental interests in their deliberations. In part this took the form of screening and "accrediting" NGO actors to UN bodies. Perhaps more than any other source, the UN World Commission on Environment and Development (the Brundtland Commission) established the context for new "multi-stakeholder" governance structures. Later, the 1992 Rio Conference on Environment and Development endorsed Agenda 21, an environmental charter that went further by specifying "major groups" or "key stakeholder" categories. These included women, youth, Indigenous Peoples, NGOs, business and industry, workers and trade unions, science and technology industries, farmers, and local authorities (Hemmati 2002, 3).

While such thinking was viewed generally as a progressive development, insofar as it broadened political debates, it also carried a potentially awkward problem of which stakeholders to sanction. The Agenda 21 list was indicative rather than binding, yet its presence in a United Nations instrument added a definite patina of prestige. Perhaps even more significant was the question of at what stage should stakeholder deliberations be inserted into a decision process? The conundrum arises from the prospect of a modified form of "pluralism," installed at the initiative of state authorities and convening a weighted forum of organized interests. Such an arrangement seems to fall somewhere between the unregulated advocacy of pressure pluralism and the more transactional solidarities of clientele pluralism. Of greatest concern, perhaps, is the danger that it reproduces, in a new guise, the flaws of its antecedents.

Water Politics at the "Netroots"

The notion of grassroots politics is well known—it involves individuals getting active on the ground, close to the level where things begin to grow. Over the past decade, however, a new political dimension has emerged in the form of the "netroots." Rather than face to face, discussion flows from keyboards and smartphones as strangers explore shared interests and differences through the World Wide Web, texting, and Twitter. Journalist Matt Bai was an early analyst of internet-driven movements in the United States, identifying such signal actors as moveon.org, America Coming Together, the Howard Dean primary campaign of 2004, social networks such as Facebook, and alternate (blog) media such as the Daily Kos (Bai 2007).

This now applies equally to freshwater politics, where it is possible to orchestrate lobby campaigns, build issue coalitions, and raise funds with unprecedented speed. Virtual political communities are now a force to be reckoned with. The animators and idea factories are the online organizations themselves. For example, blueplanetproject.net describes itself as "an international civil society movement begun by the Council of Canadians to protect the world's fresh water." The central values and cognitive "frame" for this campaign are those of water democracy. As Vandana Shiva (2002, 34–36) puts it, water is "intrinsically different—it is nature's gift and all species have a right to a share, on a sustainable basis." This leads Blueplanetproject to campaign, among other initiatives, for a UN treaty on the right to water.

Some additional examples help illustrate the potential range. In the United States, the Clear Water Network brings together more than 1,200 organizations at varying spatial scales to "keep the promise of the federal Clean Water Act." In Canada, the Polaris Institute has built its water program around an "Inside the Bottle Campaign." This opposes the commercial bottled water industry and seeks to revive and restore publicly owned infrastructure. It monitors local initiatives to ban disposable drinking water sales on a worldwide basis.

While Internet advocacy has become a formidable element in contemporary water politics, it is important to remember that watersheds still play a significant role in defining community boundaries and shaping group relations. This does not mean that resident interests predominate, but it does provide them with legitimate claims to participate. This should be evident below, as we explore a politically contested watershed in northern Alberta.

CASE STUDY: GROUP POLITICS IN THE ATHABASCA RIVER WATERSHED

To illustrate the patterns and variations of freshwater interest groups and policy communities, this section explores Alberta's Athabasca River basin. The longest river in the province, it rises at a Rocky Mountain glacier and flows 1,231 km in a northeasterly direction before emptying into Lake Athabasca. The drainage takes in 95,300 km^2, an area almost double the size of Nova Scotia. Along the way, the river flows through mountains and foothills, grazing and farm lands, and the forested north. It has been a fur trade route, a river highway, a factory feedstock, and the hydrologic foundation of a vast wilderness. The Athabasca is also a political conundrum—how can a river that rises at the Columbia Icefields in the Rockies be implicated in severe health problems of the Fort Chipewyan Aboriginal peoples, at the river's mouth? The watershed is illustrated in Map 3.1.

Beginning in the 1960s the lower (i.e., most northerly) half of the basin assumed new economic significance as a petroleum-producing region. The Athabasca oil sands represent a massive but unconventional petroleum source. Below the surface, in deposits of variable depths and hundreds of kilometres breadth, lies a world-scale bitumen resource. This has long been known to geologists but had little commercial significance until relatively recently. Alberta was already well endowed with more accessible conventional crude oil, the development of industrial technologies for separating sands and heavy oil proved complicated, and the production costs at the oil sands far exceeded world crude prices.

Map 3.1 Athabasca River Watershed, Alberta

In 1967 the Great Canadian (now Suncor) oil sands plant opened at Fort McMurray. The second producer, Syncrude Canada, followed a decade later (Pratt 1975). The OPEC-led oil price shocks of the 1970s gave added impetus to oil sands prospects but this faded with the energy price slide after 1982. However, an unprecedented oil sands rush began in the late 1990s. In what Ian Urquhart has described as "the second coming," dozens of energy consortia took up licences and announced investment plans for mines, upgraders, and refineries in the area around Fort McMurray (Urquhart 2006). This was driven, in good part, by the oil sands royalty incentives of 1996 provided by the provincial government of Premier Ralph Klein. In short order, Fort McMurray emerged as Canada's leading frontier boomtown, and incoming investment fuelled not only provincial but national GDP gains. When Prime Minister Stephen Harper trumpeted Canada's emergence as a "global energy superpower," it was oil sands production (present and future) that he had principally in mind. In short, oil sands development became entrenched in both provincial and federal economic strategy for the 2000s.

Not surprisingly, an extensive array of interests impinges on oil sands environmental policy. The earliest residents historically were the First Nations peoples of northeast Alberta whose use of the land has been acknowledged both in Treaty No. 8 and in modern Aboriginal rights law. Today the five bands in the basin (Athabascan Chipewyan, Fort McKay, Fort McMurray, Chipewyan Prairie, and Mikisew Cree) work together for political purposes as the Athabasca Tribal Council. First Nations assert interests in a variety of issues ranging from community health and welfare, business development, resource sector employment, and political advocacy. Since 2006, the Council has been a prime mover in the "Keepers of the Water" campaign to achieve public watershed governance in the Athabasca basin as part of a wider campaign in the Arctic drainage region as a whole (Keepers of the Water n.d.).

Business capital has also played a prominent role in Athabasca politics ever since the arrival of the merchant traders in the 1700s. Indeed, most of today's townsites began as trade posts at the mouths of key rivers. In the latter half of the twentieth century, however, it has been the modern resources of pulp and paper and petroleum that have predominated. Five major pulp mills operate in the upper half of the watershed, including facilities at Hinton (West Fraser), Whitecourt (Millar Western), and the town of Athabasca (Al-Pac). The Hinton pulp mill was the first to open in 1957 and Al-Pac was the most recent in 1993. An intense political debate surrounded the proposal for the Al-Pac mill—the largest in Canada at the time. The scale of the environmental impacts was intensely contested. The recommendations of a joint federal-provincial review panel were bypassed by the Alberta provincial government to speed mill construction (Pratt and Urquhart 1994). This episode, incidentally, saw the provincial cabinet overrule the recommendations of environment minister Ralph Klein, whose conversion into an all-out commercial booster can be charted from that time.

In the lower basin the oil sands hold sway. The first generation of oil sands production involves open pit mines, whose giant excavators and trucks convey raw sands to the crushing and separating plants. In 2013 there were four producing oil sands mining complexes in the Fort McMurray region (Suncor, Syncrude, Albion Sands, and CNRL) with others under construction. A second technology is used for deeper-lying oil sand deposits. This is known as in situ extraction or steam-assisted gravity drainage (SAGD). Networks of underground pipes heat the sands and convey the viscous oil to the surface for processing. At the time of writing, oil sands mining still outproduces the in situ sector, though long-term projections point to in situ as the dominant extractive technology (Oil Sands Developers Group 2012). While each firm or consortium pursues its particular corporate interests in dealing with state agencies, they can also work through industry associations such as the Canadian Association of Petroleum Producers (CAPP) or the Forest Products Association of Canada (FPAC).

Another conduit of community interests is local government. The Regional Municipality of Wood Buffalo encompasses the northeast corner of the province. Prior to the oil sands takeoff, it consisted of a half dozen small settlements. Then Fort McMurray emerged as an urban growth pole, whose population quadrupled to 31,000 in the decade to 1981 and has since more than doubled again. It is the fifth largest urban concentration in the province. In 1995 the city was folded into the new regional municipality, which enables the greater oil sands region to be administered as a common local government unit. Across the broader Athabasca watershed there are another 17 local authorities, both towns and rural munici-palities, with water interests in the basin.

The environmental advocacy sector for the Athabasca watershed combines several types of groups. An early voice was the Friends of the Athabasca, es-tablished in 1988 to demand a comprehensive environmental assessment of the Al-Pac proposal and to defend the Athabasca watershed. Given the northern and wilderness character of the region (including Wood Buffalo National Park), con-servation voices ranging from the Alberta Wilderness Association to the Canadian Parks and Wilderness Society (C-PAWS) are active. Advocating from another perspective are the groups centred on oil sands matters. The Pembina Institute is a highly regarded energy policy centre that combines research, consulting, and advocacy on sustainable energy. The World Wildlife Fund–Canada (WWF-C) is a regular partner with Pembina on matters of oil sands pollution, including the recent *Under-Mining the Environment: Oil Sands Report Card* (Pembina Institute and World Wildlife Fund–Canada 2008). Pembina is a longstanding member of the Oil Sands Environmental Coalition, along with the Toxics Watch Society of Alberta and the Fort McMurray Environmental Association. EcoJustice (formerly Sierra Canada Legal Defence) and Environmental Defence are also heavily en-gaged in oil sands advocacy.

There are also regional conservation groups based in different reaches of the Athabasca River and its tributaries. Take for example the Athabasca Bioregional Society based in the upper watershed at Hinton. The group was formed in 1997 following an acrimonious series of public hearings related to the Cheviot coal mine proposal. Founding activists sought to promote better watershed aware-ness and engagement in west Athabasca communities. In the early 2000s, the Hardisty Creek restoration project was launched, and a few years later the group drew attention to the threat posed to the Little Smoky Woodland Caribou herd by habitat loss through logging and pipelines. However, the struggle to list the herd as endangered and to set aside a protected area has been long and arduous. Regional or tributary watershed groups are not uncommon in large drainages like the Athabasca. The 2005 provincial directory of water stewardship groups listed 16 for the basin, and this is not exhaustive.

An inventory of watershed interest groups reveals a striking range of players, but how do they interact as an ensemble? As seen earlier in the chapter, the policy network concept situates groups in relation to state authorities. In a recent study of oil sands interests, Hoberg and Phillips (2011) argue that, in the initial operating decades, the shape of the policy network was closed and bipartite. Corporate actors enjoyed privileged access to provincial state authorities on industry policy matters, and nonindustry interests struggled ineffectively from the periphery. Beginning in the 2000s, however, a wider range of groups gained access, particularly through multi-stakeholder forums. NGOs drew national and international attention to oil sands environmental issues ranging from greenhouse gas emissions to watershed contamination. This was captured in a "dirty oil" narrative that by 2010 was assuming international proportions. Traditional government tactics of denying problems and dismissing socio-environmental criticisms proved increasingly inadequate. Hoberg and Phillips note the resultant shift in political tone as "'dominant actors play defence' when closed systems face the threat of conflict expansion strategies" (2011, 508). Several multi-stakeholder bodies were created in the 2000s, though they fell well short of transformative impacts. Since 2010 there have been signs of more basic political reordering. The security of international bitumen markets has been called into question by the formidable environmental opposition to the Keystone XL and Northern Gateway export pipelines. The next section describes how such changes are reflected in Athabasca watershed politics.

Oil Sands Environmental Politics

It was inevitable that an industrial transformation on the scale described above would impose extraordinary physical and social stresses on the lower half of the Athabasca river basin. The extent of the mining operations are difficult to fully convey, but it may capture the scale to note that the open pit mines and tailing ponds stand out clearly on satellite photos from space. Four dimensions deserve special note. One is the impact on the surface drainage as the mineable sand deposits are stripped of surface cover, excavated, and processed. A second is the volume of water withdrawn from the river to fuel steam separation of the bitumen, and the impact of these withdrawals on the flow regime. The third is the impact of stored mine wastes, which have been collecting in tailings "ponds" for more than 40 years and leaching chemical residues into both the groundwater and surface drainage at Fort McMurray. Finally there is the health impact of oil sands operations on downstream communities.

Surface Drainage: Since the 1970s, environmental impact assessments (federal, provincial, or jointly sponsored) have been central tools supporting policy decisions on major resource extraction projects. An EIA is generally triggered by law where a government licence is required for the project to proceed. For example, the fish habitat damage entailed in TrueNorth Energy's proposed Fort Hills oil sands mine sparked a federal Department of Fisheries and Oceans review. In this case DFO opted for a narrow technical assessment of the destruction of Fish Creek rather than a comprehensive assessment of the overall project. (This choice was challenged in federal court, unsuccessfully, by a coalition of environmental groups.) On another level, concern has been raised over the flaws of conducting project-by-project assessments as opposed to the cumulative impact of successive projects. Following a 1997 suggestion by the Alberta Energy and Utilities Board (AEUB, the powerful provincial regulator), the oil sands firms joined together to establish the Cumulative Effects Monitoring Association (CEMA). This "industry-led multi-stakeholder group" includes governments, First Nations, and environmental NGOs, or ENGOs (Urquhart 2006). However, more than a decade elapsed before CEMA was able to advance criteria for cumulative assessment, a period in which multiple oil sands projects won approval and began construction. This period of delay, or nondecision, in gearing up the CEMA structure is politically telling. In part because of this, the CEMA was widely viewed as a corporate front in the wider public context. By 2012 a long list of oil sands projects had begun construction, with another list licensed but pending, and all without a disciplined analysis of their cumulative impacts on watersheds, airsheds, and terrestrial habitats (Oil Sands Developers Group 2012).

Water Withdrawals: A second policy subsector involves water withdrawals from the Athabasca for industrial use. Bitumen production is water-intensive and production is ongoing. The oil sands mining sector accounted for four-fifths of water inputs in 2011. While both techniques recycle at least 40 per cent of industrial water, mining operations use a net 2–4 barrels (bbl) of water to extract and upgrade 1 barrel of bitumen while in situ operations use less than half that volume (Pembina Institute 2013). As the number of plants scales up, questions arise about the cumulative impacts of these withdrawals and their impacts on the seasonally variable watershed flow regime. One response was supply management, and the Athabasca River Water Management Framework was announced in 2007. Under pressure from science studies and ENGOs, Alberta Environment (in concert with federal Fisheries and Oceans) released an "interim" management framework aimed at regulating cumulative oil sands water withdrawals according to flow conditions in the river (Alberta Environment 2007). The first phase of this scheme declared that oil sands producers would be obliged to share a finite magnitude of water withdrawals and that the level would be geared to weekly flow conditions in the Athabasca. When flows met or exceeded historic levels (the green status), an apportionment of up to 15 per cent could be authorized. When conditions dropped to natural low flow levels (yellow), withdrawals would be limited, and when lows were severe, total withdrawal would be restricted.

Waste Management: A third policy concern is the polluting impact of oil sands operations on both the flowing river and the groundwater. Here attention centres on the impacts of the extensive tailings ponds, at present covering 130 km², that contain waterborne wastes from refining. The ENGO Environmental Defence estimated that more than 11 million litres leak from these "ponds" into the environment each day (Environmental Defence 2008). The most graphic of these is Suncor's Tar Island Dyke, which stands 92 metres high immediately adjacent to the Athabasca River. Because oil sands companies self-monitor groundwater contamination and the provincial government treats the data as confidential, there are at present no comprehensive site-based data on levels of toxic pollution passing into groundwater and from there on to the river. At the time of writing, scientific opinion can be described as divided. Some preliminary academic studies (Schindeler et al. 2007; Kelly et al. 2009, 2010) found evidence of mounting contamination. Yet a 2010 review sponsored by the Royal Society of Canada judged the data insufficient for firm conclusions, on water pollution at least (enhanced monitoring was, however, called for). In the past, neither CEMA nor the Alberta government disclosed their water monitoring field data to the public. Late in 2010 an expert panel appointed by the province outlined a roadmap for enhanced water monitoring on the Athabasca (Oil Sands Advisory Panel 2010). After further review, Alberta accepted recommendations for an independent monitoring agency and was joined in this by Ottawa.

Among the issues to be addressed in future is the safe storage of contaminated oil sand tailings. In 2012 CEMA submitted a proposal for long-term storage as part of restoration planning. The centrepiece is 30 "end pit lakes" that will be created in exhausted open pit mine sites. The tailings will be deposited on the bottom and will be "overtopped" by a freshwater cap, becoming a permanent feature of the landscape. Although this design is entirely untested in the oil sands and the first prototype is still under development, the industry has put it forward as a conceptual alternative to the current temporary tailing ponds (CEMA 2012).

Community Health: One final political framing process can be seen in the health threat narrative involving toxicity in the Athabasca River and the illness levels detected downstream at Fort Chipewyan. A local physician in the community since 2001, Dr. John O'Connor began to raise concerns about the apparent high incidence of cancers among his patients. The profile of illness among his 1,200 local patients contrasted significantly with the 9,000 he had serviced in a prior practice at Fort McMurray. For years, Fort Chipewyan hunters and fishers had complained about fish deformities, oil films on water, foul-tasting meat, and muskrat and duck population losses (O'Connor 2009). Beginning in 2006, O'Connor's efforts to persuade federal and Alberta health officials to launch studies was met with denial and delay. The following year, Health Canada officials launched a complaint against O'Connor with the Alberta College of Physicians and Surgeons. The allegation, consistently rejected in the community, was that O'Connor had created "undue alarm" by scaremongering among the public. In the meantime, field studies of water quality confirmed that the Athabasca carried abnormal concentrations of arsenic, mercury, persistent aromatic hydrocarbons (PAHs), and other toxins. Though no professional complaints were upheld, the continued harassment led O'Connor to relocate to Nova Scotia in 2009, though he continued to travel to northern Alberta to provide back-up service in Fort MacKay and Fort Chipewyan. Following years of punitive harassment and denial, government health officials agreed to launch studies in 2008, though the slow pace of action has been questioned. Furthermore, the Alberta Cancer Board found cancer rates 30 per cent above the norm and declared in 2008 that the health bureaucracy had been wrong to provide unsupported assurance to Fort Chipewyan in previous years (Nikiforuk 2008).

From Laggard to Leader?

In the past decade, the government of Alberta has overhauled its freshwater management system in dramatic ways. It shifted from a laggard (Premier Ralph Klein
allowed staffing at the water management branch to atrophy in the 1990s) to a
leader. The centrepieces here are the *Waters for Life* (WfL) strategy unveiled in
2003 and the *Land Stewardship Act* of 2008.

At the core of the WfL vision is the system of Watershed Planning and
Advisory Councils (WPACs) that were organized in major watersheds and sub-
watersheds (11 to date). Their mandate is to assess basin conditions and develop
plans and actions for management (Brownsey 2008). For the Athabasca, several
hundred potential stakeholders were identified and, following an initial conference,
Alberta Environment recognized and began funding the new Council in 2010.
The Council has a 15-member stakeholder board constructed on a sectoral basis,
with three persons drawn from each of the Aboriginal, governmental, industry,
NGO, and "other" sectors. WPACs are nonprofit organizations in which membership is open to any watershed resident sharing conservation goals. There are two
designated tools for council action. To begin, a state of the watershed report—a detailed technical compilation of conditions across the watershed—must be prepared.
This is intended as the foundation for an integrated watershed management plan
to guide ongoing activities. In 2010 the Athabasca Watershed Council (AWC) began work on its state of the watershed report and this continues at time of writing.

There is also a public involvement component in WfL in the watershed
stewardship groups. These are local volunteer groups that propose water improvement projects for provincial government funding by the Alberta Stewardship
Network. Many of these local groups predated the WfL announcement, but they
can qualify as stewardship groups when they are awarded financial support (of up
to $7,500 per project). Projects range from river restoration work to educational
programs and water sampling. By the close of 2010 there were over 20 such
groups identified within the Athabasca watershed.

As Alberta's flagship freshwater policy initiative, WfL outlined a new approach
that aimed to address the management of water shortages, the growing threats
to water quality, and the necessity of basin-level planning. Its implementation,
however, raises another set of challenges. The fact is that WfL was not written
on a blank page but rather imposed on top of already existing water use and
management schemes. In each watershed there was a pre-existing power grid
consisting of organized interests with embedded claims and benefits. Indeed most
of these benefits were allocated on an ad hoc or incremental basis in the period
before holistic watershed systems were recognized as relevant. Both the privileged
interest holders and their marginalized counterparts face an opportunity and a
challenge to reposition under the new regime. The dimensions of adjustment can
be illustrated in two particular ways—the manner in which water interest groups
respond to the WfL structures, and the manner in which the broader provincial
government adapts to those same structures.

In a watershed such as the Athabasca, we have seen that the range of group interests is broad: local governments, business sectors, residents, First Nations communities, ENGO groups, and even the multiple government agencies delivering programs within the basin. Groups engage in political action by many avenues, and water management is only one of these. Furthermore, political agendas are fluid—priorities rise and fall according to the sequence of events: are water levels high or low, are new users demanding major shares of river waters, is there evidence of significant contamination, is community health at risk, what is the evidence on aquatic environmental quality? Furthermore, interests may operate at different scales, ranging from the local to the watershed to the province as a whole. In short, the constellation of interested actors in a watershed can be extremely complex.

With the advent of any new political structure, such as the watershed councils after 2006, groups have a choice whether to participate or not. The multistakeholder structure of the councils, as seen above, can guarantee a seat at the table for some, and a representative voice for others. Furthermore consensus-based rules of decision-making confer potential leverage on all participants. However, the benefits of participation are limited by the functions and powers available to a council, and if political priorities fall outside of state-of-the-environment reporting, the battle must continue elsewhere. In short, a watershed council offers a parallel path for action but is only one among many available pathways.

Consider a concrete example. In 2006 a grassroots initiative, the Keepers of the Water, emerged among First Nations communities across the Mackenzie drainage area, including the Athabasca but also neighbouring basins such as the Peace, the Cree, the Fond du Lac, and the downstream Mackenzie River. The first gathering was held at Liidli Kue (Fort Simpson) in the Northwest Territories, where the Deh-Cho peoples were increasingly concerned with water quality threats emanating from the downstream tributaries. Out of this, "Keeper" groups, including the Keepers of the Athabasca, were formed in each of the main drainage areas. At the second annual gathering, participants approved a goal for "a grassroots watershed plan for the Arctic Ocean drainage basin, bringing together First Nations, local citizens and community groups" (Keepers of the Athabasca 2008a). At the fifth Keepers gathering in 2011, at Lac Brochet, Manitoba, topics included regional watershed updates, Aboriginal rights to water, sturgeon as a species at risk, clean community water strategies, cooperative water management schemes, and adaptations to climate change.

Not only does the Keepers movement predate the Athabasca Watershed Council but it functions as a nongovernmental alliance of Aboriginal peoples, environmental NGOs, and communities. Its annual gatherings discuss issues across the drainage, combining field reports and political discussions while deepening the web of contacts between civil society groups. Clearly the representative base of the Keepers movement contrasts with the Alberta watershed councils. The issue agenda for the former is broader than the latter. There are differences in funding that favour the councils, though the Keepers have drawn effectively on support from national environmental NGOs. Furthermore there is evidence that the advocacy perspectives, the issue agendas, and the ultimate watershed management blueprints will differ in the two cases.

One measure of the Keepers/Council dichotomy can be seen in their frames of reference. While the Athabasca Watershed Council is confined to the Alberta portion of the river, the Athabasca Keepers deal with the entire drainage area of the river and the lake, including the Saskatchewan portions. Another point of comparison is the difference in philosophical grounding. The Keepers' statement of principles opens with the claim that "we are guided by both indigenous elders' traditional knowledge and western science" and follows with the claim that "we recognize that significant negative cumulative impacts are compromising the health and integrity of the Athabasca River and Lake watersheds." Their declared purpose is to "build capacity for informed and effective watershed stewardship and advocacy" (Keepers of the Athabasca 2008a). In other words, the Keepers fit into the advocacy group category outlined earlier in this chapter. For its mission, the Athabasca Watershed Council seeks to "provide, foster respect, and plan for an ecologically healthy watershed by demonstrating leadership and facilitating informed decision-making." The ultimate goal is "an ecologically healthy watershed while ensuring environmental, economic, and social sustainability" (Athabasca Watershed Council 2011). This will be accomplished through the formulation of technical reports and management plans under the WfL framework. The Council has been organized and funded in a top-down fashion by Alberta Environment, and may be classified as a clientele group.

In terms of public reporting, the Keepers moved more quickly than the Council. In 2008 the *State of the Athabasca Watershed* report offered an overview of watershed conditions to spur awareness and discussion. Compiled by C-PAWS (Northern Alberta) for the Keepers of the Athabasca, it drew together "currently available sources" in a 73-page document (Keepers of the Athabasca 2008b). The AWC's "State of the Watershed" report has unfolded in several stages with a geospatial overview in 2011 and a sub-watershed ecosystem pressure rating the following year.

In 2011 the Keepers of the Athabasca launched a "Keepers Watch" initiative. Part of this involved a toll-free hotline to enable residents to report their observations of disturbances (initially in the Pembina River tributary area). Another element was the designation of a local keeper representative for each tributary and reach of the river, to extend the network for "watching, responding, and protecting" (Keepers of the Athabasca 2011). The Keepers also inaugurated an annual "Healing Walk" at Fort McMurray to observe the effects of oil sands exploitation.

Just how the existence of the Keepers movement will affect the overall prospects of the Athabasca Watershed Council remains to be seen. In many respects they are parallel organizations that, despite nominally similar purposes, display contrasting institutional features.

In the years following the Alberta WfL launch, the momentum for management planning moved in a different direction. Proclaimed in 2009, the *Alberta Land Stewardship Act* sought to fill the gaps and tie together resource management programs by a series of regional land use plans that addressed cumulative environmental effects to land, water, and air. Reflecting the political urgency of oil sands issues, the Lower Athabasca River was selected as the initial pilot region. Three years in preparation, the Lower Athabasca Regional Plan began with government research and public consultations by yet another Regional Advisory Council. The government then prepared a draft plan that invited further public input before it was revised and then reviewed and approved by the Alberta cabinet in 2012 (Alberta 2012). The principal policy tools here are three "management frameworks" for surface water, groundwater, and air quality. These schemes explicitly acknowledge the need to take account of cumulative impacts and to tie regulatory decisions to warning triggers based on indicators. The Pembina Institute characterized the plan as a "promising start" though seriously incomplete. In a preliminary assessment, Pembina highlighted many of the key development levers yet to be grasped (Pembina Institute 2012).

It can certainly be argued that, at present, the rigour of environmental regulation of oil sands business fails to meet the most basic criteria of the public interest. At the same time, ENGOs have not succeeded as advocates, despite efforts to pressure the courts and provincial and federal ministers and legislatures. Here the counterweight is oil sands capital and the critical role it has played in reshaping the Alberta petroleum industry in the new millennium.

Earlier in the chapter it was suggested that certain kinds of fundamental policy decisions are of particular significance because they define the frameworks in which later decisions will be taken. Urquhart and others have suggested that just such a commitment to maximizing oil sands production predominates not only in Alberta energy management but also in Athabasca regional environmental issues (Urquhart 2006). It was affirmed by Premier Ralph Klein's 1990s royalty and tax strategy, designed to catalyze oil sands investment on a global scale, and Alberta's extraordinary campaign of opposition to ratifying the Kyoto protocol in 2002. This points to an implicit Alberta government compromise, accepting a significant level of environmental overload in one relatively isolated frontier river basin in return for a perpetual engine of macroeconomic prosperity. Nonetheless, there is considerable evidence since 2008 of revisionary thinking in Alberta government (and oil sands industry) circles. With the overall sustainability of both the resource and the watershed being questioned in the most fundamental ways, the environmental regulatory regime is being progressively redefined. For the foreseeable future, the Athabasca basin will be the epicentre of this ongoing battle.

Conclusion

Group politics is an integral part of a vibrant water politics, and interest groups can assume a variety of forms. It is important to be sensitive to group capacities and developmental potentials. In all likelihood, a government jurisdiction or watershed hosts groups at varying levels of institutionalization and these groups are poised on different trajectories. For political purposes, groups will focus their efforts on policy issues and will seek to bring a variety of resources to bear. The target of these advocacy and clientele efforts are state agencies with the legal and administrative power to make and implement decisions.

The Athabasca watershed is a fascinating example. It hosts a variety of groups seeking to shape water decisions at multiple levels. These range from the corporate resource extractive actors that have been authorized to use and alter water quantity and quality, to the rival freshwater users in municipal and First Nations communities, to the recreational and conservationist advocates concerned with the integrity of the Athabasca system. In the case of the Athabasca, we also see a variety of watershed issues, ranging from surface water withdrawals to industrial effluent disposal to community health concerns. These issues are confronted and resolved by a combination of decision-making and nondecision processes. The regulatory issues of the upper Athabasca watershed contrast with those of the lower watershed. Where the pulp economy predominates in the former, the oil sands threaten to overwhelm the latter. The proliferation of NGOs and other civil society groups is a crucial feature of recent decades. In the 2000s, the government of Alberta was increasingly forced to acknowledge and respond to issues of watershed integrity. Part of this involved efforts to channel and co-opt civil society groups. Part of it was motivated by the need to defend the province's dominant industry against its critics, on a global scale. The new watershed regime that is emerging on the Athabasca contains some potentially transformational elements. Whether this promise is fulfilled will depend, in part, on the direction of interest group politics going forward.

4
The Freshwater State

THIS CHAPTER BUILDS A PERSPECTIVE ON the role of state authorities in the freshwater sector. In some circles, "government" is regarded as a single actor with unified characteristics. Here, however, we suggest a different approach, where the state is a complex structure of many parts and functions. The key components are discussed below, with examples drawn from the freshwater field. It is one thing to identify the state structure but quite another to appreciate its impacts. The boundaries of state authority are constantly shifting. For example, since winning majority status in 2011, the Harper government has moved aggressively to curtail Ottawa's statutory role in freshwater environmental regulation; this story is described in a section below. Finally, chapter 4 highlights the role of provincial state intervention, with a case study of the Souris River watershed in southern Saskatchewan. Not only does the case speak to the complexity of decision-making on the Rafferty and Alameda dam projects but also the interplay between provincial and federal state subsystems and organized interests.

The State System

To this point, our focus has been on politics, power, and the role of organized groups in animating freshwater governance. Such topics point to another question. On what fields and by what processes do freshwater politics play out? In large part, the answer can be found in the notion of the modern state. What, then, is the state and what does it do?

There is no ready agreement on this but most analysts would concede that the state is distinguished by the attribute of sovereignty—the capacity to make binding decisions, backed by the threat of force, for social collectivities of varying scales. Thus we can speak about a national, regional, or local "state." It is a prominent though not exclusive site where political interests converge and authoritative outputs are issued. As has already been noted, a state is also a source of political interests in its own right, and we can speak of "interests of state" in this sense.

If a state is a sovereign actor, it must be structured to exercise such authority. This includes a set of fundamental rules and procedures, agreed in advance of political engagement, to channel the process. Typically these rules are spelled out in a constitution—a foundational law of special significance—and in statute law. These rules of the political game are important for structuring the behaviour of the players.

By nature the state is a hierarchical structure that weaves together the necessary elements for sovereign choice. But how can we conceptualize a state? One useful model was advanced by Ralph Miliband in *The State in Capitalist Society*. He describes a "state system" composed of multiple subsystems—executive, legislative, administrative, judicial, regional/local, and coercive. Each of these requires particular institutions, with their own particular logics. Each offers po-tential points of access for organized interests. Varying by case, these institutions combine in distinctive ways. Thus a state constitutes a complex field of political relationships which extends well beyond the boundaries of government alone (Miliband 1973).

The challenge here is to craft an interpretation of state institutions insofar as they govern the freshwater resource in modern Canada. We can begin by exploring each of Miliband's state subsystems. This reveals a freshwater state that is predominantly bureaucratic and federal in character.

Executive

To "execute" is to carry out or to make things happen. It implies leadership and top-down direction. In a Westminster-style parliamentary system (i.e., the one Canada inherited from nineteenth-century Britain) the power to decide major policy matters falls to the collective executive of prime minister or premier and cabinet. Following an election, the leader of the largest party in the legislature is invited to assume office as first minister and, together with appointed ministers, to advise the crown. So long as this executive retains the confidence of the legislature (gauged by successful passage of major policy proposals) it continues in office. Thus when we talk of the political executive, the group that provides senior leadership, it refers to an elite group of several dozen ministers.

Cabinet is a collective executive in the sense that it acts and speaks as one, but not all ministers are equal. The first minister is pre-eminent, followed by ministers holding central coordinating responsibilities as in financial or foreign affairs. Then there are ministers in charge of "line departments" that deliver more specialized programs in functional or clientele areas. Where the discussion turns to key fresh-water departments, they tend to be middle-tier, clientele-oriented organizations such as agriculture, fisheries, natural resources, environment, and transport.

As department leaders, cabinet ministers are expected to bring major new proposals forward to cabinet for collective decisions and to inject departmental concerns into cabinet-level discussions. In addition, each minister is empowered by existing statutes to take action within an assigned portfolio area. Consider the federal *Fisheries Act*, a powerful instrument that enables the minister (on civil service advice) to regulate fisheries and fish habitats in Canadian waters. This is achieved through a massive Fisheries and Oceans field bureaucracy, deployed across six regions with a variety of regulatory and scientific responsibilities.

Which ministers matter most on water matters? The answer shifts over time. In Canada at the time of Confederation, the Department of Marine and Fisheries was prominent. Then in 1870, after Canada purchased Rupert's Land from the Hudson's Bay Company, the federal minister of the interior held responsibility for all resources in the northwest hinterland. Later, in 1882, the public right of navigation was assigned to the minister of transport through the *Navigable Waters Protection Act*. With industrialization, the dominion resources department (which included federal forests, mines, and lands) assumed a role. It has gone under many names, from the initial Department of Interior to the current Department of Natural Resources or NR Canada. The 1970 *Canada Water Act* opened a tension between the dual portfolios of Fisheries and Resources. This revolved around rival paradigms—fisheries conservation for the first and watershed management for the second. The former prevailed. Not long after, the federal Department of Environment was established and subsequently consolidated its position as a "lead" federal freshwater department. It is worth noting that the inland waters program was only one branch (alongside atmosphere and terrestrial sectors) in the new department, and that successive Environment ministers were seldom more than intermediate stars in the cabinet firmament. The situation in the provinces (the other major freshwater authority) will be discussed in a later section.

Only occasionally do freshwater issues rise to the level of cabinet priority. However, each generation seems to have at least one prominent case. In the late nineteenth century it was fisheries and in the early twentieth it was hydro-electric power. In the 1930s it involved responses to the drought on the prairies and in the post-war period it was the St. Lawrence Seaway and strategies for flood control. Industrial pollution took centre stage in the 1970s, habitat protection in the 1980s, and environmental assessment in the 1990s. The provinces were also involved. Ontario promoted a system of watershed planning authorities in the 1940s and 1950s. British Columbia embarked on a hydro-electric building campaign in its interior in the 1950s while Quebec did the same in its northlands in the 1960s. Manitoba mounted a massive works program in the 1960s, to protect the city of Winnipeg from Red River floodwaters. Finally, a concern with unsafe drinking water exploded across Canada following the deaths from contaminated water at Walkerton, Ontario, in 2000.

At most times, however, freshwater issues may fly below the cabinet radar. Existing laws offer ministers and bureaucrats significant scope for operational programming and for incremental policy adjustment, without the need to go to cabinet. Instead the key political bargaining takes place between ministers with overlapping concerns, between ministers and departmental officials, and within the policy networks linking departments and interest groups. We have already seen several cases of this, with pollution at Boat Harbour and Athabasca River monitoring in Alberta.

Legislature

If the executive role is to provide leadership and direction, the legislative role is to enact laws. Under the Westminster model, the composition of Parliament divides into "government" and "opposition" parties. On the opposition side the contrast is between the "official opposition" (the second largest party) and other smaller parties. The logic of this system is that the governing party will propose policy initiatives and the opposition parties will critically react. Through debate and close study (sometimes including expert witnesses at the "committee" stage) Parliament can clarify and improve bills before passing them into laws. Thus it has been described as a policy refinery—able to make incremental improvements to the initiatives already defined at executive levels. A legislature has at least one additional important role in democratic accountability—calling ministers to account for the conduct of their portfolios.

Is freshwater susceptible to partisan treatment? Would we expect a conservative party strongly committed to private property, capitalist markets, personal liberty, and small government to have positions on freshwater resources that differ significantly from a centrist or a left-of-centre party that sees the need to regulate markets, redistribute wealth, and manage the utilization of resources? Historically, the answer is a qualified yes. Business-oriented parties of the right have often resisted the establishment of regulatory authorities and the infringement of private property rights in the name of resource conservation. Once established, however, these principles have been embedded in modern government and the debates often shift to matters of degree. Should fishing grounds be managed by private clubs or by a public bureaucracy? Should rights of water use be regulated on a first-in-time, first-in-right basis or should rights be allocated according to social priorities? Are water supply systems (or hydro-electric power generators) better run by private businesses or public utilities?

The Parliament of Canada has been the source of key statutes that set the legal framework for water management. The *Fisheries Act* (1868) was the first of these, but others have followed, including the *Navigable Waters Protection Act* (1882), the *Boundary Waters Treaty* (1909), the *Natural Resources Transfer Act* (1930), the *St. Lawrence Seaway Act* (1949), the *Canada Water Development Assistance Act* (1953), and the *Canada Water Act* (1970). All of these will be explored in greater detail in the chapters that follow.

The modern trend in Canadian politics is toward a decline of the legislature as a decision-making body, and stronger roles for the executive and the bureaucratic subsystems (Savoie 1999). In part this reflects the vastly greater complexity of modern policy problems and the need to rely on an expert civil service for advice. It also reflects the vast expansion of "subordinate legislation" in modern government. Most statutes include enabling clauses that empower the responsible minister to formulate more detailed rules and regulations to further the objectives of the act. For example, there are dozens of sets of regulations under the *Fisheries Act* making detailed provisions for catch limits, seasons, gear, and other fishing conduct; water pollution standards for polluting industry; and habitat protection rules. These are formulated by departmental officials and approved at cabinet by means of order-in-council. They can be altered by subsequent order without the need to return to Parliament for formal amendments to the act.

Before entirely dismissing the role of legislatures and their members, however, it is important to make some important qualifications. First, although a majority party enjoys a dominant position as government, relying on the support of its MPs to carry the day, this does not apply in a minority situation. Instead, when the largest party holds fewer than half of the seats in a legislature, it must attract support from opposition MPs to pass bills and maintain the confidence of the House. This obliges the government to be more pragmatic and open to compromise if it wishes to survive. Since half of the federal elections since 1957 have returned minority Parliaments (including those of 2004, 2006, and 2008), this is a familiar situation in Canadian national politics.

A second qualifier involves the role of House of Commons committees. These specialize in designated policy fields, and their membership reflects the party proportions in the House of Commons. Committees can examine proposed government bills and have the capacity to call expert witnesses ranging from ministers and bureaucrats to interest group spokespersons. When conducted effectively, they can enrich the policy debate and improve the draft legislation. Committees can also identify policy issues for investigation and go to the field to hold hearings and issue reports. For example, the House of Commons Standing Committee on Fisheries has published notable reviews of that resource on all three coasts, as well as reports on fish farming or aquaculture. In 2005, the Senate Committee on Energy, Environment and Natural Resources flagged the emerging water crisis in western Canada and probed the scope of the problem (Canada 2005).

The final qualifier involves the role of individual MPs as advocates and champions for local interests in their constituencies. This is sometimes described as an ombudsman role between citizens and governments. One ultimate test of policy is its impact on the ground at local levels. Here an elected member has the opportunity to assist in the resolution of local problems that will not otherwise reach the minister's (or deputy minister's) desk. This may involve winning funds for local works such as bridge repairs, water treatment or sewage facilities, or water monitoring or testing studies. It may involve grants to local water NGOs or getting administrative field staff to prioritize local concerns. While these are far from the high profile "big picture" projects preferred by ministers, they can be invaluable in community settings and can lead to tangible results.

Administration

The German social theorist Max Weber was a founder in the study of bureaucracy. Writing in the early twentieth century, he outlined an "ideal type" of modern administrative organization. Weber cited attributes of hierarchical control, specialized roles, rule-governed activities, and impersonal operations as secrets of bureaucratic efficiency (Weber 1947). While bureaucracy has been part of many state forms, it assumed greater prominence in nations such as Canada following World War II, when commitments to new and complex social programming required larger and more capable civil services.

As seen above, the federal administration of freshwater has been split among several functional departments. In 1971, however, the creation of the first federal Department of the Environment (DOE, now known as Environment Canada) opened the possibility of more systematic water programming. The department began with a merger of a half dozen "organizational orphans" assembled from various departments and dealing with air, fisheries, land and forest, water, and pollution (Doern and Conway 1994). Of these, the fisheries branch brought the most powerful legislative tool in the form of the fish habitat provisions of the *Fisheries Act* and a field staff that spanned the nation. By contrast, the inland water branch arrived at DOE from the federal mines and resources department, heavily based in water science studies, with a headquarters' focus and a mandate for federal-provincial collaboration under the *Canada Water Act*.

The contrasting logics and cultures of these respective units was evident early on. The DOE sought to frame an approach to regulating pulp and paper effluent, which accounted for more than half of all industrial releases into inland waters. The fisheries branch pushed an approach based on best available treatment technologies at the end-of-pipe, with national minimum standards. By contrast, the inland waters branch favoured site-based regulations based on the assimilative capacities of receiving waters, to protect against biophysical damage (Parlour 1981). This was a "political" choice that shaped Ottawa's approach to waterborne effluent for decades to come.

Although such organizational differences may seem trivial at first glance, they are politically significant. Here they highlight the origins of the DOE as a balkanized agency that struggled to instill a uniform philosophy and organizational culture. Graham Allison and others have made such "bureaucratic politics" a central variable in policy studies. Built on the premise that program mandate and staff professional outlook will tightly shape the organizational interests of a department or agency, this theory can be summed up in the phrase "where you stand depends on where you sit" (Allison 1971, 176). Put slightly differently, how you define an issue depends on where your desk is located, in organizational terms. Some government agencies are, by design and recruitment and mandate, highly disciplined while others are fragmented and less coherent.

Since the 1970s, the trend in Canada has been to vest the administration of crown water powers in departments of environment. This includes both instream flows and groundwater. However, it does not normally include all water-oriented impacts of terrestrial commerce ranging from forests to mines to farms. As a result, the wider picture for freshwater-related policy is more complicated. In 2006 for example, 22 federal departments and agencies were identified as having water responsibilities, including the big five of Environment Canada, Fisheries and Oceans, Natural Resources Canada, Agriculture, and Health Canada.

The situation is similar in the provinces, where departments of the environment administer crown title, license rights of water use, and monitor water for quantity and quality. A stand-alone department for water is rare (the Manitoba Water Conservancy is an exception and the Saskatchewan Water Security Agency is a crown corporation). However, a water branch within a department of the environment (or natural resources) is common. The dilemma is that no single department controls the full range of water-related programs. While an environment department can play a lead role, effective management requires coordination on a larger scale. In Nova Scotia, for example, the Department of Environment chairs a provincial government water task force that includes nine additional departments, ranging from transportation, agriculture, and fisheries to municipal affairs, natural resources, energy, and health (Nova Scotia 2002). There is also the matter of provincially owned hydro-electric corporations. These massive firms are intimately tied to their parent governments, giving the companies significant political leverage on water policy issues.

Each water management bureaucracy has its own institutional history. Consider Environment Canada. Following an initial surge of activity, the federal DOE slipped into a decade of quiescence beginning in 1976. This is explained in part by the political distractions posed by successive energy crises and the 1982 economic recession, when green concerns took a back seat. Prospects began to improve again during the first Mulroney government, the final phase of a 20-year syndrome that Doern and Conway (1994, 12) describe as "the rise and fall and rise of the DOE." To galvanize a water agenda, a Federal Water Policy Inquiry was announced in 1985 (Pearse et al. 1985). Its report, *Currents of Change*, outlined an ambitious program that was partly reflected in Ottawa's 1987 *Federal Water Policy.*

The 1987 policy declared freshwater to be a scarce resource that could only be properly managed if its commercial value was accurately determined. Freshwater programming would no longer be simply reactive—in response to problems. For the future, the overriding policy objective was to use the resource "in an economically efficient and equitable manner consistent with socio-economic-environmental needs of present and future generations" (Canada 1987). It pledged Ottawa to take the lead, albeit in cooperation with the provinces. Among the five broad "courses of action" for its achievement were water pricing, science leadership, integrated planning, legislation, and public awareness. For greater guidance, 25 statements of specific policies were included.

This new approach could have put Canada on the forefront of global freshwater management. It has been described as "visionary for its time" (Corkal et al., 2007) and Pearse and Quinn (1996, 335) characterized it as "the high water mark" in federal water policy. However whatever political urgency propelled the 1987 policy was soon exhausted, and for this there may have been several reasons. First, the Mulroney Government's Green Plan of 1990 was an all-encompassing program in which water policy had to vie with other priorities. Second, as the lead freshwater administrative authorities, the provinces had their own ideas about management priorities that did not include a renewed federal presence. In fact, several provinces were soon drawn into disputes with Ottawa over new dam and reservoir projects, as in the Souris River case discussed below. Third, efforts by the Chrétien government to eliminate a record budget deficit led to severe program cuts in Environment Canada after 1994. Staff were lost, field offices were closed, and water funding was slashed. The net result was that, by the end of the decade, Ottawa's 1987 commitment was a dead letter, lacking both the political will and the program capacity for bold new action.

Shadowing the travails of Environment Canada was the emerging regulatory domain of "environmental assessment." This was a signature initiative of 1970s environmentalism, which called for systematic review of the environmental impacts of proposed new development projects—terrestrial or aquatic—before licences or permits were granted by the responsible agencies. The goal was to ensure that proponents included environmental impacts in the planning of their projects, a matter often ignored in the past. In this way negative impacts could be detected and avoided or mitigated before construction and operations began. The logic of environmental assessment (EA) was to document baseline (i.e., pre-project) conditions and weigh the impacts of a project proposal to assess the degrees of negative impact. Water development projects were often at the forefront of environmental assessment (Houck 2006).

In Canada this began in 1974 when Ottawa announced the Environmental Assessment Review Process, or EARP regime, with responsibilities vested in a new agency. Over the next decade or more, the provinces followed suit. In this parallel federal and provincial EA regime, the potential for conflict was high, as the Souris case illustrates below.

Federalism

Federalism is usually defined as a situation where sovereign authority is divided between national and subnational governments. It is commonly found in nations made up of diverse social and spatial interests that, it is hoped, can be accommodated by assigning the more "local" responsibilities to the provinces while maintaining common responsibilities at the central level. In practical terms, a federal system multiplies the number of authorities with constitutional autonomy. It opens possibilities for tension and conflict and highlights the need for coordinating mechanisms.

For freshwater politics, as in most policy domains, an overriding question involves the division of powers. Jurisdiction over freshwater resources—their ownership, use, and management—is split between the federal and the provincial authorities. Ottawa has a strong foothold by virtue of its jurisdictions over fisheries, international treaties, navigable waters, and interprovincial water flows. While this ensures a federal presence in several key dimensions of freshwater management, provincial governments have an even larger position, based on their ownership of public lands and resources, along with their jurisdictions for property and civil rights and local and private matters. The meaning of these provisions has evolved over time, shaped by judicial interpretation and by federal-provincial negotiation, and has also evolved with the changing roles of freshwater in Canadian society and economy. Still, if there is a basis for general water management, it tilts toward the provinces rather than Ottawa. As Saunders put it, there is today "de facto acceptance of the primacy of the provinces in most areas of water policy" (Saunders 2006).

If the provinces occupy the central regulatory and management roles, the government of Canada has devised several mechanisms to remain influential in water federalism. Some of these are conveyed by statute, as with fish habitat protection under the *Fisheries Act* or river regulation under the *Navigable Waters Protection Act*. Another source that has been particularly significant since World War II is the federal spending power, which allows Ottawa to spend money in areas extending beyond its jurisdictional competence. Under the *Canada Water Conservation Assistance Act* of 1953, Ottawa offered to share the capital costs of approved conservation works. It was under this program, for example, that the Winnipeg floodway was financed. In a similar vein in 1970, the *Canada Water Act* opened the way for a substantial federal effort in aquatic science as well as for joint spending programs such as the federal-provincial water resource management plans. The federal government also plays a crucial role in international water flows. The Canada-US Boundary Waters Treaty and the *Boundary Waters Act* of 1909 established the International Joint Commission as a continuing panel for the investigation of shared watersheds. Today there are many cross-border watershed councils operating under its auspices. Within Canada, the federal government played a key role in fashioning the Prairie Provinces Water Board in 1948 to deal with intensifying demands on the Saskatchewan River system. It later played a similar role in the Mackenzie River Basin Board in the 1990s (Saunders and Wenig 2007).

Another mechanism for joint or coordinated federal-provincial action is through intergovernmental machinery. These are ongoing bodies for continuing consultation at the ministerial or officials' level. The Continuing Committee of Ministers of Environment (CCME) is one such structure that includes freshwater in its mandate. The ministers meet occasionally to set working agendas and to receive policy recommendations. In the periods in between, committees of expert bureaucrats convene to advance the technical work of the CCME. Here also, the ebb and flow of policy priorities can be observed. In the early 1990s, the CCME's Advisory Committee on Water was abolished—a stark signal of declining interest. However, the Walkerton crisis served to draw the CCME quickly back into drinking water protection after 2000.

In 2010 the provincial and territorial premiers gave at least symbolic recognition to freshwater priorities. At the annual meeting of the Council of the Federation, meeting in Winnipeg that year, leaders approved a "Water Charter" that pledged all governments to a "best efforts" commitment to water conservation, efficiency, monitoring, technology innovation, and municipal planning. Whether this amounts to more than a motherhood gesture can be questioned. No concrete measures or projects were stipulated, no timetables were set, and no follow-up reviews were mandated. Rather, the leaders agreed "to take all timely measures in our respective jurisdictions and, when appropriate, work together" (Council of the Federation 2010).

Law and Judiciary

Water law is a combined product of legislative output and judicial review. The courtroom can be viewed as a field of political engagement as well as a venue for dispute settlement. Thus it is important to factor the role of judges into water politics. There are a variety of potential disputes that can arise. Some are between persons and corporations, often involving property, contracts, commerce, or criminal law. Others are between citizens and the state, involving the delivery of government programs and the application of legal regulations. Still others are between governments, involving questions of jurisdictional powers. All of these are areas where legal disputes are resolved by judges.

There are several sources of law that contribute to water politics. Common law is often described as "judge-made law," as it is derived from the reasons that judges enunciate for their decisions. In the English tradition, judges draw upon precedents from prior judgments—particularly those of senior courts of appeal—insofar as the case at hand shares similar characteristics. The common law of water emerged from disputes in England between landowners and commoners. For example, the 1830 case of *Rex v. Inhabitants of Oxfordshire* provided the legal definition of a natural watercourse as "water flowing in a channel between banks more or less defined." Furthermore it was decided that water in free-flowing form cannot be owned or possessed, even though the beds below the flow can. In another example, riparian law spelled out certain terms of use by virtue of a property right of access from the bank. Persons with land rights adjacent to the flow enjoyed strong rights to use the watercourse for domestic purposes and also for secondary "reasonable" uses so long as flow and quality downstream are unaffected. Should an owner hold both banks, a structure can be erected provided that flow is not altered (Atlantic Development Board 1969).

Through most of the nineteenth century, these common law rights guided Canadian judges as well as English. However, a rival source of law is found in statutes enacted by legislatures; in cases of direct conflict, statute law prevails and common law rights are subordinated. Thus when Canadian authorities began to assert crown title to flowing water around the turn of the twentieth century, it marked a significant political turn. In Nova Scotia, for example, the *Water Act* of 1919 vested title in the provincial crown. Until that point, small rural landowners suffering burdens from dams and impoundments enjoyed considerable success in gaining compensation under common law. However the 1919 statute created a new Water Commission with licensing authority over future dam and reservoir projects, by which the government intended to make hydro-projects more accessible. This worked to the advantage of industrial capital but at the expense of small riparian holders as it obliged judges to alter the calculus in settling disputes (Nedelsky 1990). Today most provinces assert crown title through some form of water act that confers crown title and licensing authority for flowing streams, lakes, and beds. It is important to note, however, that where statute law is silent, common law continues to apply.

Constitutional law is another field in which water law is framed. This involves the interpretation of the meaning of constitutional texts and the settlement of disputes pertaining to them. While all terms of a constitution are potentially open to litigation, those affecting freshwater have centred on the federal-provincial division of powers. In other words they ask which level of government holds the power to act on particular activities. Only a few decades after Confederation, for example, some provinces challenged the national government's fisheries power on the grounds that provincial crown title to river banks and beds should carry over to the fish in the water column. The highest court of the day sided with this argument in 1898. An administrative solution was concluded, to delegate administrative control to consenting provinces.

The 1982 *Constitution Act* served to dramatically expand the scope of judicial review by entrenching a series of citizen rights and freedoms. For example, section 35 affirmed constitutional recognition of all existing treaty rights and aboriginal rights in Canada. Within a few years the Supreme Court heard the case of *R. v. Sparrow*. Here Ronald Sparrow's conviction for fishing with an illegal net was challenged on the basis that he enjoyed an Aboriginal right to fish that superceded the statutory *Fisheries Act*. Put another way, Sparrow argued before the Supreme Court of Canada that the Indian Food Fishery Regulations infringed on his right, exercised since time immemorial, to fish for domestic purposes. In its 1990 judgment the Court found in Sparrow's favour, thereby triggering a historic revision of the federal fisheries policy toward Aboriginals (Sharma 1998). More generally, Aboriginal rights to water continue to be contested in judicial settings (Phare 2009).

Examples such as these illustrate ways in which the courtroom can become a forum for resolving political conflicts. Rulings in the senior courts of appeal are authoritative and final. They can either uphold or invalidate statutes, regulations, and the programs that underlie them. At the same time, it is important to appreciate the defining characteristics of legal politics. The process can be expensive and slow. The Sparrow case took six years from initial charge to final decision on appeal. In addition, arguments must be framed not in declarative political terms but according to the vocabulary and the logic of the law. Furthermore, decisions are zero-sum in nature—a plaintiff or defendant either wins or loses—and there is little room for the compromising style that can characterize legislative or bureaucratic politics.

Regional and District State Structures

While the "senior" levels of constitutional government enjoy the strongest legal foundation, no discussion of the freshwater state would be complete without mention of the many types of regional and district structures. Here we refer to institutions based on spatial or functional mandates related to water. They exist at the discretion of senior governments and can be modified or terminated by their sponsors. At the same time they should not be confused with well-established local or municipal institutions, though the latter may be important partners in area management. There are several rationales for regional and district units. One is to formulate and deliver a newly defined program. Another is to aggregate pre-existing authorities into larger units for joint action. Although they are not confined to natural resource management, such structures are familiar in this sector. They may be charged with planning or coordination or project management or research and education. They may be purely administrative in the sense of organizing and delivering public programs, or they may involve direct or indirect constituency representation. Outputs from district water governing bodies may be incorporated into statutory programs, or statutory powers may be delegated in part to district units. A common property is that they are established to overcome the limitations of standard jurisdictions and bureaucracies and to establish closer contact to local conditions.

The watershed scale is particularly suited for this level of government. As already seen, there is a coherence to drainage basin landscapes that can coincide with administrative mandates. In the 1930s the US government established the Tennessee Valley Authority with legal powers to promote economic growth in a hitherto degraded region. Following World War II the government of Ontario established a statutory system of conservation authorities by grouping munici-palities into special-purpose planning bodies according to watershed boundaries. In recent decades, the prairie provinces have been leaders in establishing water councils or basin authorities to address licensing, monitoring, and ecosystem is-sues on tributary basins and main stem rivers. Since 2000, Prince Edward Island has declared a community watershed organizing program that seeks to have management plans for all significant streams.

In addition to watershed-scale units, there are many schemes that established special-purpose bodies on a more localized basis. These include irrigation dis-tricts, where farmer-owned authorities build and operate water delivery works; flood control districts, where floodplain damage reduction plans are applied; groundwater management districts, in which withdrawal rights are geared to sustainable recharge; drinking water protection districts, where special regula-tions govern human activity in proximity to supply reservoirs; and drainage districts, where surface water collection schemes are implemented in a coordi-nated way.

Note should also be taken of authorities established to oversee interjuris-dictional watersheds between provinces and territories. The Mackenzie River Basin Board has responsibilities for the Peace-Athabasca-Mackenzie drainage while the Prairie Provinces Water Board covers the Saskatchewan and Churchill drainages. The Lake of the Woods Control Board covers northwestern Ontario and eastern Manitoba. These institutions tend to be technical and administrative in both design and decision-making, with far less popular grounding than the special districts mentioned earlier. Finally there are regional watershed boards that operate under the authority of the International Joint Commission to link Canadian and American portions of cross-border watersheds.

Taken together, the sections above show that the Miliband's state subsystems can highlight key structures of freshwater politics. In concrete disputes, it is com-mon for these systems to interact in different ways. In part this explains why the outcomes of water conflicts can be unpredictable. Organized interests can select from an array of institutional venues in pressing their claims, or they can combine actions on multiple fronts. If one venue proves resistant, attention may shift to others. Alternatively, developments in one venue may alter the prevailing ar-rangements in others. It is important to appreciate the entire state configuration in tracing a freshwater controversy. Sometimes the state system itself is called into question and its boundaries are redefined. The next section describes Ottawa's efforts to draw back the scale of environmental regulation in recent years.

Federal Restructuring of the Freshwater State: 2012

Earlier we noted that the boundaries of state authority are constantly changing. A dramatic example of this arose in 2012 when the Harper government redrew the shape of its freshwater mandate. Through the enactment of two key statutes, the federal Conservatives imposed the most significant transformation of Ottawa's environmental role in a generation. Central to this was a retreat on legal protections for watercourses in the face of commercial development. It was accomplished by curtailing the application of key statutes and narrowing the scope of federal environmental review.

In the spring of 2012, the Harper government launched a bold restructuring of federal regulatory regimes for natural resources and the environment. The timing was not by accident, coming less than a year after the Conservatives won their first majority electoral mandate. The mechanism was carefully chosen as well—a 420-page "omnibus" bill that began with implementation measures for the 2012 budget but added to it a sweeping set of amendments, repeals, and substitutions to more than 60 nonbudget statutes.

Part 3 of the omnibus budget Bill C-38 was titled "Responsible Resource Development." It was designed, in the words of Natural Resources Minister Joe Oliver, to install a "twenty-first century regulatory system." The thrust of this legislation was to lighten regulatory burdens faced by resource developers. This could be achieved in three ways—by eliminating existing regulations, by redefining the requirements in more developer-friendly ways, and by federal withdrawal from regulatory activities by delegating authority to the provinces. Each of these played a major role in C-38.

One of the most graphic examples involves the federal *Fisheries Act*, which we have seen has been a central management statute since the time of Confederation. It will be recalled that federal fisheries policy was expanded significantly by the habitat policy released in the 1980s. In particular, section 35 sets out what are known as the HADD provisions—making it illegal to harmfully alter, disrupt, or destroy fish habitat. This reflected the awareness that the health of fish populations turned, critically, on the health of host aquatic habitats. Section 35 equipped federal fisheries officers with strong powers to review development projects for potential HADDs and to require adaptations to secure the required permits. In addition, where the minister authorized a project involving a HADD, it came with an obligation to replace the lost habitat to ensure that there is "no net loss."

Part 3 Division 5 of Bill C-38 changed some key terms of the habitat provisions. The HADD section is replaced with a clause prohibiting "*serious* harm to fish that are part of a commercial, recreational or Aboriginal fishery, or to fish that support such an industry." In addition, serious harm is defined as the "death of fish or any *permanent* alteration to, or destruction of, fish habitat." Taken together, these Harper government amendments have the effect of narrowing the definition of habitat damage (harmful "disruption" is eliminated), narrowing the definition of harm (to cover only "serious" cases, however they are defined), and narrowing the scope of habitat damage (to cover only "permanent" alterations). In addition, the narrower definition of fish as species in use (or fish that "support" useful fish) means that nonharvested species are no longer covered. Another significant effect of the exclusion of temporary habitat alteration or destruction from the serious harm test is to ignore incremental or cumulative impacts that might eventually have permanent effect. Finally, there is a provision for the cabinet to designate certain "Canadian Fisheries Waters" as exempt from the amended section 35.

The federal government's intentions here are clearly to redefine the environmental balance point between fish habitat damage and resource development impacts, in favour of the latter. The advocacy of petroleum, mining, pipeline, and hydro-power interests in favour of such changes is well documented (Galloway 2013). At the same time, the fish habitat amendments in the 2012 budget bill were also challenged from several angles. More than 600 scientists signed an open letter to Harper and Minister Keith Ashfield in March 2012, arguing the need to strengthen rather than weaken the habitat provisions in the *Fisheries Act* (Schindler et al. 2012). Two months later, an extraordinary public statement by four former fisheries ministers (two Conservative and two Liberal) conveyed "our serious concern regarding the content of Bill C-38 and the process being used to bring it into force." Tom Siddon, David Anderson, John Fraser, and Herb Dhaliwal called for full examination of the proposed amendments at a parliamentary committee, and greater clarification from ministers on the rationale for change and on the role of corporate lobbying in the process. The four former ministers declared that "a strong *Fisheries Act*, a competent science establishment and vigorous enforcement programs are essential to protect fish stocks and the habitat on which they depend" (Siddon et al. 2012). Ultimately, neither this nor other political criticism led to a single amendment, and C-38 received assent during the summer of 2012.

Months later, in the autumn of 2012, the Harper government introduced a second omnibus bill, C-45. This time the *Navigable Waters Protection Act* was a prime target. Originally enacted in 1882, the NWPA ranked alongside the *Fisheries Act* as one of Ottawa's most substantial regulatory statutes. At its core is the protection of a public right of navigation that was originally defined in common law. As Transport Canada put it, navigable waters are defined as "all bodies of water that are capable of being navigated by any type of floating vessel for transportation, recreation or commerce" (Transport Canada 2013). Because many of the most serious threats to navigation involved obstruction (such as dams, bridges, booms, and causeways) or pollution (such as debris or material dumping), the statute also took on an environmental dimension. No physical "work" could be located in a navigable water without ministerial approval (there was a "minor impact" power of ministerial exemption). When the *Canadian*

Environmental Assessment Act (CEAA) came into effect in the 1990s, its review terms encompassed the NWPA along with other designated federal legislation. As a result, ministerial approvals triggered CEAA assessments.

Earlier, in 2009, the minority Harper government had made amendments to the NWPA to curb what were perceived to be excessive waterway regulations. A tiered classification of waterways was defined with only certain tiers subject to the NWPA. Also, by ministerial decision, certain classes of works could be exempted from statutory approval (and as a result would be exempt from CEAA processes). The public notification and consultation provisions for exempt projects were also eliminated. In short, the scope of the NWPA was narrowed by limiting the range of waters and of projects to which approval and assessment applied.

In the Fall 2012 omnibus act, the NWPA was more radically amended. First, the name was changed to the *Navigation Protection Act*, to underline a retreat from environmental protection and a focus on navigable conditions alone. Second, application of the statute was confined to a designated list of waterways that included 3 oceans, 97 lakes, and portions of 62 rivers. The rationale here, according to Transport Canada, is "to focus TC resources on the country's most significant waterways" (Ecojustice 2012). Third, for all other nonlisted waterways, there is no need for approval for "works," no legal authority to remove obstructions, and no need for proponents to provide public notice. There is also provision for Ottawa to delegate its continuing navigation protection powers to other governments (i.e., provinces). It should be noted that six months earlier, Bill C-38 had exempted major pipelines and power lines from the NWPA and assigned navigational safety for these facilities to the National Energy Board.

So far as nonlisted waterways were concerned, the amended act declared that common law rules would still apply. In other words, private parties could seek remedy for navigation injuries by launching court action against the agents of the injury. In political terms, however, this transformed the power relations from one of ministerial protection of a public interest under law, to one of private citizen initiatives through the courts. Where the NWPA process was proactive, the common law route is inherently reactive and post facto. Where the onus under the NWPA was to prove no damage, the onus under the common law of nuisance is to prove damage. In addition, the costs of compliance are shifted largely from navigational waterway modifiers to navigational waterway users. There are also significant implications for Aboriginal rights. The crown duty to consult on actions that may affect Aboriginal rights or title does not extend to private interests such as corporations, so the scope of the crown duty is radically narrowed to the listed waterways. As one critic put it, "this is the ultimate in 'privatization' of Canada's navigation regulatory regime" (Ecojustice 2012). In a similar spirit, the Harper program also carried major amendments to the *Canadian Environmental Assessment Act* and the *Species at Risk Act*.

In sum, the 2012 package has the effect of narrowing and lessening certain standards of legal review, increasing ministerial responsibility in triggering reviews, and redefining key terms, while increasing the prospects for Ottawa to delegate decisions to the provinces. The Harper government policy of 2012 reflects the interconnected elements of the modern freshwater state. Cabinet decisions were translated into legislative format and attached to the budget bills. On the strength of the Conservative majority, key statutes were amended to curtail their scope and bureaucratic application. Future court challenges will be weighed against the 2012 statutory terms. And a potential shift of initiative, from Ottawa to the provinces, has been set in play.

CASE STUDY: THE SOURIS RIVER WATERSHED AND THE RAFFERTY-ALAMEDA DAM DISPUTES

A classic example of the freshwater state acting on multiple levels is the dispute surrounding the proposed construction of the Rafferty and Alameda dams in southeast Saskatchewan. Over more than a decade of conflict, all elements of the state were engaged before the projects were completed in the mid-1990s. The case illustrates the multiple complications that can arise when a major water development project is launched, as well as the many distinct political venues in which organized interests are expressed. Of particular note are the cross-border alliances and tensions, the strategies of legal challenge by citizen groups, and the federal-provincial dimensions of project approval.

The Souris River features a surprising level of geopolitical complexity for an intermediate-sized watershed. The river rises near Weyburn and flows 700 km to its confluence with the Assiniboine River in Manitoba. Three of the source tributaries point in a southeast direction and join at Oxbow. As the Souris, it continues toward the US border and enters the state of North Dakota where it gains added flow. After passing the city of Minot, the river turns north and re-enters Canada, this time in Manitoba. Here the "lower" Souris basin (a separate southeast Saskatchewan watershed that flows directly into Manitoba) joins the main stem, which continues northeasterly to intersect with the Assiniboine River and flow onward to Winnipeg. Thus the Souris not only transects the Saskatchewan-Manitoba boundary but also twice crosses between Canada and the United States. It is a heavily engineered basin, including some 40 dams, 4 of them major. The entire watershed is illustrated on Map 4.1.

The Souris River watershed depends completely upon seasonal precipitation. This means that its flow patterns vary sharply from the spring melt to mid-summer drought, punctuated by random seasonal cloudbursts. In an arid part of the prairies, where dryland farming is the rule, water is a key limiting factor and water "management" assumes a different cultural form than elsewhere. Marc Reisner's comment on the United States applies equally to Canada—as he puts it, "in the east, to 'waste' water is to consume it needlessly or excessively. In the west to waste water is *not* to consume it, to let it flow unimpeded or undiverted down rivers" (Reisner 1986, 12). In this sense, dam-building is perfectly

Map 4.1 Souris River Watershed, Saskatchewan

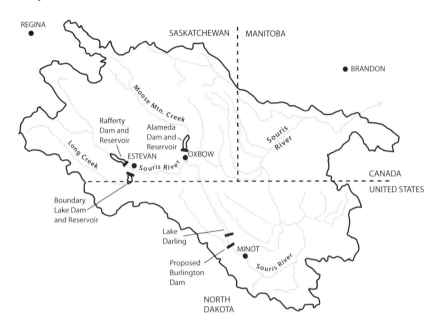

in keeping with water conservation. Yet on the Souris, water scarcity combines with water excess. The North Dakota city of Minot has been the victim of major floods, repeatedly in the 1970s and most acutely in 2011. In effect the Souris is defined by both water shortage and overabundance, which complicates any regulatory efforts.

Farm residents of southeastern Saskatchewan have long sought a form of river management but this has been frustrated by physical and political factors. As early as 1940 the province of Saskatchewan pressed for a formal agreement on apportioning water between the three jurisdictions in the Souris basin. The International Joint Commission (IJC) concluded that insufficient data existed at that time—a decision that, by perpetuating the status quo, implicitly favoured North Dakota, where the Army Corps of Engineers had already built multiple dams. The issue was revisited in 1959 when it was agreed that Saskatchewan could retain 50 per cent of the flow and the International Souris River Board of Control was established under the IJC.

This Saskatchewan share was never fully used. The Boundary reservoir was built to cool a local coal-fired power plant that supplied half of the provincial base electrical load at the time. However, the push for hydraulic works was stronger on the American side. In response to the Minot floods in the 1970s, the US Army Corps of Engineers proposed the Burlington dam as a "dry dam" that would fill in the spring and empty as summer progressed. This American proposal was killed when a political deadlock developed between anti-dam farmers and pro-dam Minot residents.

This opened the way for a different approach in the 1980s, when new political leadership took control in both the province and the state. The concept was to regulate the Souris by means of two new Saskatchewan dams, with tie-ins to electricity generation in the province and water supply in North Dakota. In 1985 the Saskatchewan Power Corporation proposed the Shand coal-fired power plant with the Rafferty dam and reservoir as its water source. With Minot increasingly anxious about flood protection, the Alameda dam was added as an upper-basin floodwater storage structure, with the hope that US authorities would co-finance the project.

The Rafferty dam site is on the Souris River main stem upstream of Estevan, where the Shand coal-fired power plant is located. An earth-filled dam of 20 m height, it creates a reservoir 57 km long that stores 440,000 m^3 when full. A 10-km diversion was also proposed to enable excess water at the Boundary Reservoir to be diverted to Rafferty. Further east, the Alameda dam is sited on the Moose Mountain Creek tributary. Located just above Oxbow, the Alameda is a higher (38 m) earth-filled structure that impounds a 25 km reservoir storing 105,000 m^3 when full. The Alameda dam was completed in 1994 while the Rafferty followed in 1995.

Given the transboundary watershed, a binational agreement was required to set out the details of the intended flow regime. It is telling that the detailed terms were hammered out by technocrats from Saskatchewan Power and the US Army Corps of Engineers, and then approved by Ottawa and Washington in a 1989 agreement (Redekop 2012). This century-long deal spelled out the allocative terms, with specific obligations for Saskatchewan not only to hold back spring flows but also to guarantee levels in Lake Darling on the American side (Canada and USA 1989). For Minot, the flood protection scheme was geared for a 1-in-100-year flood, whereas the earlier Burlington design was for 1-in-500 years. It was decided, at political levels, that the IJC and the Souris River Board would play no role in the design or negotiating process, thus sidelining the most authoritative sources of watershed expertise.

The Saskatchewan party system of the time was polarized between the New Democrats (who governed until 1982 and again after 1991) and the Conservatives (in power from 1982 to 1991). The NDP was unsympathetic to the Souris River proposal during the opening phase, but Conservative leader Grant Devine (an agricultural scientist whose constituency included Estevan) was its champion (Hood 1994). In the run-up to an election in February 1986, Devine announced that the twin dams would be built, subject to environmental impact approval and a US contribution to the capital costs. A new crown agency known as the Souris Basin Development Authority (SBDA) was put in charge of project design and construction, including the job of navigating its pathway through some 25 licence and permit processes.

As we have seen, the premier (or prime minister) heads the cabinet and the executive subsystem. But Premier Devine's enthusiasm for the Rafferty-Alameda project was not shared by all elements of the provincial, and federal, states. In Saskatchewan, various line departments resisted. At cabinet, other ministers harboured doubts that later hardened into silent opposition. So long as Environment Minister Eric Berntson was at the table, the SBDA enjoyed strong political support, but after his departure in 1989, other ministers and senior departmental officials became bolder and more openly hostile. This intensified as the environmental court battles (detailed below) intensified in the 1989–93 period.

The federal government was also a significant player by virtue of the cross-border waters dimension. Not only did federal officials co-chair the International Souris River Board of Control (under the IJC), but the federal minister of the environment also held responsibilities under the *International Rivers Improvement Act*, requiring a federal licence for a major work within Canada on any boundary river. This proved to be a key political pressure point for anti-Rafferty forces, which successfully challenged the adequacy of the environmental assessments undertaken by Environment Canada.

On the Saskatchewan side of the Souris watershed there was skepticism about how project costs matched up with benefits. The Alameda dam came in for particular criticism, as local farmland stood to replace the Burlington project and protect Minot against floods. Indeed the Alameda reservoir was often described by critics as "America's Lake" (Redekop 2012). Such concerns were dismissed impatiently by Conservative politicians and SBDA officials. Nevertheless, concerned citizens came together early in 1988 to form SCRAP: Stop Construction of the Rafferty-Alameda Project.

The Rafferty-Alameda project appeared at a moment when environmental assessment law was still at a formative stage in Canada. The principle of compulsory assessment of major project impacts was widely accepted, but the procedures and techniques were still germinal. The federal government published its first "Guideline" in 1974 (revised in 1984), obliging departments and agencies to perform assessments before licensing decisions. However this "regime" was not specified in fine detail, leaving officials considerable discretion of execution (Hood 1994). In Saskatchewan the NDP enacted the province's first *Environmental Assessment Act* in 1980, though few regulations had been finalized under it by the time that the Rafferty-Alameda project was referred to an assessment board in 1987. In some respects, state agencies were still in the process of occupying this potentially massive new field of regulatory politics. In any case, development agencies tended to regard EAs as formalities. The initial Saskatchewan review was completed in little more than a month. The initial federal review, when it was judicially compelled, took less than a month (Houck 2006).

In all, six judicial actions were launched on behalf of comprehensive environmental review. A citizen challenge to inadequate provincial public consultation failed; a SCRAP challenge to the adequacy of the provincial review also failed;

an action by the Canadian Wildlife Federation to force Ottawa to undertake a federal review was successful (and sustained on appeal); another CWF action to require a comprehensive panel review was also successful; an action by Ottawa for a judicial order to stop construction during the panel review failed; and a citizen action to force a federal review of the Alameda project after the site was shifted succeeded (though the project was completed while the review was underway).

Through repeated litigation, project opponents successfully exploited a series of legal ambiguities and procedural irregularities, delaying project completion by half a decade (Stolte and Sadar 1993). At the same time, these challenges led Canadian courts to strengthen the status of federal environmental assessment policies. The legal vagaries of the federal EARP Guidelines Order cried out for judicial challenge by environmental advocates, and the Rafferty-Alameda project provided the spark (Tingley 1991). The 1989 action by the Canadian Wildlife Federation, at the Trial Division of the Federal Court of Canada, succeeded in quashing the initial licence under the *International Rivers Improvement Act* (IRIA) and ordered the federal minister of environment to fully comply with the EARP guidelines. Where the courts hesitated was in their willingness to halt the project until adequate reviews were completed. By the time the EARP hearings were finished, the major engineering works were largely in place.

There followed a complicated series of steps and countersteps over several years, requiring repeated court challenges and policy miscues (Tingley 1991). Following EARP hearings in 1989, construction resumed and the Rafferty dam was largely complete by November. Then federal court Justice Muldoon quashed the "second" IRIA license on the grounds that full EARP compliance still required a panel inquiry. Saskatchewan sought financial compensation from Ottawa for the ensuing delay, and it was only in 1992 that the way was cleared for final construction (Canada 1991).

It should be evident that the Rafferty-Alameda project became a lightning rod for a variety of political issues. Provincial officials argued that a provincial development scheme was being held hostage by central Canadian environmentalists and by design defects in a federal policy that had little to do with the project. Critics of the scheme questioned the coherence of the two-dam design, the credibility of the capital cost estimates, and the apparent contradictions in combining water supply, flood storage, and recreational purposes in the manner proposed. In addition, both federal and provincial authorities were willing to exaggerate the perfidy of the other to the point that water project particulars were sometimes lost from sight. Ultimately the Souris River controversy and the dam/reservoir debates serve as an intriguing example of the complexity of project politics and the capacity for them to permeate all avenues of the modern freshwater state.

The legacy of the twin dam/reservoir projects can be found in the ongoing functioning of the watershed, as detailed in annual reports by the International Souris River Board. The ultimate capital cost exceeded the original estimate of $80 million by several orders. As a result, the American contribution of $40 million dropped to less than 20 per cent of the total. It is estimated that flood management actions saved Minot from flooding in 1999, 2001, 2005, and 2009. But events in June 2012 overshadowed these successes. Heavy rains the previous fall left soils saturated within the watershed and winter snows in 2011–12 were double normal levels. These factors combined with acute spring rain events to send a 1-in-500-year flood into North Dakota, inflicting unprecedented damage on Minot. This prompted a binational review of the 1989 Canada-US operating plan, which continues at the time of writing.

Conclusion

It is evident that freshwater policy issues permeate the modern Canadian state. At any point in time, significant questions are under consideration at multiple levels. Authority over these matters is dispersed and lines of accountability are far from clear. Indeed, a challenge for interest groups is how to accurately "read" the state structure and deal strategically with it. The questions are many: when to lobby a government minister (and if so, at which level); when to mobilize opposition party efforts in a legislature, or appear at committee deliberations; when to press concerns with bureaucratic officials and with which bureaucracy; whether a court challenge offers prospects for policy influence? In later chapters we will encounter these questions in a variety of freshwater settings.

What are some of the lessons to be drawn from the Rafferty dam experience? The importance of ministerial leadership and cabinet solidarity is amply evident, if policy intent is to be realized over time. Also the long duration of a dam and reservoir project can be seen in the sequence of stages from proposal to formal acceptance to design and construction. When a watershed flows between jurisdictions (much less countries), the political process will involve multiple sovereign authorities and be more complex for that fact. In recent decades, the growing importance of water conservation and ecological interest groups has also become clear. Finally, the courts offer an important avenue for NGOs and other interests seeking to overturn an unfavourable decision by blocking it.

PART TWO

Fields of Engagement

5
Fisheries and Pollution

WHEN FRESHWATER IS CONSIDERED AS A "host" environment for living organisms, attention usually turns to fish. This chapter explores some of the leading political dimensions of freshwater fishing and fishery management. Among the significant variables are the interests of fishers and the conflicts that may arise among them, the status of fish stocks and the challenges of conservation and restoration, the allocation of jurisdictional authority between federal and provincial levels, and the ongoing threats from the pollution of aquatic environments. The chapter continues with a case study of the Miramichi watershed in New Brunswick and the status of wild Atlantic salmon in particular. The politics of salmon has been prominent in this watershed since first contact. Today, salmon management offers a classic illustration of the challenges facing fisheries more generally.

In Canada, the freshwater fish resource is distributed across five drainage basins that encompass tens of thousands of rivers and lakes. Each is a potential host for one or more fish populations. Despite this massive freshwater estate, the range of fish species is surprisingly narrow. From a fisheries point of view, fewer than 30 species figure in terms of major catch importance. Heading the list on both the Atlantic and Pacific coasts is salmon, long regarded as the king of the game fishes, an anadromous species whose life cycle combines freshwater and saltwater habitats. Regionally prominent are pickerel, perch, trout, whitefish, char, and others. But in a comparative context the natural range is not diverse. Canada holds only one per cent of the 20,000 global freshwater species (Pearse 1988, 23).

Each province has its own particular profile. In Nova Scotia for example, 17 native species have been present since the last ice age. This is not the whole story, however, as another 26 fish species have been introduced over the past three centuries of settlement. Further variations are found at the spatial level, where the size and mixture of populations varies by body of water and drainage basin. Even the same species can face markedly different conditions from one watershed to another, as the Atlantic salmon will attest.

This underlines the fundamental challenge in understanding, much less managing, the fisheries resource. Overall, the endowment and the value of Canadian fisheries are substantial. But individually, the stocks found in particular lakes and rivers range from abundant to scarce, from commercially valuable to negligible, and from ecologically sensitive to resilient. The dilemma of freshwater fisheries programming stems in large part from its character as a localized resource on a national scale, with occasional international dimensions. Under these circumstances it has been very difficult to undertake sufficient surveys, at the appropriate scale, to fully understand the resource. Commercial value has normally dictated research priorities. But even with prominent species such as salmon, knowledge has been elusive and management has been of questionable effectiveness. On the Atlantic coast the salmon stocks that were so abundant in pioneer times hit rock bottom in the early 1980s. On the Pacific, salmon have been in crisis for the better part of the last generation.

The Politics

The politics of the fisheries begins, however, with the interests that arise from the social appropriation of the wild resource. To put it another way, differences begin when rival claims are made on the access, capture, and utilization of different sorts of fish. It is not simply a question of "who" but also of "what" and "how."

In Canada, Aboriginal cultures have relied traditionally on fish to support their domestic economies. Fish were speared and netted, smoked and dried, consumed and exchanged as part of precontact life. Fishing sites were frequented by particular band and tribal groups, and fishing seasons were often the occasion for social gatherings. Later, with European settlement, opportunities arose to trade or sell fish commercially as well. During these times, a premise of permanent abundance prevailed.

However, by the nineteenth century this premise was already being challenged and distributional conflicts broke out in many directions (Newell 1993). Some of this was culturally driven, as white colonists resented and resisted the efforts of Native fishers to maintain traditional access. It took the form of settler landowners invoking private land rights to exclude Indians from riparian access. It also involved denying or dismissing treaty rights. Finally it took the form of attacking Aboriginal fishing practices. For example, in Maritime Canada, white anglers took strong exception to Mi'kmaq night fishing with flambeaux—blazing torches fixed to the ends of canoes to draw fish to the surface where they could be speared. In the eyes of colonial gentlemen and military men, this was deemed unsporting (Parenteau 1998). As a result, the angling lobby pressed the federal Fisheries Department to outlaw Native practices.

Another form of conflict arose between fishers located at different sites along a river system. Upstream residents saw their fisheries restricted by intensive harvesting by downstream rivals. The use of nets and weirs at river mouths interrupted fish movement upstream and jeopardized the return of spawning salmon stock. Inland communities regularly petitioned the authorities for protection. Colonial authorities responded by the mid-nineteenth century with regulations to prohibit spearing and netting on spawning beds. Another tool for fisheries administration, still used widely in Quebec and New Brunswick, involved the crown leasing reaches of river to sports associations for their exclusive use, maintenance, and—it was thought—fish protection (La Forest 1960).

As time progressed, the cleavage between two sets of white fishers— commercial and sport anglers—deepened. The philosophy of angler responsibility for conservation underwrote not only river leases but private guardianship arrangements against "poaching," and elite tourism became a profitable seasonal industry. In the rural areas of upper river systems, the practices of spearing, netting, and torching were adopted by whites. For the Maritimes, Parenteau reports that "the annual Atlantic salmon run produced a series of confrontations each season between anglers, private guardians, government wardens, and local fishing populations from 1867 to 1914" (Parenteau 2004).

In the twentieth century commercial fisheries expanded on major water bodies like the Great Lakes and Lake Winnipeg. Catch levels were enhanced by technological adaptations such as freezers, steam power, and larger and better nets. Ten thousand people were employed in the Great Lakes commercial fishery by 1900 (Bocking 1997). The decades following World War II saw the dramatic rise of angling as a recreational pursuit. This generated new tensions over shares of the fishery, particularly where stocks were depleted and habitats fouled. A third sector, the Aboriginal subsistence fishery, remained important in some regions and for some species, such as salmon. After decades on the defensive, this sector received a dramatic boost as a result of the 1982 constitutional recognition of "treaty and aboriginal rights," a provision that the Supreme Court of Canada later applied to fishing rights. By the mid-1980s, the "allocation question," as it came to be known, was being fought politically in watersheds from the Fraser to the Miramichi, from commercial fisher lobby groups to sport fishing conferences to tribal councils and in federal and provincial management offices (Tuomi 1985).

Much of this conflict was concentrated on shaping the legal regime for fisheries and particularly on securing an entrenched advantage within it. In his 1988 review of freshwater fisheries policy in Canada, Pearse points out that fisheries "management" can be directed at three distinct targets: managing the fishing, managing the habitat, and managing the stock (Pearse 1988, 109). The first is where disputes among fishers predominate: how many fish of various species will be taken, who in particular will take which share, at what time of year and in what location, and with what gear will the fishing take place? Fisheries legislation can be quite detailed in nature, setting out open and closed seasons, bag limits, numbers of licensed participants, permissible instruments, and other terms. The federal *Fisheries Act* and regulations were used in the late nineteenth century to restrict Aboriginal fishing. A century later, they were used to phase down commercial fishing in maritime river estuaries. Not that state interventions were always effective—poaching has always been a major issue and conflicts between rival fishers were often pursued and resolved outside of the law.

Managing the habitat involves protecting and restoring water quality in rivers and lakes so that fish stocks have the best chance of survival. The process of industrial manufacture involves the production of wastes and the alteration of waterflows. Dams and holding ponds will block stream flow and, unless ameliorated by fishways, will prevent fish migration to and from spawning grounds. Mill wastes disposed into streams and rivers can degrade water quality and river bank and river bed conditions. Chemical pollutants from land runoff or direct disposal can be toxic to aquatic species across food chains and cause dramatic fish kills (Ross and Amter 2010).

Prior to the 1970s, untreated effluents were routinely discharged from factories and waste facilities with little concern for the damages. A glib slogan of that time summed it up: "The solution to pollution is dilution." The pulp and paper industry, Canada's largest manufacturing sector for decades, accounted for half of all aquatic pollution (Sinclair 1990). The industrial chemical industry and municipal sewage disposal accounted for much of the rest. It was only with the dawning of the age of environmentalism that the government of Canada squarely confronted the problem. Under the authority of the *Fisheries Act*, the federal government issued the Pulp and Paper Effluent Regulations of 1972. They set new standards for effluent loadings but, significantly, excluded plants already operating before that date (a practice known as "grandfathering"). In effect this was a compromise approach that required new installations to treat industrial effluent to a high standard, while allowing older facilities a longer period for adjustment (Clancy 2004).

An alternative approach to pollution protection is to focus on a watercourse as a habitat for aquatic life. In 1986 the Department of Fisheries and Oceans took a significant step into this form of regulation, by announcing the federal fish habitat protection policy. In many ways this reflected the growing impact of conservation biology and ecological science. The new policy sought to change the policy framework by asserting the essential value and continuing need to defend host environments in the round. Central to the fish habitat regime was the principle of "no net loss" of habitat due to development impacts. Damaged habitat required restoration or substitution of similar quality (Canada Department of Fisheries and Oceans 1986). This habitat regime was the target of legislative change in 2012, as detailed in the previous chapter.

Managing fish stocks is the third and in some ways most challenging goal. An indispensable tool for understanding population dynamics is fisheries science, and even here the task is daunting. For each body of water there are complicated relationships between biophysical capacities and species characteristics to take into account. In addition are the trophic relations of energy that run between species. Natural reproduction can be augmented by hatchery cultures, but the effects of these can be uncertain. Also, naturally occurring stocks can be jeopardized by the introduction of exotic species capable of disrupting prior patterns. A contemporary policy tool that reflects an appreciation of the value of species per se is the species at risk regime. In cases where a population has been severely diminished or even extinguished in a host environment, there are technical and legal instruments available for designation and remediation. This will be explored below in greater length in relation to salmon.

Fisheries Law and Management

In Canada's federal form of state, "sea coast and inland fisheries" were assigned to the national government by section 91(12) of the *British North America Act* of 1867. The first dominion *Fisheries Act* was passed the following year, drawing heavily upon the prior statute in the Colony of Canada. The act remains one of the most powerful federal statutes, vesting extensive authority in the federal fisheries minister. However, this policy field is anything but straightforward. Pearse remarks that "the inland fisheries may be one of our most complex cases of divided jurisdiction" (Pearse 1988, 37).

Fish are a wild resource inhabiting a body of water. In terms of property ownership and constitutional authority, the living fish can be distinguished from the water column and from the riparian banks and beds that enclose water. Wild fish may not become property until they have been caught, but those wild fish may still be an object of public policy by those with responsibilities for the water resource. Furthermore, the right to fish may be determined by the riparian rights holder or the water title holder.

Toward the end of the nineteenth century, several provinces mounted judicial challenges to the federal jurisdiction over inland fisheries. The provinces argued that their jurisdiction over property and civil rights (including riparian rights) and public lands (vested in the provincial crown) necessitated provincial jurisdiction over modes of fishing and the allocation of fishing privileges. The appeal courts found for the provinces in several cases, and this led in 1899 to a negotiated arrangement by which Ottawa delegated the administration of inland fisheries to Ontario and Quebec (Parisien 1972). As a result, the licensing of fishers and the enforcement of harvest regulations are normally handled by provincial authorities, while Ottawa retains its roles in freshwater fish science and habitat protection. This modern arrangement has been described as "a complex patchwork of freshwater fisheries jurisdiction, ranging from full federal delivery to delegation in whole or part" (Canada Department of Fisheries and Oceans 2010).

What was the state of freshwater fisheries policy by the 1970s? The signals were not positive. Great Lakes stocks had suffered severe declines. Pulp and paper and other toxic industrial pollutants imposed extensive damage on river and lake habitats. One of the most infamous impacts involved the English and Wabigoon Rivers of northern Ontario, where facilities associated with the Reed Paper plant released mercury into the water. As it bioaccumulated in the downstream fishery food chain, it poisoned many Ojibwa peoples who contracted the debilitating Minimata disease (Troyer 1977). By the 1990s, the damaging impact of persistent chemicals, and their intergenerational legacies, was recognized more generally (Colborn, Dumanoski, and Myers 1996).

The urgent need for a freshwater fisheries policy modernization was set out by Peter Pearse in his 1986 report to the Canadian Wildlife Federation, *Rising to the Challenge*. He described the freshwater fisheries decline as a "creeping crisis," reflected in the slow but insidious decline of fish stocks for decades (11). This went unnoticed because of its localized incidence—individual stocks in particular water bodies were collapsing and declining year by year. Pearse highlighted overfishing and habitat damage as twin causes. He also offered a glimpse into the relative shares of the three fisher categories in 1985, where the Aboriginal sector accounted for 5 per cent of the total catch by weight, the (declining) commercial sector 28 per cent, and the (fast growing) recreational sector 66 per cent.

This relative ordering was about to change in another direction, as the meaning of the 1982 amendment on Aboriginal treaty rights was worked out in the courts. Previously there was little governmental affinity for Aboriginal fishers, at either federal or provincial levels. The prevailing stance was that treaty guarantees had either lapsed or been superceded by post-Confederation laws of general application (such as the *Fisheries Act*). This view also found expression in the lower courts in the pre-charter era. In 1990, however, the Supreme Court of Canada reversed this in *R. v. Sparrow*, which confirmed an Aboriginal right to fish for food. This forced a reworking of federal regulations to accord allocative priority to Aboriginal fisheries (Sharma 1998). Seven years later, *R. v. Marshall* opened the same prospects for Mi'kmaq treaty right holders in Maritime Canada (Wicken 2002).

Threads of Fisheries Science

Louis Agassis is often considered the father of ichthyology—the zoology of fishes. After pioneering work on Amazon fish and a coordinating role in zoological classification, Agassis moved to Harvard University in 1848 where he spent more than 20 years teaching and writing for the next generation of fisheries specialists. It was not until the 1870s, however, that the US Fish Commission became the first federal government research agency (Pisani 1984). Despite the fact that science and management are closely interwoven today, field science came relatively late to the management field. Laws, licensing, and enforcement systems were well established by the time science made its appearance in the late nineteenth century. This was the case in Canada as well. A fisheries Board of Management was established in 1898, and the first two field stations, staffed by summer university researchers, opened at St. Andrews, NB, and Nanaimo, BC, in 1908. Full-time scientific staff were taken on in the 1920s, but their policy impact remained limited.

It seems fair to say that the practical (commercial and political) and the scientific (method-driven research) perspectives on fisheries moved on separate tracks that occasionally intersected. For example, when fish hatcheries were first advanced as a solution to declining wild stocks such as salmon, the bureaucratic promoters invoked scientific authority. Controlled breeding could provide stock that would compensate for natural decline. Over time, however, scientific opinion began to question the universal efficacy of artificial stocking (Taylor 1998). This hints at some more basic dilemmas of state involvement in fisheries science. Should the priority be foundational (i.e., "pure") science or applied science? Can the latter be achieved without the former? Are the universities the appropriate place for basic fisheries inquiry? Is contract research the preferred tool for management support? As mentioned, the federal government established a Board of Management in 1898 for a new Marine Biological Station, a floating research barge that could be moved among sites on the Atlantic coast. Several fixed stations followed at Georgian Bay, St. Andrews, and Nanaimo. The early research output tilted toward pure fisheries science. In 1912 it was reorganized as the Biological Board of Canada, with greater financial and policy autonomy from the Department of Marine and Fisheries. Following the war, the Board was redirected toward more applied and technical problems (Johnstone 1977).

More generally, turn-of-the-century fisheries administration was driven by concrete material interests. These included the domestic and commercial demand for fish products, the rival claimants for fisheries access, and the potential revenues to be extracted from licences, fines, and business spinoffs. In the government sector, this was an era of licences and rules. Parenteau's fascinating accounts of New Brunswick salmon policy during this time contain virtually no mention of science inputs.

Distinct from the study of particular fish species is the study of aquatic systems. The late nineteenth century saw the rise of limnology as an integrated study of inland waters (lakes and rivers). This embraced physical conditions as well as food chains. Here a pivotal figure was Francois-Alfonse Forel, whose pioneering fieldwork took place at Lake Geneva. In 1922, the International Limnological Society (SIL) was founded to link scientists worldwide.

Provincial governments inherited the federal administrative focus on licensing fishers and seem to have felt less need of science inputs unless pushed by crisis. In 1920, the Ontario Department of Game and Fisheries (Lands and Forests after 1946) began supporting inland fisheries work by biologists at the University of Toronto. The Ontario Fisheries Research Laboratory was the instrument here. There was a defining angle, for, as Bocking notes, "researchers generally focused on the dynamics of fish species of importance to commercial or sportfishers" in their studies of population sizes and dynamics and fishing impacts (Bocking 1997, 157–58). By the 1960s the provincial fisheries science staff began to grow but academic limnologists continued to play a key role.

One of the milestones of government-supported freshwater science in Canada was the creation of the Experimental Lakes Area (ELA) in 1966. It speaks to the importance of state sponsorship in establishing unique research settings and in paving the way for new research paradigms. Equally, the ELA's recent demise as a federal science centre is revealing about the politics of government-hosted science.

The origins of Experimental Lakes lay in pressing public policy needs. In 1964, the International Joint Commission was directed to examine Great Lakes pollution. Out of this came the establishment of the Freshwater Institute (FWI) in Winnipeg. It was the FWI that launched a new permanent facility for "whole lake" or "whole ecosystem" studies. The FWI secured federal financial support, and the government of Ontario agreed to set aside the lands and waters and take back the timber licences then in effect. The site, in northwestern Ontario, included 17 small watersheds and 46 lakes. The first research program, covering the years 1968–75, centred on lake eutrophication. This responded to concerns about blue-green algae blooms in Lake Erie. In policy terms it led to recommendations that made Canada the first country to ban phosphates from laundry detergents (which accounted for more than half the phosphorus supply in many lakes) and the compulsory removal of phosphates from municipal sewage discharges into lakes. The next major ELA program, extending from 1972 to 1992, explored the processes of lake acidification. Beginning in the 1990s, an initiative was launched on the effects of reservoir creation and flooding.

The 1980s and 1990s saw continuing debates over ELA mandates and outputs, but new operating agreements were negotiated in 1983, 1993, and 2000. The founding generation of scientific leaders moved into new careers in the public service and the universities, and federal budget constraints also posed difficulties. One ELA scientist referred to the 1990s as a decade of "troubles" for the ELA. Despite its past distinctions, there were as many as five attempts to phase out the program in recent decades.

The 2012 budget by the Harper majority government included a broadside of cuts to environmental science. This included scientific staff in departments ranging from DFO to Environment Canada and Parks. In early May, ELA employees were notified that Ottawa was terminating support for whole lake ecosystem research, effective in March 2013 (Smith 2013). This prompted a letter-writing campaign by scientific and ENGO groups in Canada and abroad, protesting the loss of a unique experimental setting for applied environmental research. It also triggered the formation of a protest campaign by the newly formed Coalition to Save the ELA, which succeeded in keeping the issue in the news during the transitional nine months (Saveela n.d.). The Harper government's contention that whole lake ecology no longer fit with expressed federal research priorities was fiercely challenged in many scientific quarters. In 2013, newly selected Ontario Liberal Premier Kathleen Wynne announced that the province would provide funding to maintain the ELA.

In sum, over the course of half a century the Experimental Lakes Area figured in a variety of policy narratives. It began as a bold environmental field venture and evolved successively into a confirmed contributor of frontline policy-relevant science, a questionable science infrastructure expense at a time of tight budgets, and finally an obsolete federal facility. In different eras, it has been caught up in a variety of scientific, administrative, and partisan debates. Most recently, it has become part of the debate about whether the Harper government has declared war not only on environmental advocacy groups, but on publicly supported science in the public interest.

Clearly there are many science dimensions of fisheries and aquatic habitats. But if there is one fisheries issue that exemplifies both the influence and the limits of limnologists in public policy, it is the documentation and explanation of acid precipitation that so gravely damaged the lakes and rivers of eastern Canada. This is the subject of the following section.

Acid Rain

One of the most profound threats to freshwater fisheries in eastern Canada comes from the chemical transformations of lakes and rivers due to acid rain. The story of its origins, impacts, and eventual policy responses is very revealing of fisheries politics.

The scientific building blocks are not new. As early as 1727 there was awareness that precipitation could wash acidic (particularly sulphuric) particles from polluted air. A century and a half later, Robert Smith coined the term "acid rain" in the British midlands, where coal fuelled the industrial revolution. However, given coal's indispensability for manufacturing growth, the pollution was seldom questioned seriously. As recently as 1952 London experienced a dense five-day smog that caused over 4,000 deaths, as people inhaled acidic water droplets. This was a powerful catalyst for the UK's 1956 *Clean Air Act*. There were parallel European findings of acidifying lakes, particularly in Scandinavia where prevailing winds carried UK emissions from high towers. In Ontario the work of University of Toronto biologist Harold Harvey revealed the acidity of lakes in Killarney Provincial Park near Sudbury. This raised questions about the link to smelter emissions by the copper-nickel industry.

By the 1970s acid rain was recognized as a complex four-step phenomenon. First of all, sulphur- and nitrous-oxides (SOx and NOx) were produced from coal plant combustion and nonferrous smelters. These were then transported over long distances by prevailing winds, especially from superstacks (almost 400 metres high at Sudbury) that released emissions at altitude. Third, these pollutants were transformed by precipitation into particles of sulphuric or nitric acid—H_2SO_4 or HNO_3. Finally they were deposited as rain or snow and altered the chemistry of soils, forests, and waters according to the "buffering" capacities on the surface. The key variables were the volumes of emissions, measured in millions of annual tons of SOx and NOx, and the nature of receiving environments such as vegetation, soils, rocks, and waters. Where acid reduction capacities are low (especially on the rock shield), river and lake acidity can increase quickly and heavy metals can leach from soils (Howard and Perley 1980).

In waterways the key measurement is the pH level of surface waters. The pH scale measures the concentration of hydrogen ions, with 0 representing maximum acidity and 14 representing maximum alkalinity. On this scale, 7 is seen as a neutral solution and 5.6 is considered clean water in equilibrium with atmospheric CO_2. In the northern hemisphere a range of 4 to 7 is normally found, with the 4s downwind of major industrial emitters and the 7s and above in alkaline prairie soils. It is important to bear in mind that since the pH scale is logarithmic, a reading of 5.5 is 10 times more acidic than a 6.5 figure. For fish scientists, waters with a level in the low 6s can be considered a point of prospective damage, with some species starting to die at pH 6.2. Under 5.2 the natural buffering potential is exhausted and waters will be very slow to recover. For Atlantic salmon, pH 5.0–4.7 can kill half the salmon eggs and up to a third of fry. The spring acid reading on Nova Scotia's Mersey River centres in this range.

By the late 1970s, there was general agreement on the nature and scope of the problem. However, scientists were chagrined by the political positions reflected by the emitting industries in North America. This involved varying degrees of evasion. Initially the predominant expression was to deny that there was a problem, suggesting that certain lakes are naturally acidic. Later as the scientific evidence mounted, the argument shifted. Polluters conceded that there was a problem but denied that industry was chiefly responsible, since there were multiple contributors including duck droppings and forests. Finally, as the evidence became overwhelming, business accepted a causal responsibility while contending that it was too late to make meaningful change (Smol 2002).

Acid rain policy would never be determined by industry alone. Beginning in 1970, governments began confronting the problem. Initially they acted in isolation, though a level of coordination emerged in later stages. The 1970 UN Conference on the Environment in Stockholm identified acid rain as an emerging priority, and environmental advocacy groups in Canada took up the cause. That same year, the province of Ontario issued an executive order for INCO's massive mine complex at Sudbury to cut its SO_2 emissions from 6,000 tons/day to 750 tons/day by 1978 (a deadline later extended to 1984). The goal here was to reduce acid pollution at the source.

Recognizing that the Great Lakes region was an acid polluting region on both sides of the border, the government of Canada developed contacts in Washington. This began with research consultation in 1978. Two years later came a Memorandum of Intent to work on a trans-boundary pollution agreement. The election of the Reagan Republicans killed this initiative, with the business-friendly White House declaring that more research was needed. Working groups were formed in 1981 but little progress was made during the Reagan years. It was not until 1990 that the first President George Bush signed *Clean Air Act* amendments for a 50 per cent SO_2 cut by 2000.

Meanwhile, there were federal-provincial collaborations of some substance in Canada. Environment Canada took the lead in proposing a maximum 20 kg per hectare per year maximum load for "moderately sensitive" ecosystems. Federal and provincial environment ministers agreed on 50 per cent reductions from 1980 levels by 1990. In 1984 this target was decoupled from American pledges and made unilateral by 1994 (MacDonald 1991).

Over 30 years, then, acid rain reduction policies became a rare but legitimate success story in North America. But what impact did it have on the freshwater fish stocks of affected regions? For Atlantic Canada the total SO_2 emissions at source dropped by 32 per cent by 1995. The deposition of acidic sulphate also declined in this period. However, data to 1998 (Beattie and Ro 1998) indicated that most of the region still received deposition greater than the critical load (that which maintained a pH above 6). Nova Scotia watersheds were the hardest hit.

The most dramatic impact has been in Maritime salmon rivers. In Nova Scotia, the highest depositions of acid rain have been in the western region and in the Atlantic shore drainages. On the Atlantic shore, pH levels range from 5.3 to 4.6, the latter making natural reproduction impossible. Of particular damage is the "plug" of acid accompanying the annual spring melt. Salmon have disappeared completely from 14 Nova Scotia rivers and declined by 90 per cent in 20 others. Thirty more are classified as threatened. The Atlantic Salmon Federation calls for a further reduction of SO_2 emissions by 75 per cent (Atlantic Salmon Federation n.d.).

A 2006 appraisal concluded that while precipitation acid loadings will return to balance over the next three decades, the cation loadings will take more than a century to disperse. An experimental project to lime sections of the West River in Halifax County in 2002 has shown positive results, but the prospects for broad-scale liming of the dozens of most damaged rivers has yet to be seriously considered (Atlantic Salmon Federation and Environment Canada 2007). Acid rain may be the best known environmental threat to Atlantic Canadian rivers and fishes but it is far from the only one. In this chapter's case study, Canada's most famous salmon angling watershed—the Miramichi River—is explored.

CASE STUDY: SALMON IN THE MIRAMICHI WATERSHED

The Miramichi in New Brunswick remains one of the great wild rivers of eastern Canada. It has an axial length of some 250 km from source to mouth and drains almost one-quarter of the provincial area. Its complex system of tributaries creates 13 sub-watersheds and covers more than 14,000 km^2 of forested land (Chadwick 1995). The two main branches are the Northwest Miramichi and the Southwest Miramichi, each flowing in an easterly direction before converging at Wilson's Corner for the final 20 km flow to the estuary in the inner portion of Miramichi Bay. This watershed is the second largest in the province, half the size of the Saint John but twice that of the Restigouche. The dispersal of sub-basins in the upper reaches also contributes to the resilience of the overall watershed. In addition, most of the terrestrial drainage is heavily forested, a physical feature that has closely shaped relations between humans and nature. The second dominant natural resource is salmon. The Miramichi is a spectacular salmon habitat, fished continually for centuries and the most important Atlantic salmon spawning ground on the east coast today. Among the sub-basins, the Northwest, Southwest, Renous, and Little Southwest provide the most extensive and important spawning grounds.

Considering its area, the Miramichi drainage is only sparsely inhabited. The population of about 45,000 is divided between Miramichi City near the estuary, a series of lumber towns located along the Southwest Miramichi, and rural residents scattered throughout the basin. Map 5.1 sets out the main tributaries and settlements.

Prior to the 1760s, European interests had little presence on the Miramichi, and Mi'kmaq fished a variety of species including bass, trout, eels, smelts, and sturgeon as well as salmon. The standard techniques included weirs, spears, traps, and nets, depending on species and season. A decisive change was marked by the 150 mi^2 land grant to William Davidson and John Cort in 1765, upstream of the confluence of the Northwest and Southwest Miramichi. This resulted in a fixed net salmon fishery and export business as well as the sale of riparian land to settlers. When the Davidson grant was revoked some 20 years later, colonial authorities transferred much of the best land to settlers. As a result, Mi'kmaq peoples found themselves under pressure at their village sites of Metepenagiag (Red Bank) and Natoaganeg (Eel Ground). Despite a Mi'kmaq river land licence

Map 5.1 Miramichi River Watershed, New Brunswick

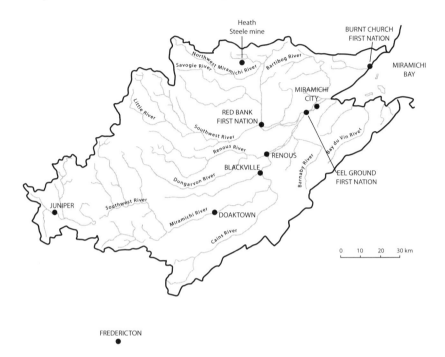

from Governor Parr on the Northwest above Red Bank and several reserves being established below that point, the nineteenth century saw sustained campaigns
to open Indian lands and squatter actions on those same lands (Hamilton 1984).
Ultimately three Mi'kmaq reserves were confirmed on the lower Miramichi
at Red Bank, Eel Ground, and Esgenoôpetitj (Burnt Church), amounting collectively to less than one-third of the original Davidson grant.

Not surprisingly, given its forested hinterland, the Miramichi has also figured
strongly in the province's industrial history. In many ways the history of northeast
New Brunswick is the history of the Miramichi. In early colonial times, two
towns grew up near the mouth of the river. Newcastle was established as the shire
town for Northumberland County in 1786. Located near the confluence of the
two main branches, the Northwest and Southwest Miramichi, it began as a commercial centre for the masting, shipbuilding, and lumbering industries as well as a
key port of export. Part of this trade was a thriving business in catching, pickling,
and exporting barrelled salmon. Slightly downstream on the opposite bank was
Chatham, a parallel town most prominently associated in the nineteenth century
with the shipbuilding and lumbering interests of the Cunard family. In 1825
the Great Fire burned a quarter of the province's forest cover while decimating
Newcastle. It was one of the epic natural disasters of the century.

By the mid-nineteenth century the cumulative impact of the commercial fishing and export trade registered in the first historic salmon stock decline. Although the long distance fish trade never recovered, local communities still relied heavily on salmon as part of the regional economy, and a massive system of shore net fishing continued. By the 1850s a third sector began to expand as sport fishers discovered Maritime salmon rivers. While angling was pursued across the Maritimes, the Miramichi was understandably famous and attracted seasonal sport fishers from all over the continent and beyond.

The rise of the timber economy affected the salmon resource in many respects. Early logging began at the riverbanks and advanced upstream. Not only did the loss of riparian forest cover tend to raise water temperatures (to which salmon were sensitive), it could also encourage soil erosion and siltation. Even more severe was the impact of spring log drives to transport logs downstream, scouring riverbeds and destroying spawning habitat in the process. Add to this the impact of local sawmills. Their dams and mill ponds blocked the fish runs, and although fish ladders were often mandated by law, these were often ignored. Solid wood wastes were also disposed into streams in the forms of wood chips and sawdust.

The Atlantic salmon run in the Miramichi was historically the greatest on the east coast. Even with its relative decline in modern times, this watershed remains the most important in eastern North America. The riverbeds of the many tributaries offer massive spawning grounds and rich habitats for juvenile fish. The young fish hatch out in May or June. During the first few years in local waters, adequate forest cover and supply of leaf detritus are keys to health. After an initial two to six years of life in the river, the surviving smolts leave their freshwater nurseries and head downstream to the sea. Their internal organs adapt to salt water and they spend one or more years in the ocean growing rapidly in size. The subsequent return of grilse (one year at sea) or adult salmon (two or more years) to their native rivers for autumn spawning involves a reverse adaptation. The demographics of salmon survival are stark. By one estimate, for every 7,000 salmon eggs laid, 70 smolts reach the sea and of these, four return to their original river where three spawn successfully (MREAC and ACAP 2007, 52). Although numbers of return spawners are vastly diminished with each cycle, Atlantic salmon can spawn as many as six times. It is the upstream and downstream migrations that afforded extraordinary opportunities for the subsistence, commercial, and recreational salmon fisheries.

The regulation of salmon fishing is a complex and many-sided story. The federal government was pressed on several fronts to favour the interests of rival harvesters. Commercial operators concentrated on the lower river and estuary while local residents defended their domestic fisheries wherever they lived. Aboriginal fishers continued traditional practices on the river while the increasingly lucrative tourist anglers and lodge owners pushed for a sport-dominated harvest. Despite the guarantees for traditional harvesting pursuits that were central to the eighteenth-century Mi'kmaq treaties, the colonial and Canadian courts tended to subordinate Indian hunting and fishing rights to the authority of provincial crown land, forest, and water title (Wicken 2002). As seen earlier with

Boat Harbour, the federal government had a strong jurisdictional claim after 1867 through its mandate for Indian Affairs. In practice, however, the federal fisheries power became the fulcrum of government intervention. In the decades following World War II, the sport salmon sector became more formally organized, with several angling groups at both the watershed and the regional level. The result, discussed later in this section, was a far stronger voice for salmon conservation.

A key factor shaping politics among rival harvester interests was the licensing system. Beginning in the mid-1800s, when spearing and netting were first prohibited in spawning grounds, the colonial crown in New Brunswick and Quebec began leasing salmon fishing rights on designated river passages to private individuals and angling clubs (Parenteau 2004). In return for exclusive rights, lessees were obliged to install private guardians to monitor and protect their holdings. This system was carried over to the federal freshwater regime and was later transferred to provincial administration. By the 1890s more than 100 prime salmon stretches had been disposed in this way, with affluent foreigners joining Canadians as angling lease holders. Not surprisingly, the private lease system provoked widespread tensions with rural residents who held to customary local use rules. Parenteau describes the history of legal and cultural conflicts around fisheries patrolling, subsistence fishing, net fishing bans, and poaching on salmon watersheds like the Miramichi. It was notoriously difficult to secure and uphold convictions among rural magistrates and juries, even for violent crimes such as arson and assault. Such community tensions are what James Scott (1990) refers to as everyday forms of local resistance, of which only a portion rises to the level of visible politics.

One activity that fell beyond the grasp of salmon conservation, however, was the commercial forest industry. New Brunswick hosted one of Canada's premier lumber industries, and the pulp and paper sector came to rival it in the twentieth century. Both, however, lay under provincial government jurisdiction and Fredericton was tightly committed to the logging and milling economy. One of the most spectacular instances of this involved the chemical spray campaigns that covered the province for 40 years after 1953 (Sandberg and Clancy 2002). Maritime Canadian forests were prone to cyclical (20–40 year) infestations of the spruce budworm, which killed massive swathes of softwood stands. During the 1920s outbreak, the budworm damage was treated as a natural and inevitable process that would end when the insects ran out of food. By the time of the next cycle in the 1950s, neither government nor industry contemplated widespread timber losses with equanimity. An unprecedented joint enterprise was organized for the comprehensive, multiyear aerial spray of insecticides across the New Brunswick forests. Beginning in 1953, the chemical DDT was applied by a private air force assembled by Forest Protection Inc. (FPI) and millions of hectares were covered in peak years. This was not without ecological cost. Almost immediately, ground evidence pointed to the damaging impact to fish and birds, with much of it also documented by field studies at the federal fish research station at St. Andrews (Keenleyside 1959). The Atlantic Salmon Association publicly opposed the spray campaign as early as 1956. It also figured, dramatically, in Rachel Carson's 1962 bestseller, *Silent Spring*. Juvenile salmon populations declined sharply in the late 1950s and early 1960s.

What makes the DDT spray program so significant ecologically was its breadth and duration. For 15 years, FPI applied an industrial chemical to New Brunswick watersheds such as the Miramichi, with virtually no officially expressed concern for its collateral effects on wildlife or humans. The absence of integrated resource programming is politically revealing. Crown forest agencies dealt with the budworm as a forest management matter, while crown wildlife and fisheries agencies had very little influence on the key decisions, despite the ecological implications for birds and fishes. While one federal agency (the Canadian Forestry Service) was a partner in New Brunswick's spray campaign, another agency (the Fisheries Research Board) was documenting the environmental degradation. It is a telling comment on political priorities that the Miramichi fisheries research program was discontinued in 1968 by federal government decision.

Dramatic as the forest spray campaigns have been, it would be wrong to ignore other industrial impacts. In the postwar period, a promising base metal find was made near the Temogonops River, a tributary of the Northwest Miramichi. The Heath Steele mine, a copper-lead-zinc operation, was opened in 1956 by a joint venture of American Metals Inc. and INCO. By one account, during the spring that followed the first dumping of untreated waste water into the stream, returning salmon tried to reverse their course to the spawning grounds and exit the fish box at the entrance to the Northwest (Weeks 1968). While the mine property changed hands several times and was periodically closed when markets slumped, production continued until 1999. Over a 30-year operating life it released heavy metal and acid contaminants into the river and depressed pH levels to the point of eliminating native fish from the Temogonops tributary. Remedial work has continued at the site since 2000.

The sulphate pulp mill near Chatham was an added source of organic pollutants for decades until its closure in 2005. Similarly a wood treatment plant in Newcastle accounted for persistent aromatic hydrocarbons (PAHs) before its closure in the 1990s. Sewage treatment systems in Newcastle and Chatham added bacterial pollution to the lower river before their recent upgrades, as did Canadian Forces Base Chatham before its closure. It is not an exaggeration to state that, by eliminating the major effluent contaminants, the de-industrialization of the Miramichi watershed over the past two decades has brought significant improvements to water quality. Even in the estuary, where contaminated sediments have been deposited for over half a century or more, the government of Canada's decision to cease dredging a shipping channel has prevented the release of accumulated toxins. As a whole, this has led to a local assessment that while stresses remain, "the state of the Miramichi River is generally good" (MREAC and ACAP, 2007, ii).

Returning to the salmon resource, the 1970s and 1980s were decades of concern, characterized by the continued decline of spawning numbers. Several conservation measures followed. In 1984, commercial net fishing was closed across the Maritime region including the Miramichi. That left recreational and

Aboriginal fishing. In another wild salmon conservation measure, the sport fishing regulations were altered in favour of catch and release (as distinct from catch and retain) fishing. Today on the Miramichi, this occurs through a combination of licence conditions and bag limits, delineated by stretches of the river. Large adult salmon (>63 cm) can be fished on a catch and release basis only. Small adults (<63 cm) can be retained on the basis of one per day and eight per season, while catch and release are limited to four per day. In the years before the *Sparrow* decision, Aboriginal fishing did not attract policy priority but this began to change in the 1990s and accelerated after the *R. v. Marshall* decision in 1999 (Coates 2000). For salmon, a combination of gill netting, angling, and trap netting is authorized, subject to catch limits, under collective licenses negotiated with First Nations.

The initial conservation impulse, then, lay with regulating fisher behaviours. Parallel to this, an expanded program of population monitoring and science work was launched. The combined freshwater and seawater life cycle made salmon a very complicated species to model for management purposes. One dimension is population abundance. The overall Atlantic salmon stock with at least one sea year peaked in the 1970s as high as 1.7 million fish. In the 1980s the total dropped below 1 million, and in the 1990s the range was .6 million to .8 million. By 2009 the estimated total was again .6 million salmon. For the Miramichi River system, the average adult population in the early 2000s was 54,200, down about one-third from the previous decade (Canada Department of Fisheries and Oceans 2010b). Another key dimension is adult escapements and sea returns. Here data are measured by trapnet and headwater barrier counts. In 2012, the estimated return population was 21,640, a decline of one-third from the previous five-year average (Canada Department of Fisheries and Oceans 2013). A further key dimension is spawn concentration, which has been measured by egg deposition in prime spawning areas. For the Miramichi basin, the "conservation limit" has been defined as a rate of 2.4 eggs per m^2 in wetted rearing areas. Eggs met the conservation level in 7 of the 15 years to 2007. In 2012, eggs met only 72 per cent of the conservation level (before harvest), with a higher level on the southwest than on the northwest arm (Canada Department of Fisheries and Oceans 2013).

The trends described above are only a few of the population parameters that are modelled in basins like the Miramichi. Taken as a whole, the picture is one of a population running at the lower end of a 30-year trend, and with a significant drop from trend in 2012. There is regional variation as well, with three of the key tributaries (Little Southwest, Renous, and Southwest) on the southwest arm having higher counts on certain criteria than the northwest. Such findings have heightened the already elevated concern among sport fisher groups, conservationists, and government managers. In the short term, consideration can be given to lessening sport fish retention levels by bringing all adult salmon under catch and release. There have also been suggestions about negotiating a suspension of gill net salmon fishing by First Nations. Although either of these may come to pass, they would require a shift in the implicit political bargain that seems to underlie the harvest management regime—that both angling tourism and First Nations interests deserve a continuing if declining share of an adult salmon fishery.

At the same time, the expanded science database points to new areas of concern. As seen above, federal and provincial jurisdiction is concentrated in the freshwater phase of the salmon life cycle, as bounded by salmon fishing area 16A. Yet the past two decades have also underlined the vulnerability of adult salmon to intensive fishing in the ocean phase of their life cycle, or as the science literature terms it, "marine intercepts." Declining survival rates at sea are reflected in declining adult salmon return rates and the resulting declines in freshwater spawning on rivers such as the Miramichi. Of particular concern recently has been the West Greenland salmon fishery, where an estimated 80 per cent of the stock comes from Atlantic North America. Here the political regime is entirely distinct, dependent upon negotiated agreements among sovereign states, to limit catch and effort in the North Atlantic. The North Atlantic Salmon Conservation Organization, founded in 1984, succeeded over a decade in reducing the West Greenland ocean salmon fishery by 85 per cent to about 213 tonnes (80,000 large salmon). This evolved into a far smaller "subsistence" fishery, taking 10–25 tonnes (3,000 to 7,500 salmon) per year in the 2002–09 period. However this harvest rebounded to 35 tonnes in 2012. Furthermore, at the time of writing, Greenland talks about more than doubling this harvest in years to come (Burke 2013). The fact that the Greenland salmon landings are still less than the combined Canadian sport and First Nations harvest has made it difficult to deny the Greenlanders claim to an expanded share on grounds of equity (Taylor 2013). As DFO put it in 2009, the department's policy effort on salmon has been "persistent, expensive and consistently challenged by new or emerging threats to their [salmon] survival" (Canada Department of Fisheries and Oceans 2009).

Challenges of Managing a Species under Stress

One political interest that has only recently gained recognition is the wild species itself. The notion of natural species put at risk from human society, and deserving of protection on such grounds, began to find policy expression in the 1970s. As the legal regime expanded, species at risk (SAR) policy held the potential to alter the balance among organized interests. Even after the recent Harper amendments, state authorities are required to intervene where scientific evidence points to high levels of threat. While Miramichi salmon have not yet been designated in the endangered category, other Atlantic salmon stocks have.

The plight of wild Atlantic salmon became a public concern in the 1980s and has continued to the present day. Studies suggesting population declines coincided with reports from fishers about field conditions and landings. One important consequence was the expansion of field research. Historically, the Atlantic salmon occupied a range along the eastern seaboard from New England in the south to east Hudson's Bay in the north. An estimated two-thirds of that population lay in Canada. The economic importance of this resource was un-questioned. Yet three decades later, the total population has fallen by half. In this section we examine why this has occurred.

One of the early findings was to caution against generalization. For species at risk purposes, 16 distinct salmon segments or units have been identified in Canada, each consisting of multiple rivers where the fish shared genetic and behavioural traits. Some have been designated stable or *not at risk* throughout the past three decades, in northern Quebec, Labrador, and most of Newfoundland. At the same time, five units have been designated *endangered*, along the Bay of Fundy, Nova Scotia's Atlantic coast, and Quebec's Anticosti Island. On the south coast of Newfoundland, salmon fall into the less urgent classification of *threatened*. In the southern Gulf of St. Lawrence, along with the lower St. Lawrence River and Quebec's north shore, salmon are *of special concern*. And in Lake Ontario, wild Atlantic salmon have been *extinct* for over a century (Canada 2010a).

These categories—extinct, endangered, threatened, of special concern, and not at risk—are part of the continuum established by Canada's species at risk regime. Passed in 2001, it consists of a series of interconnected decision-processes aimed at identifying, protecting, and remediating the conditions of vulnerable species. As far as salmon are concerned, the Miramichi watershed is part of the southern Gulf of St. Lawrence unit, where the classification is "of special concern." This means that ongoing monitoring is required, though active habitat intervention is not. At present, the policy focus is on the "endangered" units mentioned above. What might a SAR strategy involve, if conditions deteriorated further in the Miramichi? The inner Bay of Fundy unit (iBoF) was first designated endangered in 2001. It was placed on the "at risk" list in 2003 and a recovery plan was formulated. The iBoF unit was reas-sessed in 2006 and 2010 with similar conclusions. For the other four units that were assessed as endangered in 2010, the process is just beginning (Canada 2010b). At the time of writing, the minister is still assessing the technical endangered status report. When it comes, the ministerial response may involve DFO science-based recovery potential assessment, further public consultation, and a socioeconomic cost report on the impact of listing. Following all of this, the minister will go to cabinet with a recommendation on the listing question. Thus any prospect of a recovery plan is a matter for the future. Not surprisingly, the salmon sport fishing advocacy network has expressed frustration with the slow pace of government action in this field.

It may be thought that the federal government's tardiness in launching a frontal SAR strategy for salmon recovery is irresponsible. The evident lack of urgency does raise significant questions. However, the evolution of scientific thinking helps to illustrate multiple dilemmas. It is natural to concentrate on the freshwater conditions in spawning and juvenile growth phases. Here attention has been drawn to the negative impacts of dam barriers, industrial contaminants, and overfishing. In the 2000s, however, the question of reduced marine survival also came to the forefront. This includes matters of farmed fish impacts, diseases, increased predators, illegal fishing, and ocean ecological changes (Canada 2010a). The nature of the conservation problem, then, has been changing. As a result, the particular mix of assessments and responses will vary by population unit. Along Nova Scotia's Atlantic shore, acid rain is central. In Newfoundland and Labrador, illegal fishing leads the list. In the Bay of Fundy, it is salmon farms and ecology.

Contemporary Politics and the Salmon Policy Network

Historically, government agencies and organized social interests have been closely involved in legal and regulatory decisions for salmon. But the discussion above suggests that patterns of society-state interaction have become more formalized in the modern period. Today the policy community for fisheries management, on the Miramichi and elsewhere in Atlantic Canada, consists of several organized interests, both state and nonstate, that are connected in complicated ways. Several features are worth noting. First, the nonstate players operate on spatial scales ranging from the local to provincial to international. This applies particularly to sport fishing and Aboriginal interests. Second, the range of activities now extends far beyond conservation advocacy. NGOs in the Miramichi now operate fish hatchery facilities, maintain water quality testing networks, and sponsor scientific studies and consultative meetings independent of government. First Nations negotiate fisheries agreements with DFO and have access to the courts when administrative options fail. Third, this has developed against a backdrop of salmon stock declines in recent decades, which places greater pressure on state fisheries agencies at a time of diminishing fiscal capacity. Not unrelated to wild salmon regulation is the expansion of the salmon farming segment since the 1980s. Finally, since 1990 judicial decisions have elevated the status of Aboriginal fishing activities in the management hierarchy and forced a reordering of priorities.

The policy community that surrounds salmon conservation suggests a combination of pluralist and clientelist relations. In the early phases sport fisher groups had to campaign to attract government attention. This seems to have worked best when the salmon lobbies were able to combine residents within the watershed and seasonal sport fishers who lived outside it. As time progressed, the groups that demonstrated staying power were enlisted as allies and partners for certain purposes. At times, alliances of salmon groups spanning the entire Atlantic coast have managed to push a wider agenda to protect salmon in the North Atlantic and Europe.

There were voices for organized sport fishing from the middle of the nineteenth century, but the modern story begins in 1953 with the formation of the Miramichi Salmon Association (MSA). This was formed by anglers to defend the health of the salmon stocks. Its members are distributed across the watershed and beyond. Long an advocacy group, the MSA underwent a qualitative shift in the late 1990s. It assumed ownership of the federal salmon hatchery in South Esk when the DFO announced its closure. It hired the first permanent staff in 2000 when former federal biologist Mark Hambrook assumed the role of president.

For a voluntary sector group, the MSA has wide coat-tails and deep pockets, reporting a $923,000 expenditure budget in 2012. Each autumn it hosts $1,000-a-plate dinners in Montreal, New York, and Chicago. It partners the government of New Brunswick in the crown fish tract licensing program, has begun a "First Cast" program for young anglers, and holds a seat on virtually every Miramichi watershed working group. It runs a summer Conservation Corps with Mi'kmaq youth from the Red Bank and Eel Ground reserves. The MSA also supports vigorous measures (including poisoning) to eliminate the invasive small mouth bass (a non-indigenous species and competitor to salmon, introduced in 2005) from its foothold at Miramichi Lake (Miramichi Salmon Association n.d.).

The sport salmon lobby has a wider grasp than a single watershed, and its provincial voice is the New Brunswick Salmon Council. It brings together 26 local conservation groups, including the MSA and its subsections. This body has been the collective voice of wild salmon conservation and a lobbyist for more effective New Brunswick salmon policies. It has campaigned for the prohibition of all gill net salmon fishing, pressed for a shift to land-based salmon aquaculture, and called for the expansion of catch and release rules to include all age classes of salmon in critical areas. The Council closely monitors DFO salmon programs and quickly highlights and condemns any contraction of federal effort (New Brunswick Salmon Council n.d.).

The New Brunswick Salmon Council also serves as one of six regional affiliates of the umbrella interest group known as the Atlantic Salmon Federation (ASF). The roots of the ASF lie in the Atlantic Salmon Association formed in 1948 in Montreal (ASF, n.d.). Thirty-five years later the Association merged with the science-oriented International Atlantic Salmon Foundation of St. Andrews to form the ASF. In 1987 it hammered out the protocol known as the Matapedia Accord that formalized the respective roles of the Federation and the regional affiliates. In effect, the ASF focuses on political and policy action while the regional councils or associations concentrate on resource enhancement and field projects. Thus we can see a three-tier associational structure combining advocacy and operations.

Returning to the watershed level, a leading citizen group today is the Miramichi River Environmental Assessment Committee (MREAC). It originated in 1989 in response to the federal government decision not to conduct an environmental assessment of the pulp and paper mill expansion at Newcastle in Miramichi Bay. The MREAC undertook the study anyway, with financing provided by the mill itself. Once done, the group moved on to the question of watershed health. Its final report was released in 1992. On the base of past achievements, the MREAC was a natural candidate for the Atlantic Coastal Action Program (ACAP) and was so designated in 1993. As seen in chapter 3, ACAP support is designed to elevate a group to higher operational levels, with a full-time director and ongoing project funding. At the same time, the ACAP guidelines require that affiliates function as stakeholder forums with ties to a variety of regional water groups. The first

Miramichi action plan was released in 1994. The 2007 state of the watershed report, mentioned earlier, is an important sequel.

The second key stakeholder bloc in the Miramichi salmon policy network are the First Nations peoples. By virtue of the treaties, the Constitution, and the court decisions, they hold a distinct legal status based on Aboriginal food fishery rights. First Nations fishery rights extend to a wide variety of species and sectors, particularly those with commercial potential. Yet, as seen earlier, salmon fishing rights have been asserted along twin tracks—direct political action in cases like the Big Hole Tract dispute of 1995 and negotiated fishing agreements with DFO in the post-Marshall period (Adlam 2002). Wild Atlantic salmon have a key role here, given Mi'kmaq history on the Miramichi. In addition, estimates put First Nations food fishing at approximately half of the total Atlantic regional annual harvest, with angler retention making up the rest.

Today no established interests deny a First Nations' legal right to salmon, but there remains a continuing policy controversy over the conservation aspects of this fishery, covering both gear types and harvest levels. Gill nets are widely used by Aboriginal fishers and entail very high mortality for both salmon and trout, whereas trap nets and angling make it possible to select food fish by age and sex and further the salmon recovery goal. For Mi'kmaq the choice of fishing method is seen as integral to the right to fish and to manage the fisheries. For non-Mi'kmaq the elimination of salmon gill netting is considered a crucial conservation measure, albeit one that must be negotiated with Aboriginal rights holders. In the neighbouring Cascapedia (Quebec) watershed, the Gesgapegiag First Nation implemented a voluntary suspension of gillnetting on a trial basis. One possible avenue is to negotiate agreements between state conservation agencies and First Nations that enable the latter to limit gill netting as part of a Band salmon management policy.

Other organized interests play roles in the salmon policy network. These include industrial interests in the forest and mineral sectors. Although leading facilities have been closed over the past decade, there are environmental legacy issues to be addressed here as well as the prospects for new industry. For example, the shale gas sector (discussed in chapter 9) has identified geophysical potential in the upper regions of the Miramichi watershed. More stable economic sectors include the commercial fish camp operators and the tourist segment more generally. The municipality of Miramichi City is also a major stakeholder in the estuary region.

These threads can be drawn together to characterize the salmon policy network on the Miramichi. It includes multiple departments of the governments of Canada and New Brunswick, the relations between departments at each jurisdictional level, and relations between the two levels. For example, salmon stock assessment falls to federal Fisheries and Oceans, while species at risk policy is based in Environment Canada. First Nations fishing rights involve both federal Indian Affairs and DFO. Fish licensing is administered by New Brunswick Natural Resources while tourism and environment play roles, too. The organized interests

Figure 5.1 The Salmon Policy Network for Miramichi

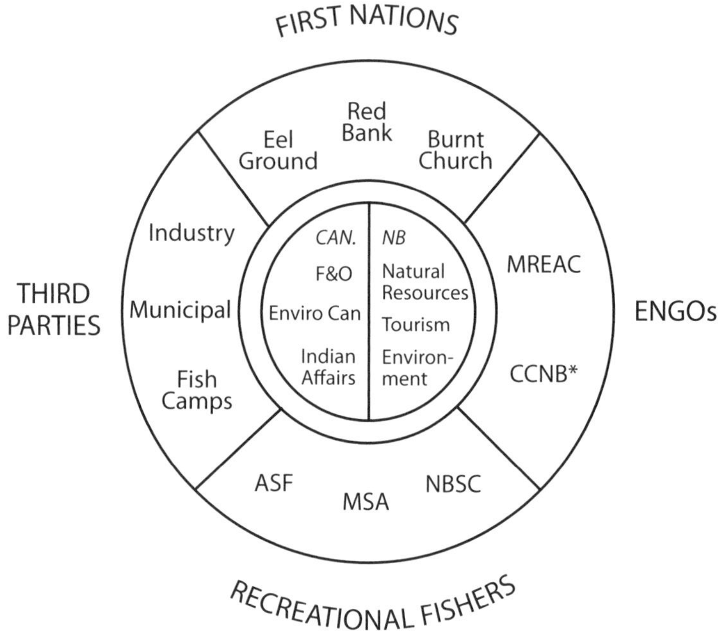

FIRST NATIONS

Red
Bank
Eel
Ground
Burnt
Church

Industry

CAN.
F&O

NB

Natural
Resources

MREAC

THIRD
PARTIES

Municipal

Enviro Can

Tourism

ENGOs

Indian
Affairs

Environ-
ment

Fish
Camps

CCNB*

ASF
MSA
NBSC

RECREATIONAL FISHERS

*Conservation Council of New Brunswick

can be grouped by category as well. In the sport salmon category, the network is predominantly one of pluralist advocacy. In the First Nations category, by contrast, relations are decidedly more clientelistic. Overall the salmon policy network is best described as a hybrid. Figure 5.1 illustrates the various layers.

Conclusion

Freshwater fisheries constitute a complex field of politics and management in Canada. This is partly due to the diversity of species, stocks, and habitats that can be found across the country. There is an equally complex network of interest groups, ranging from local fish and game groups to provincial and national associations, including particular representation for key species like Atlantic salmon. Fisheries policy can target many variables: it can regulate the fishers themselves or the fish-sustaining habitat or the health of fish stocks. Much of nineteenth-century fisheries politics was driven by conflicts among different fishing segments. Distinct harvester groups—commercial, recreational, and Aboriginal—compete for political priority and management support. In contexts of resource depletion, this can lead to zero-sum contests.

The period following World War II brought attention to fish stocks, and the period since 1980 elevated habitat in the policy mix. The scope of freshwater fisheries programming has expanded markedly in the past half century, particularly with mounting social awareness of the threats of aquatic pollution, the realities of lost habitat, and the complex ecological relations that embed fish in food chains. Since the 1980s, another dramatic transition has attended the judicial confirmation of Aboriginal fishing rights. Major gaps persist, in both biophysical and sociopolitical knowledge. In addition, freshwater fisheries policy is subject to an issue-attention cycle that features periods of activism but also quiescence. If senior governments choose to disengage on fisheries questions in the current age of austerity, community stewardship may be challenged to fill the vacuum. Certainly such trends are reflected in the salmon sector of the Miramichi watershed.

6
Irrigation Politics

IN WESTERN CANADA, THE GREATEST DEMAND for freshwater is made by agri-culture, and irrigated farming is the most water-intensive variety. This chapter explores how water has been organized and used for purposes of irrigation. It is a story almost as old as the nation, but it has evolved in response to new technologies, organized clienteles, and government policies. Broad-scale irrigation involves river regulation and the construction of extensive storage and transport structures. Once established, such works alter waterways in definitive ways, and the interests associated with irrigation facilities become substantial political players. In the classic era of irrigation development, producer interests enjoyed politically dominant positions. Eventually, however, the logic of growth and expansion confronts natural limits, and by the 1980s these limits began to register both physically and politically. A variety of new interests, both within and beyond the affected watersheds, challenged the development coalition in southern Alberta. Our case study of the Oldman River tributary basin offers a striking case in point. First with the construction of the Three Rivers Dam and later with the new mandate for water management in the South Saskatchewan River basin, the fundamentals of irrigated farming have come under review in recent times.

Irrigation can be defined as farming by use of water greater than what is available from natural rainfall. While irrigation is practiced in most provinces, Alberta is the leader, with British Columbia and Saskatchewan a distant second and third. Together they account for 85 per cent of irrigated agriculture in Canada, with most of the balance found in the market garden areas of Ontario and Quebec. Whether the location is southern Alberta, the Okanagan region in the BC interior, or central Saskatchewan, farmers depend heavily on irrigation if they seek to cultivate anything but dryland crops.

Irrigated farming is a world phenomenon. Indeed three-quarters of such operations occur in the developing world. On a global basis, 17 per cent of agricultural production was produced on irrigated land in the 1990s, but irrigation generated more than double that as a share of overall food production (Ongley 1996).

An irrigation system requires the engineering and construction of elaborate systems to collect, transport, and deliver water. This means dams and reservoirs, canals, pipelines, and water compression systems. Equally, an irrigation system requires a sociopolitical regime to decide questions of who builds and owns the infrastructure, who allocates the water, and what the water is worth. Irrigation is integral to watershed management systems as well, as large-scale continuous withdrawals can trigger water shortages in local drainages.

Excessive water withdrawal is now a prominent question in many parts of the world. Unmanaged water takings can radically diminish downstream flows as well as affect groundwater levels. The question of nonpoint (diffuse source) water pollution is also of major concern in this sector. This is because irrigation water passes through land and returns to the waterflow via canals and natural drainage. Often this drives up salt and nitrate counts downstream. High field fertilizer use adds to the chemical load. One of the most severe cases of dysfunctional irrigation is found in the Aral Sea region, located on the border between Kazahkstan and Uzbekistan. During the Soviet period, irrigation was pursued relentlessly to support a cotton industry. The major rivers feeding the Aral Sea (once one of the four largest lakes in the world) were dammed and the flows diverted to cotton farms. By 2000, the Aral had declined to one-tenth of its former size, and both waters and lakebeds had heavy concentrations of salt and chemicals (de Villiers 1999). In the West today, sustainability questions are now being posed systematically to irrigated farming. Both state authorities (through departments of agriculture) and industry interests (farmers and irrigation suppliers) are closely involved in licensing, standard setting, and certification systems for environmental performance.

Historical Origins

In the early 1890s, disparate interests came together in southern Alberta to promote a new form of agriculture. The principals included railway and coal promoter Elliot Galt and Charles Ora Card, a Mormon community leader from the United States. A closely aligned third party was the national Department of the Interior, whose officials administered crown title over natural resources. Because land grants usually accompanied railway charters, Galt was eager to attract settler immigrants to the semi-arid frontier west, and it was Card who convinced him that farming rather than ranching was the key to prosperity. The Mormons had demonstrated this in Utah, where they had perfected a farm system based on irrigated fields. A group of American Mormons planned to emigrate and take up hundreds of thousands of acres leased from Galt's Alberta Rail and Coal Co., but the deal faltered amidst the economic depression in 1893. The plan was revived a few years later as a swap of land and cash in return for the Mormons' building of the first St. Mary canal (den Otter 1982). Later came the founding of towns, the extension of railways and further canals, solidifying a new form of prairie agriculture (den Otter 1988). Today more than 60 per cent of the irrigated farming in Canada is located in the three major tributary basins of the South Saskatchewan River in Alberta: the Red Deer, the Bow, and in particular the Oldman.

The practice of irrigated farming is far from new. In Asia, the ancient rice economy was based on elaborate systems of water control and distribution that were maintained by state authorities. In North America, the Anasazi Indians of the southwest stored and distributed freshwater for desert agriculture in precontact times (Cech 2003). And it is said of the Mormons that the advance party to Utah in the 1840s laid out farmstead boundaries on the first morning and began to dam and dig the first ditches in the afternoon. California qualifies as the most heavily engineered irrigation state, where 85 per cent of all freshwater consumption goes to agriculture. Although private irrigation schemes began there in the nineteenth century, intensive irrigation took off after World War I, driven by new centrifugal pumps that lifted groundwater together with generous financial subsidies from the US federal Bureau of Reclamation (Reisner 1986). Two particular concerns of this chapter are the political interplay of societal interests and state policy, and the impacts of irrigation agriculture on associated watersheds.

The 100th meridian of longitude provides an approximate dividing line between the well-watered eastern region of the continent and the semi-arid west where annual precipitation is less than 50 cm (20 inches) per year. Certain forms of dryland agriculture can flourish here—livestock grazing on short grass ranges for example, and field crops such as wheat, oats, sorghum, and sunflowers along with some grasses and hays. But for most other crops, a steady supply of water is necessary to supplement natural rain and snowfall. Among these crops are corn, beans, other vegetable and fruit crops, and intensive livestock operations. This water can be extracted from the ground, as it is in the plains states that overlay the giant aquifers, or it can be diverted from natural waterflow into field watering. Alberta is part of the latter group.

In the case of irrigation, the challenges of development involve an interplay of physical engineering and sociopolitical organization. To illustrate this we consider the politics of irrigation at its epicentre in southern Alberta. This highlights a variety of property rights to land and water, the roles of private and public capital, the roles of respective governments, the design of specialized institutions such as irrigation districts, and the problems of water allocation that accompany extensive irrigation. A case study of the Oldman River basin completes the discussion.

Designing and Maintaining an Irrigation Regime

Building a new economy is never a simple matter. It involves a synthesis of ideas, material interests, and action. Often it relies on a screening process of trial and error, fits and starts, as many experiments are launched and a few prove out. Invariably this involves conflicts of interests among prospective winners and losers. The terms of advantage and the coalitions of interest inevitably shift over time. Because the irrigation economy of southern Alberta has evolved for more than a century, it can be examined in several phases (Topham 1982).

Irrigation on the Settlement Frontier

In Alberta, the first projects tended to be sponsored by private rail and land owners, who had a joint interest in attracting settler-farmers to the region. In this they were joined by purveyors of technical knowledge in hydrology and engineering. On this basis, "watered farming" joined ranching and dryland cropping as agricultural techniques on the prairies. For a water-scarce and drought-prone region, where the nineteenth-century surveyor John Palliser laid out his massive "triangle" of apparently non-cultivatable lands, irrigation offered dramatic possibilities to transform the natural environment. Consequently it was promoted in the pre-World War I period, principally by private capital. River flows were held up by the construction of weirs—in-stream barriers that hold back some waters while permitting a surplus overflow. Canals were then dug to carry the behind-weir water to farm limits.

This would not have been possible, however, without facilitative measures of state policy. In 1894 the Parliament of Canada (which exercised state jurisdiction over prairie lands and waters until 1930) passed the *Northwest Irrigation Act*. It asserted crown title to stream beds and stream flows, displacing the previous riparian system that vested use rights in adjacent landowners. This enabled the federal Department of the Interior to survey and license water withdrawals from river channels, independent of the riparian landlords. This regulatory power made the Dominion government a central party to the promotion of irrigated agriculture, offering any assistance short of direct spending on the construction of fixed works (Mitchner 1965). By 1900 there were 112 projects, large and small, serving 80,000 acres (Raby 1965). Today, there are almost 3,000 individual irrigation projects under license by Alberta Environment, totalling some 310,000 acres or about one-fifth of total irrigated farmlands (Alberta Agriculture and Rural Development 2013). The balance of irrigated farmland is served by group projects.

A prominent example of large-scale irrigated land enterprise was the St. Mary Project, begun in 1901. Launched by Galt and the Mormons, it began with a weir and headgate on the St. Mary River, which fed a canal to the Magrath and Lethbridge areas. The system unfolded as a series of connector flows from the canal to creeks and coulees, using natural features wherever possible. At the farm boundary the landowner took control and built a system of ditches to bring water to the fields. By the time the project passed to the Canadian Pacific Railway (CPR) in 1908, some 4,000 acres were irrigated. The potential for ever wider application drove promotional campaigns to attract further settlers. Posters proclaimed "Every Man a Rainmaker!" and "No Drought Here!" Lethbridge town described its environs as "The Garden of the West." By the close of World War I, the CPR had water agreements for over 100,000 acres (SMRID n.d.).

The Emergence of Local Irrigation Bodies

Around the time of the Great War, the province of Alberta found its way toward a more assertive promotional role. This was expressed in the *Irrigation Districts Organization Act* of 1915. It targeted the supply and distributional end of the irrigation chain by enabling a form of alternative enterprise to the private company. In effect, it adapted the municipal model to a special purpose authority for irrigation works. This had been pioneered in the United States, as a solution for the supply of water to farmers lacking riparian (on-stream) rights. The irrigation district offered a means for such farmers to join together to construct a delivery infrastructure to their landholdings. The first California statute was passed in the

1880s (Worster 1992). An irrigation district (ID) has farm owner or lessee members with assessed irrigation acreages on which they pay annual rates. Members contract with the ID for water delivery to an assessed annual level at a stipulated rate. To build the infrastructure, the province of Alberta offered financial support to newly formed irrigation districts, through bond guarantees to underwrite construction and maintenance. By the time that crown land and water jurisdiction passed from Ottawa to Alberta in 1930, there were six such IDs to go along with the four projects owned by private land companies. By 1960 there were 12 IDs, and today they number 13.

The Alberta *irrigation Districts Organization Act* represented a crucial step forward. Not only did it provide indispensable financial support to the new organizations but it did so in a manner consistent with the ethic of farmer-run enterprise that was so central to the times. Moreover, the irrigation districts were farmer-, not government-, owned though they certainly advanced Alberta government interests. The act also standardized the fiscal and governance procedures for irrigation districts. The first five IDs were established in the region of the St. Mary water scheme and drew upon it for water supply.

Whether the irrigation enterprise was corporate or district, certain physical and social features were the same. A system that relied on taking off water from natural streams was constrained by the flow patterns of those rivers. In snow-fed basins like those in southern Alberta, this meant that flows would peak in late spring and hit bottom in the winter months. This imposed complicated supply problems as farmers coped with declining water levels as the crop year unfolded. An obvious alternative was to redesign the flow pattern, to store large volumes in reservoirs and lakes for release throughout the year. But the design, construction, and financial challenges here were beyond the capacity or inclination of early irrigators. Although the CPR built the first major storage dam on the Bow River at Bassano in 1914, it proved to be the exception.

If aggregate water supply was the "macro-political" dilemma, then individual farm needs fuelled the "micro-political" turmoil. Each farmer faced the challenge of managing that farm's water, and the problem was invariably one of adequate supply. Situations of shortage, whether due to seasonal drought or distributional biases, had the capacity to trigger quarrels in communities and send rival parties to court.

In addition to marking the province's commitment to irrigated farming, the design of the ID system created powerful new institutions in rural southern Alberta. By 1948 there were a dozen irrigation districts. Having been created by provincial statute and supported financially by the Irrigation Branch of the provincial department of agriculture, the IDs enjoyed a positive clientelistic relationship with the government of Alberta. As a further measure of political maturation, the IDs joined together in 1948 to create an associated voice for their collective concerns (Alberta Irrigation Projects Association n.d.). While they came under financial stress during the Depression (with the consequences described below), they survived to play a renewed role in the modern period. Today they account for more than 1.3 million acres or almost 80 per cent of irrigated farm lands in the province (Alberta Agriculture and Rural Development 2013).

The Era of State-Sponsored Projects

As with much else in prairie agriculture, the Depression triggered a heightened state presence. The federal government had scaled back in 1930, following the transfer of resource jurisdiction to Alberta and Saskatchewan and the retrenchment of the once-mighty Department of the Interior. Five years later Ottawa was back, however, in the role of reclaiming dust-bowl agriculture. The mechanism here was the newly formed Prairie Farm Rehabilitation Administration (PFRA).

Initially the new authority concentrated on promoting reclamation on dryland farms—through new plowing techniques to minimize erosion, tree planting for windbreaks, and the use of dug-outs to store on-farm water. Local water control structures in the form of weirs or small dams were also built at sites in western Saskatchewan. During the 1930s, however, the PFRA was pressured by farmers to sponsor larger projects in aid of land recovery. Surveys and engineering plans were made on several southern Alberta rivers.

Momentum grew following World War II, when political support was lent to larger water supply projects as part of federal reconstruction work. This served the dual roles of evening out water supply bottlenecks and enabling expanded service to farms. Among the new generation of major dam-reservoir impoundments that were promoted and financed by the PFRA was the St. Mary dam and reservoir. Approved in 1946, the project opened in 1951. It included a low-line main canal that ran easterly for several hundred kilometres to Medicine Hat, with several additional dam/reservoir structures installed along the way. In the decades since initial construction, this network has been upgraded continually and increased its carrying capacity to cope with the more intensive needs of pressurized sprinkler watering systems. In 1974 the PFRA transferred ownership of the headworks assets to the government of Alberta, while the distribution system has been managed by the St. Mary River Irrigation District, created in 1968. Today it is the flagship of farm irrigation projects, servicing over 327,000 acres (SMRID n.d.).

The biggest of all prairie impoundment schemes, however, was the South Saskatchewan River Project. It was first investigated by the PFRA after World War II and a dam site was selected in 1947. At a stroke, it would capture a far larger share of irrigated agriculture for Saskatchewan. The scale and the cost of the proposed scheme, to dam the flow and create a new reservoir around the confluence of the South Saskatchewan and the Qu'Appelle rivers, was vast (PFRA 1980). The federal government, whose financial support was indispensable, referred the question of cost-benefit calculations to a Royal Commission. In 1952, the commission advised against proceeding. This drew stinging rebukes from the government of Saskatchewan, which felt that equity considerations compelled a major irrigation public work to match Alberta's.

Six years later, with a Conservative government in office in Ottawa and native son John Diefenbaker as prime minister, the South Saskatchewan River project was approved. A cost-sharing agreement between Canada and Saskatchewan was quickly agreed. It was a multiple-use project that called for the irrigation of 500,000 acres. Ottawa would build the dam while the province would finance most of the power plant and the irrigation works. A second, smaller dam was built on the Qu'Appelle River to close the new reservoir at the southeast end. With total costs of $120 million, the project was completed in 1968. The main dam was named after Jimmy Gardiner, a former Liberal premier and federal minister who was an energetic champion of the project, while the reservoir was named Lake Diefenbaker.

By this point a policy network had solidified around the promotion of irrigated farming, and it has continued to strengthen over time. At least five sectors come together in this "productivist" alliance—the farmers themselves, the equipment and supply industry, the irrigation districts, and the provincial and federal departments of agriculture. The core developmental agenda is to advance irrigation prospects in all directions: technical improvements, scientific advances, additional irrigation districts and water supply systems, irrigated crop diversification, and environmental awareness.

Basin Planning and Management

A time lag separated the expansionary years of irrigation infrastructure and the policy recognition of watersheds as resource management units. In southern Alberta, rural resource management was defined in terms of farm improvement through most of the twentieth century. The supply of water was treated as a factor of production and little more. How did this policy system operate and what accounts for its eventual evolution? In some respects it is a story of rival use-claims, asserted on a variety of scales and leading eventually to a recognition that scarcity necessitated planning.

The growth of irrigated agriculture in southern Alberta in the twentieth century has been the strongest influence on regional water licensing. Here the provincial government joined with farmers and water works providers in the durable political alliance described above. With the exception of some hydro-electric projects in the upper foothills of the Bow River sub-basin and a couple of municipal water systems, irrigation has dominated water management activity. Moreover, with the federal government's withdrawal following the transfer of crown resource title in 1930, regulatory initiative shifted to the province. The fact remained that the vast prairie watersheds were interjurisdictional in nature. In recognition of the interprovincial contours of the Saskatchewan and Nelson basins, and the interdependencies of upstream and downstream users, a proposal arose in 1930 for the establishment of a Western Water Board. However, it foundered when Ottawa decided not to ratify the concept.

It was almost two decades later when this notion was revived in the form of the Prairie Provinces Water Board Agreement (PPWB) of July 1948. Board members were nominated by the three prairie provinces along with the federal government, with a mandate to gather data on water flows and existing works and, on referral from a member, recommend water allocations and report on projects. The most significant feature here was the emergence of a new management forum with a potential basin-wide reach, as the Board's concerns ran from the Rockies to Hudson Bay. However, the Board had an advisory function only, and final decisions remained with cabinet officials in the respective originating jurisdictions. In institutional terms, then, the original PPWB would fall into the category of "weak" coordinating bodies.

In a 1964 commentary, Stewart Raby concluded that the PPWB's commitment to a basin-wide framework remained unfulfilled. Baseline surveys had yet to be done. Provincial authorities concentrated on protecting and advancing their respective "sovereign rights" and showed little commitment to comprehensive watershed planning (Raby 1964). A case in point was the struggle between Saskatchewan and Alberta that began in 1951, when the South Saskatchewan River Project proposal was referred to the Board for comment. As seen earlier, this was Saskatchewan's first mega-storage prospect for a multipurpose dam and reservoir, and its scale dwarfed all previous prairie schemes. The Alberta delegate to the Board refused to let deliberations proceed on this proposal, unless it was combined with consideration of an alternative scheme advanced from Edmonton. The latter became known as the William Pearce Scheme (Mitchner 1965). It involved a complex of canals and reservoirs that would divert water from the Red Deer River to sub-basins further east. The Alberta plan also involved the diversion of waters from the North Saskatchewan River, to support new irrigation districts on both sides of the Alberta-Saskatchewan border. From the Alberta government's point of view, the Pearce Scheme captured uncommitted waters from the Red Deer basin for the benefit of arid lands within the province (500,000 acres) while offering a shared benefit with western Saskatchewan (200,000 acres).

Clearly the two provinces were jousting for the spoils of irrigated farming, for which water rights were the prerequisite. Despite its nominal mandate, the Prairie Provinces Water Board was unable to apply a basin-wide perspective in 1951. The Board lacked the powers, the tools, and the will to make an impact. Instead, governments fell back on traditional pressure tactics: instructing their delegates to the Board, log-rolling support for rival projects, prevaricating with a commission of inquiry, and depending upon factors of partisan advantage in the end. The disposition of the South Saskatchewan project demonstrates the absence of integrated water planning capabilities in the 1950s and early 1960s.

As it turned out, Alberta was just beginning to grapple with inter-basin diversions. In 1965 the provincial water resources division announced a new master plan known as PRIME—the Prairie Rivers Improvement, Management, and Evaluation Program. It called for a systematic review of diversion possibilities to augment the freshwater flows in Alberta's southern basins. As the government put it, "About 89 per cent of the total water flowing through Alberta is carried by … northward flowing rivers. The remaining 11 per cent which flow through the southern populated areas of the province must service 85 per cent of the population. The logical solution to this problem of distribution is to divert northern waters southward where they are more urgently needed" (Bocking 1972, 121). Despite the enthusiasm of the Social Credit government of Ernest Manning to support his electoral base in the rural south, the idea of transferring Alberta waters across a continental divide proved controversial. "PRIME is a crime" became a campaign slogan by the opposition. When the Lougheed Conservatives took power in 1971, PRIME was officially abandoned, although the government of Alberta remained vigorously committed to river development projects. Today there is a legislative prohibition on water transfers among the seven large Alberta basins. However sub-basin to sub-basin transfers are still possible within a major drainage basin (Beveridge and Droitsch 2008). As recently as 2011, a Red Deer River diversion proposal was advanced that recalled, on a smaller scale, the 1951 Alberta scheme (d'Aliesio 2011).

The completion of the Gardiner dam, on a hitherto undeveloped part of the South Saskatchewan watershed, underlined the need for more sophisticated basin planning going forward. In 1969 the PPWB sponsors approved an important new planning tool, the Master Agreement on Apportionment. Central to this was the principle of "equitable apportionment," which defines eligible shares of cross-border waterflows. Each province is entitled to the use, or "net depletion," of 50 per cent of the "natural flow" on entry to its jurisdiction (defined as the volume that would flow in a watercourse in the absence of human interference or intervention). Several schedules spelled out the details of Alberta-Saskatchewan and Saskatchewan-Manitoba flows. The adoption of this apportionment regime served to elevate the Board staff to the status of a technical authority on measurement and monitoring matters. It also offered a macro-framework in which the respective provinces agreed to regulate internal uses. As put by the master agreement, provinces "are free to pursue long-term plans as long as they abide by the water-sharing formula" (PPWB 1969). Disputes about the meaning or effect of the agreement are to be referred to the Federal Court of Canada.

In a variety of ways, the master agreement marked a higher stage of collaborative deliberation. Each government authorized the deal by cabinet order-in-council. The master agreement described the Board as being "reconstituted" by its terms. It also acknowledged the need for "consultation and cooperation." Henceforth the Board members would be tasked with administering an intergovernmental agreement of fixed proportions. They were also supported by a deeper technical staff. Fourteen border monitoring stations were assigned to monitor stream flow, and more than 90 sites have been designated for data gathering toward modelling the natural flow, especially in the South Saskatchewan and Qu'Appelle basins. During the 30 years since the master agreement, the Board has extended its work through three technical committees, covering hydrology (flow volume), water quality, and groundwater (to delineate and regulate cross-border groundwater aquifers). In 1992, additional schedules joined the master agreement to cover water quality and groundwater. The operational work of the Board was financed half by Ottawa and half by the provinces while the federal government financed all monitoring programs.

Over the past 30 years, the PPWB has emerged as one model of transboundary water regulation. Its strengths were recognized in the 1985 Inquiry on Federal Water Policy, where the authors observed that "the most significant interjurisdictional water management arrangement in Canada is the Master Agreement on Apportionment" (Pearse et al. 1985). However, it has not been duplicated elsewhere, and the closest parallel organization, the Mackenzie River Basin Board, has not yet advanced far enough to address the apportionment question. Both boards have their limits on the governance side. Staffed and financed by senior governments, and restricted in membership, there is little public space or visibility and little civil society engagement. (The MRBB does include a First Nations delegate from each participating jurisdiction.) Although the sponsoring governments could argue that civic involvement is better focused at the sub-basin and tributary basin levels, leaving whole-basin issues to the attention of the board, there is an obvious democratic deficit in the current structure. This issue will surface again in chapter 10.

The above discussion makes clear that broad-scale irrigation transforms host watersheds in basic ways. The escalating demand for water deliveries can stress the flow regime. Once begun, the political logic of water withdrawal is relentless. Prior to the 1970s, the provincial electoral politics of southern Alberta facilitated expanded irrigation, and few questions were raised on the supply side. This applied not only to Alberta sub-basins but to the South Saskatchewan River system as a whole. What happens, though, when rival users sense that water licensing has fallen out of balance? This question is explored in the case study that follows.

CASE STUDY: OLDMAN BASIN AND CONTEMPORARY WATERSHED CONFLICT

As seen above, the South Saskatchewan River system consists of three main tributary basins in Alberta. Each of these catchments involves not only a physical basin but also a distinct community of users that shape its watershed profile. The most northerly of the three, on the Red Deer River, drains from Rocky Mountain sources in an easterly direction. It passes through the city of Red Deer and gains from several tributaries before joining the South Saskatchewan as it exits Alberta. At present the Red Deer River basin is the only one that is not over-allocated for purposes of withdrawal. A second catchment, on the Bow River, descends from the mountains to supply several hydro-electric sites, service the city of Calgary, and support several of the larger irrigation districts in Alberta. The Bow River was the epicentre for the devastating Calgary flood of 2013. It is in the Oldman River basin, however, that irrigated agriculture figured as the hegemonic political and economic bloc through much of the twentieth century. This section examines water politics in the Oldman sub-basin in a period of significant political re-ordering. The case highlights a collision between traditional management practices and more contemporary approaches and the deep-rooted conflicts this engendered.

The Oldman River has a main stem length of 362 km and drains an area of 23,000 km² (almost double the size of the Miramichi). It delivers almost half of the flow to the South Saskatchewan at Medicine Hat. The population of the basin is currently about 210,000, with the city of Lethbridge accounting for somewhat under half of the total (Oldman Watershed Council 2010). There is a striking level of landscape variation from the mountains in the west to the prairies in the east. While the upper reaches in the forests and foothills run free, the lower parts of almost all tributaries are heavily regulated with dams, reservoirs, and canals. One other defining feature is that the available waterflow in the Oldman basin is fully "allocated" to existing licensees. There is no surplus.

Such are the internal variations that the tributary basins to the Oldman are grouped into five distinct categories. The "Mountain" tributaries are, not surprisingly, the upland regions where forest and grassland make up the dominant land covers and angling is a significant activity. These rivers flow strongly in the first half of the year, as snowmelt and spring rains prevail, but moderate in the second half when they depend on groundwater base flow and rainfall. The three main tributaries converge at the Three Rivers dam, discussed more fully in the pages below. The "Foothills" tributaries, which lack mountain sources, are shallower in depth and warmer in summer temperature. They run through grasslands with forest cover, and agriculture (ranching and farming) is the leading activity. These tributaries feed the main stem of the Oldman below the dam.

The "Southern" tributaries rise in the mountains of Montana and flow northerly to join the main Oldman stem near Lethbridge. These are heavily regulated rivers, with the first dam built in 1899 and 11 reservoirs now storing water, principally for irrigated farming. Eight of the 13 Alberta irrigation districts draw water from the southern tributaries. For several of these IDs water is diverted into watersheds across the height of land to the east. This includes the St. Mary Main Canal system that links the St. Mary River waters to farms as distant as Medicine Hat. The "Prairies" tributaries run through the classic landscape of extreme temperatures and aridity. These rivers depend heavily upon feeder flows from upstream, whether by river or canal. The Prairies also benefit from diversions between tributary basins. Since 1899 there has been a flow diversion from the Bow River watershed into the Oldman watershed near High River. Here waters from the Highwood are partially diverted by means of a canal-dam-reservoir system into the Little Bow River, where they are released as the summer unfolds. The even more significant role of the St. Mary canal has already been mentioned. The fifth category is the Oldman main stem below Lethbridge.

Not surprisingly, physical and social conditions vary greatly within the Oldman basin. One overall assessment of watershed conditions, by the Oldman

Watershed Council, rated the Mountain tributaries as "good," with the Foothills and Southern tributaries and Oldman main stem "fair," and the Prairie tributaries varying between "fair" and "poor" (Oldman Watershed Council 2010). Map 6.1 illustrates the Oldman drainage.

By the 1960s there were 10 irrigation districts in the Oldman basin as well as hundreds of private operators, with Lethbridge as the social epicentre. The ongoing prospects for irrigated farming were uncertain, however, for several reasons. The water delivery infrastructure was aging, and the water volume demands of the new pressurized field watering equipment were increasing. Both federal and provincial governments had ownership stakes in the dam-reservoir-canal systems. Finally, Alberta agreed in 1969 to an upper limit on its withdrawals from the South Saskatchewan system at one half of the natural flow, as noted above.

None of this deterred the irrigation farm community, however, which was among the most organized of farm sectors. Nor did it discourage the political class in Edmonton.

The rural south of Alberta was electorally strategic, a traditional bedrock of the Social Credit Party, in power since 1935. When Peter Lougheed's Conservative Party won the election in 1971, its strength lay chiefly in the large cities. Although

Map 6.1 Oldman River Watershed, Alberta

they initially had no seats in the "irrigation belt," the Conservatives were highly solicitous of the rural south.

During their first term, the Conservatives took ownership of previously federal-owned irrigation works in the province, and surveys were launched for potential new dam sites on southern rivers. In 1975 Lougheed won 9 of 12 irrigation belt seats, in part by promising renewed infrastructure and new storage works in the Oldman basin. This was confirmed with the 1975 release of a new policy declaring the priority of "water management for irrigation use." In 1976 the provincial Environment Department rated nine potential sites for a dam in the Oldman watershed, giving preference to the Three Rivers site at the confluence of the Crowsnest, Castle, and Oldman Rivers. Although it was ranked only sixth on environmental impact grounds, it placed first overall for its proximity to the giant Lethbridge Northern Irrigation District (LNID). Water would flow by gravity into the upgraded LNID canal system. Significantly, an alternate offstream storage system could have been built at one-eighth of the cost, but it did not find favour with either the irrigation lobby or the government. The Three Rivers announcement launched a 15-year sequence of events in which commercial agricultural priorities consistently overwhelmed environmental considerations, though not without a prolonged political challenge (Glenn 1999).

Almost immediately, criticism of Three Rivers arose from a constellation of other river-using groups. Anglers opposed the loss of prime fishing grounds. Several dozen farmers with land in the Three Rivers area opposed the inundation of their holdings. Downstream from the proposed dam site lay the Peigan Indian Reserve No. 147, which straddled the river. The band wished to protect burial grounds, reassert treaty rights to the water resource, renegotiate the status of the 1923 weir/canal diversion that had been built on their reserve, and profit from an alternate dam site on their lands. To the ongoing frustration of local irrigation boosters, several years elapsed while the province prepared further site studies. It was not until 1984 that the Three Rivers site was confirmed by the province, opening the way for detailed project work. In 1986, construction work began.

By any standard, the Oldman dam was a major project. It began in 1986 with the construction of two 900 m long diversion tunnels that would take the river flow around the dam site during construction. Two years later construction commenced on the main dam structure, whose capital cost had tripled to more than $300 million. This earth-filled structure is the central control work, impounding a reservoir of almost 500,000 cubic decametres that backs up 42 km of the valley and feeds a canal system into the LNID and beyond. The dam was built under contract to the provincial Department of Public Works, but ownership was transferred to the Department of Environment in 1994. In 2003 ATCO Power opened a modest 213 MW hydro-electric unit at the outlet of the east diversion tunnel operating seasonally from May to September.

Over the 1976–93 period, the Oldman dam became synonymous with environmental dysfunction. As the project sponsor, the government of Alberta

pursued it singlemindedly, exploiting provincial crown title and statutory powers to ignore, defy, and ultimately overwhelm its opponents. For its part, the
government of Canada was a passive and timid presence (de Loe 1997a, 1997b).
It seemed caught between its mandates to freshwater management and navigable
waters and to Aboriginal peoples—which the project clearly triggered—and a set
of national political priorities like constitutional renewal, where progress would
require Alberta's goodwill.

Over the next several years, however, a series of challenges were mounted
by opponents of the Oldman dam. The year 1986 saw the beginning of protests by the Peigan First Nation, who claimed rights to the natural river flow
through their reserve. Particularly prominent here was the Lonefighter group.
Led by the charismatic Milton Born-with-a-Tooth, they protested the project
by direct action, using heavy equipment to try to re-route the riverflow around
the existing weir on their reserve. This culminated in an armed stand-off between the Lonefighters and their Band member allies and the RCMP, followed
by arrests and prosecutions.

In 1988 it was the turn of the environmental group Friends of the Oldman
River (FOR). In addition to hosting a huge music festival, the Friends took legal
action to halt construction until an environmental assessment was conducted under federal law. Opponents of the dam accepted that the provincial government
was determined to advance the project against all objections. But the opponents
placed more faith in the federal environmental assessment procedures to ensure
a balanced review. When it became evident that Ottawa was unwilling to flex its
regulatory muscle (authority derived from its fisheries, Indian Affairs, navigable
waters, or environmental assessment powers), the anti-dam coalition headed for
the courts.

Possibly no water project in Canadian history has attracted a greater volume
of litigation than the Oldman dam. While the details cannot be fully reviewed
here, there were essentially two lines of court action. One was launched in 1986
by the Peigan band (now known as the Piikani First Nation), asserting treaty and
self-government rights to the water flowing through their reserve. Another action
was begun by the Friends of the Oldman River in 1987. The Friends argued
that provincial and federal licensing procedures had been violated. Perhaps the
key action arose in 1989 when the FOR asked the Federal Court of Canada to
quash Ottawa's approval of the dam because the federal environmental assessment
review guidelines order had not been applied. Two months later, in a separate
case described in chapter 4, the Federal Court ordered Ottawa to conduct an environmental assessment on the Rafferty-Alameda dam project in Saskatchewan.
Given several parallel attributes, the Oldman dam also appeared to be in trouble.
However, the federal trial court judge, James Jerome, ruled that since there was
no explicit directive for a review under the relevant federal legislation, it was not
required. Jerome distinguished the Oldman from the Rafferty case on the basis
that, as an international watershed, the latter was subject to federal environmental
review in a way that the former was not (Glenn 1999).

In March 1989, the Federal Court of Appeal overturned Jerome's ruling and ordered the federal ministers of transport and fisheries and oceans to comply with the federal environmental assessment review order by convening a formal assessment. Although further construction work without federal approval breached the law, Ottawa commenced the review without halting construction. This was justified on the ground that there was a public safety risk in leaving the dam project partially completed. The environmental review continued throughout 1991. Its May 1992 report found that "as presently configured, the project is unacceptable" and advised the decommissioning of the dam by opening the low-level diversion tunnels (Federal Environmental Assessment Review Office 1992). As an alternative, 22 specific recommendations were offered to mitigate the impacts, including a settlement with the Peigan band. In the interim, the broader policy question—whether Ottawa's EARP guideline order had full force of law (as distinct from being a discretionary directive)—was addressed by the Supreme Court of Canada. It found that the EARP had full legal force, thus requiring a navigable waters review by the department of transport.

The Oldman dam struggle was not yet over. In 1993, a further Federal Court decision gave Ottawa the discretion to select from among the 22 recommendations on offer and the government then announced that it would not decommission the now-operational dam. Transport Canada granted approval in the fall of 1993 despite the fact that a settlement with the Peigan Band was not agreed for another eight years. Also in 1993, the federal and Alberta governments signed an agreement to cooperate on future environmental assessments. The practice of holding joint or combined federal and provincial environmental assessments became more common from that point forward. Five years later, all federal and provincial governments signed an Environmental Harmonization Accord, in an effort to avoid jurisdictional overlaps in future. This deal served to curb the scope of federal environmental assessments in the future.

In sum, a complex, heavily mediated political process unfolded between 1984 and 1993. The decision sequence involved technical analysis, site assessments, network alliances, and bilateral negotiations between state agencies and organized interests. It also involved judicial challenges, electoral commitments, and direct citizen protests. The process was far from linear; indeed the terms of advantage shifted frequently during the conflict years. While the Oldman project was ultimately achieved, it was the last of the big dam and reservoir projects to appear on southern Alberta rivers and it came at a cost.

The political scars remained for years. In some respects they were self-inflicted. On the Oldman project, the government of Alberta proved rigid and combative. The government of Canada proved timid, conflict-averse, and even derelict in its responsibilities. In the absence of balanced deliberation, southern Alberta's farm commerce bloc anchored a development coalition that dismissed environmental considerations and accentuated the political contradictions. This in turn drove Aboriginal and environmental activists to increasing degrees of opposition. In the process, the provincial reputation in water management suffered a serious black eye while the federal government's retreat from the spirit of its 1987 water policy was clear for all to see. The opportunity to update or overhaul the management regime in the South Saskatchewan basin was lost for more than a decade.

Some lessons were learned from the Oldman conflict, however. When the Pine Coulee storage reservoir project was proposed for Willow Creek, a joint federal-provincial environmental review was struck to review the plan. After deliberation, the panel approved the project and it was installed by 1999. A major proposed expansion of the Little Bow River diversion was similarly reviewed and approved, with conditions. That project was installed by 2006. It is now accepted that any new dam and reservoir project must be managed to include rigorous environmental assessment (Rood, Samuelson, and Bigelow 2005).

More generally, the failures of Alberta freshwater management were evident by the time the Oldman dam was operational in 1992. Particularly in the South Saskatchewan River basin (SSRB), supplies were overcommitted. There was no social consensus on management objectives, and the necessary conceptual and technical tools were not available. The new Alberta *Water Act* of 1996 began the process of revision (Heinmiller 2013). It recognized the need to plan on a watershed basis and it recognized that some basins were at or beyond maximum withdrawal levels. In 1999 the province launched the SSR water planning process, and in 2002 the South Saskatchewan River Basin Plan (Part One) confirmed a major change in policy outlook. It authorized the transfer of water licence rights as well as holdbacks of water for conservation purposes. It also declared several southern rivers in the Oldman sub-basin (the St. Mary, the Belly, and the Waterton) closed to new water allocation applications. Part Two of the plan involved further scientific studies along with public consultations leading toward a formal management strategy (Alberta Environment 2003). In 2006, the new basin-wide plan was put in place for the South Saskatchewan River (Alberta Environment 2006). This plan was, in part, a product of recommendations by four basin advisory committees (including one for the Oldman). The point of this plan was to provide new advice to senior crown water officials. The minister of environment is empowered to determine, by means of a crown reservation, how to use any unallocated water—for in-stream flow needs, storage of peak flow, licence applications in the future, or First Nation needs. The plan also stipulates the "matters and factors" that must be considered by regional directors in the future assessment of water licence and certificate applications.

One of the significant results of water planning in the SSRB was expanded stakeholder engagement in the sub-basins. The Oldman River Basin Advisory Council joined with a prior water quality monitoring initiative to form the Oldman Watershed Council (OWC) in 2004. With a 16-member board and a small staff, the OWC has produced a report, *The State of the Watershed*, as well as a draft priorities plan for future management in the basin. Work is organized through volunteer "teams" for rural, urban, science, and integrated watershed management concerns (OWC 2010, 2011). Almost 90 per cent of the Council's

$400,000 financial budget came from the provincial environment department (although another $400,000 was recorded as in-kind contributions in 2012). On another scale are the community organizations tied into the Council through board representation. These include NGOs, government departments, industry, agriculture, municipalities, and First Nations as well as members at large. As the OWC turns its attention toward integrated planning, it aims to connect upward (toward the SSRB plan) and downward (toward tributary sub-basins). The Council reports that one of its continuing challenges is to access water-related data lodged in government agencies but not publicly available. In this it echoes the experience of community programs across the country. Indeed, data-sharing protocols may serve as a keen test of whether governments view stakeholders as advocacy voices only or whether a place will be made available in clientele circles.

In sum, over the past decade a new water management regime has been installed in the Oldman sub-basin and in the South Saskatchewan River basin more generally. This includes new legislation, new policy frameworks, and new regional institutions for consultation, deliberation, and priority-setting. The new civil society links include the Oldman Watershed Council, a multi-stakeholder body. First Nations will also play a considerably more prominent role, as provincial water management adjusts to the new Aboriginal rights doctrine of the crown's duty to consult.

This does not mean that all water allocation questions have been resolved. Far from it. A moratorium on new water licenses will exacerbate the political tensions among some watershed interests. On scales ranging from the local drainage to the sub-basin to the watershed as a whole, differences will arise over policy priorities, optimal policy tools, and lines of accountability. For example, the government of Alberta prompted controversy in 2011 with a proposal to divert flows from the Red Deer River sub-basin to provide water to adjacent drainages in the arid Special Areas further east. Not only did this revive memories of the William Pearce and PRIME schemes of old, but it also suggested that the manipulation of freshwater as a development tool was alive in the south. However, it seems fair to say that the stresses imposed by water shortage in southern Alberta basins in recent decades have set the stage for innovation and renewal at the political level (Rojas et al. 2009).

Conclusion

Irrigated farming originated alongside prairie settlement, and today it is most widely practiced in the western provinces. Irrigation regimes require capital, structural works, and management institutions, and they can assume several forms as demonstrated here. Such works have a common aim—the capture and impoundment of water and its distribution to farm properties. So intensive are the supply needs that irrigation has created its own set of policy issues—how to regulate the allocation across a watershed, how to avoid over-commitment of available waters, and how to deal with farm runoffs and degradation of water quality.

Irrigation brings a particular set of political interests to a watershed, including water suppliers, water users, and the local governments whose prosperity depends upon their continuing success. Since flowing waters are held predominantly by crown authorities in Canada, governments (mainly provincial) confer water rights by licence and these in turn are monetized as part of agricultural enterprise. In this way policy networks of impressive resilience take form. At the centre of these networks are the government irrigation agencies, the local irrigation districts, and the farmers themselves. The stakes are high, as a guaranteed supply of water is essential and there will always be a demand for new irrigable land. Moreover, a freshwater licensing regime based on "first in time, first in right" is likely to confer senior status on some irrigation interests. So formidable is the irrigation policy network that the Alberta government's initial response to water scarcity in the 1960s was to investigate the potential to divert north-flowing rivers into southerly basins.

It is only recently that watershed-scale planning has entered the picture, and the southern Alberta situation offers a striking example of the new challenges. It seems evident that the hegemony of irrigation has slowed the water management revolution in the province. This is well illustrated by the Oldman dam controversy. An intersection of political forces—including organized irrigators, regional boosters, and governing party cohorts—underwrote the Oldman project in the 1970s. Events progressed with little regard to noncommercial interests including Aboriginal peoples, recreationists, environmental advocates, and downstream interests.

Eventually new paradigms took root. In Alberta this may have happened under the combined pressures of political fallout from the Oldman battles, apportionment deliberations by South Saskatchewan River authorities, and climate change revelations tied to future flow forecasts. A "new politics" of irrigation has emerged, involving a wider range of stakeholders including ENGOs, First Nations, and the general public. The new policy instruments include watershed management plans, basin councils, and state of the river reporting.

7
Flooding and Flood Control

THIS CHAPTER INVESTIGATES FLOODING AS A geophysical and a social phenomenon. Treated in some cultures as an inevitable part of a natural cycle, and in others as a hostile threat to civil life, floods are integral to most watersheds to some degree. The political question is how do communities respond to flood realities? In earlier chapters we have seen that flood management became an integral part of river engineering, with efforts to tame wild waters and harness them to social need. Such developments were not spontaneous or inevitable, however. They depended upon key policy choices that were influenced by coalitions of organized interests. In other words, flood policy has an important political dimension. Who promotes flood control measures, who resists them, and who carries them out? What are the overriding ideas in flood management? Here as elsewhere, policy interventions have consequences that feed back into the political equation and alter the paths going forward. After discussing these matters, the chapter explores one of the most flood-prone watersheds in Canada. The Red River basin has experienced acute floods for its entire recorded history. By examining the interplay of physical and social forces within this watershed, the politics of flood disturbances can be seen. It is sometimes said that the Red River has two problems—too much water and too little. This captures both the tension and the irony of the flood control subsector more generally.

Floods in Modern Life

Writing of traditional German approaches to flowing water, David Blackbourn observes that "nature was usually seen as a servant or an enemy" (Blackbourn 2006, 182). This characterization applies to much of Canada's water history as well. In the previous chapter we saw an example of its servant role. Here we deal with nature as an enemy.

The phenomenon of flood is one of the natural and in some places inevitable aspects of the hydrologic cycle. Extreme precipitation events interact with the physical landscape and the water table to lift watercourses beyond their channels and inundate adjacent lands. Some flood patterns are seasonal and prone to repetition. In Canada, they follow predictable climate patterns and may be linked to accumulated winter snowmelt and runoff, or rain-on-snow precipitation, or flash rainfall from summer storms, or ice jams at breakup time. The first three types accounted for two-thirds of the 168 flood disasters identified between 1900 and 1997. Although major floods can occur in almost any geography, more than three-fifths of the list just mentioned took place in Ontario, New Brunswick, Quebec, and Manitoba. Not surprisingly, in light of the above facts, 40 per cent of these major flood events occurred in the months of April and May. A map of flood events in twentieth-century Canada shows sites in all provinces and territories, many of them repeat events (Shrubsole et al. 2003).

While all floods are wrenching experiences to the communities involved, some are truly exceptional (Environment Canada 1993). Take, for example, the "century floods" on Manitoba's Red River in 1950 and 1997, or the Mississippi "Great Flood" of 1993, or Hurricane Hazel—it dropped 2.1 metres of rain on Toronto on October 14–15, 1954. A smaller but equally intense shock hit Rapid City, South Dakota, on June 9, 1972 with devastating results. The Saguenay flood of 1996 is another epic case, as is Calgary in 2013. Such cases point to a distinguishing feature of flood politics. Disruptions of great magnitude can shock the policy system and trigger urgent reviews and policy responses. However, there is nothing inevitable in this. As one study notes, "there is … no guarantee that the nature of the policy issues raised by a major flood disaster will offer anything more than post-event response and recovery" (Johnson et al. 2005, 561). Often the urge to set things right can exhaust the political energies of policy elites.

The flood phenomenon is social as well. It is a topic of biblical provenance, with the 40-day flood detailed in chapter 7 of the Book of Genesis. Indeed, the role of the Creator continues to be bound up with flood events in the Christian west. Sudden and profound disasters can be viewed as "acts of God"—responses by divine providence to the machinations of people on earth. Gradually it seems that the term became secularized to apply to a "natural" event of the physical world that could not be prevented by human action: a hurricane, tornado, drought, or flood. The historian Ted Steinberg contends that the Johnstown, Pennsylvania, disaster of 1889, in which heavy rains combined with a faultily constructed earth dam to kill thousands in the Conemaugh valley, marked a turning point. Postmortem blame ranged from an act of Providence to a failure of human artifice, making the event "a post-modern disaster in a pre-modern world" (Steinberg 1996). Perhaps most critically, there could be no legal responsibility for an "act of God."

Flood politics has a much deeper history, however. In Europe, projects to contain wild rivers began in the Middle Ages. By 1800 hydraulic engineering had congealed as a field of practical science. As mentioned in chapter 2, Johann Tulla played a major part in this movement. Having founded a school of engineering at Karlsruhe in 1807, he drew up a plan in 1812 for redesigning the entire Upper Rhine River. What made this so bold was the sweeping nature of the scheme—not an assemblage of projects so much as an integrated plan to modify and control an entire drainage. In a series of treaties that stretched over several decades, authorities in Tulla's home state of Baden and its neighbours along the river agreed to successive sets of projects that were more or less consistent with the blueprint (Blackbourn 2006). Following Tulla's death in 1828, the work continued for almost half a century. By 1900 Germany was recognized as the leader in the discipline of hydraulic engineering, with tens of thousands of trained, well-organized professionals at work across Europe and beyond.

Much of the political and economic imperative behind Tulla's work on the Rhine, and the work of his successors in other drainage basins, was prompted by the threat of flood. Floodwaters inundated not only low-lying farmland but also towns and villages. Furthermore, in the aftermath of floods the watercourse was often altered, with banks eroded and buildings swept away. Often the answer to flood control lay in the tributaries rather than the main stems of giant rivers. It was in the upper sub-basins that flash summer storms or sudden spring melts could magnify the swell and launch damage downstream. Flooding is, in essence, an extreme instance of the fluctuating water levels that characterize most river basins. The engineering response is to better control those water levels and buffer the variations. A variety of tools are available here, ranging from dams and reservoirs that absorb the pulses and slow their progress for orderly release, to dikes and levees that aim to confine maximum river flows within planned channels, to canals that divert floodwaters away from a natural watercourse. While this can be pursued incrementally, on the project-by-project basis often favoured by political authorities, hydraulic engineering is based on more holistic analysis.

A parallel process emerged somewhat later in the New World, with distinct policy and institutional attributes. In nineteenth-century America, government flood relief thinking was tied to the twin imperatives of commercial development and engineering knowledge. Not only was the Army Corps of Engineers (and its offshoot, the Corps of Topographical Engineers) involved in surveying western lands, but it was also the leading edge of engineering knowledge on river navigation and flooding. The Humphreys-Abbot study of Mississippi River hydraulics, published in 1861, was a path-breaking contribution to the understanding of river flows. Significantly for the Corps, the study generated a new planning paradigm that relied on levees (floodplain dikes) alone for flood defence. For decades, as Congress became increasingly concerned with inland river and harbour works, this doctrine determined the entire engineering strategy on the lower Mississippi (Reuss 1985). Only with the massive 1927 flood was this paradigm dislodged to make way for new measures like floodways and reservoirs that took hold in the 1930s.

The "structural" approach to flood protection continues today, albeit amid more complex institutions. With the breakdown of the "levees only" doctrine at the Corps of Engineers, the way was opened for larger dam/reservoir and diversion/spillway projects to join the mix. The bureaucratic rivalries among the Corps, the Bureau of Reclamation, and the Soil Conservation Service (SCS) were manifest in differences over where and why to build (Clarke and McCool 1996). The SCS focused on small dams on upstream channels that protected agricultural lands against normal floods, while the Bureau and Corps gravitated to large dam and reservoir works downstream to protect populated areas. All versions benefited from the terms of the 1938 *Flood Control Act*, by which the federal government took the financial lead (Costa 1978). Subsequent acts in 1944 and 1954 served to expand the federal role.

Distinct coalitions of flood control interests coalesced to entrench and extend structural approaches to flood defence. As soon as a town or city was exposed to the havoc wreaked by floods, its population demanded protection. This began as early as the Middle Ages in continental Europe, and parallel pressures began in North America in the mid-nineteenth century. Similar calls for protection came from farm and rural interests, which settled in lowlands and intervales near river systems. A related question was who would finance and maintain flood works. If damages were local, the onus might fall on local authorities to take action. Alternatively the responsibility could fall on more senior governments, particularly if flood planning was to be conducted on a watershed basis. Business bloc organizations are often local or regional, and they can apply strong leverage to the need for flood protection. Much depends also on the intellectual frameworks through which floods are apprehended.

One of the effects of these engineered measures was to reduce the frequency of floods, by eliminating low-level risks and engendering a social sense of floodplain safety. This complemented the commercial development inclinations of state and local governments that sought to maximize land use and property tax yields. Put simply, the "flood-proofing" of low-lying areas was good for business. Furthermore, to the extent that senior governments covered the capital costs of flood control works (the cost-sharing provision was eliminated from the US federal statute in 1938), this option proved even more attractive. In this way, local governments along with their commercial and real estate industries and property owners coalesced behind the protective works philosophy of flood control. It was a powerful coalition of material interests equipped with a durable cultural outlook.

The challenge eventually came from the cost-benefit calculations around structural defence strategies. While levees and dams were normally effective against modest floods, sometimes for generational intervals, it was the impact of the exceptional events that undermined the model. Despite massive capital investments, damage from major floods mounted in the decades following World War II. So did outlays for damage compensation.

A major change began in the United States through the work of a Congressional task force. It continued with the *National Flood Insurance Act* of 1968, which subsidized 90 per cent of the cost of flood insurance for inhabitants of communities subject to prescribed federal flood plain management rules (Carolan 2007). This involved a 1:100 design level of risk. Though take-up on this program was initially slow, an incentive was added in 1973 when compliance with those same rules was required for communities to be eligible for federal flood structure assistance.

Flood Policy and Politics in Canada

There is a long history of water channel works in Canada. The Acadian settlers of the 1600s built dikes to protect their coastal lands from saltwater. In the process they developed an ingenious device known as the *aboiteau* or water box. Built into a dike, *aboiteaux* allowed the impoundment of freshwater at high tide and its release at low tide, helping to desalinate coastal soils in the process. Sea dikes (the

Canadian term for levees) were also common in British Columbia, where sea dike districts were being organized for collective action in the 1870s.

When dams began to emerge on Canadian rivers, however, they were connected to hydro-electric power more than flood control. For the late nineteenth and early twentieth centuries, flooding was viewed for the most part as an uncontrollable risk. In contrast to the United States, there was no strong national government commitment on flood control.

As late as the 1930s the forces of nature were left to themselves in the most flood-prone parts of Canada. The critical recipe for severe floods combined sustained heavy precipitation with broad river valleys. In British Columbia, the Fraser River flooded on average every four years, though extreme events occurred in 1894 and 1948 (Evenden 2004, 142). Manitoba's Red River (profiled in detail below) was even more flood prone, including landmark events in 1852 and 1950. The Saint John River experienced major flood events in 1887, 1923, and 1936.

It was in southern Ontario, however, that the balance of political forces supporting engineered floodworks first took hold. Here, in a series of rivers that drained farming basins into the Great Lakes, the combination of rural and urban land damage provided a catalyst. Almost from the turn of the century there had been municipal and business concerns about the extent of flooding along the Grand River that runs through Waterloo, Kitchener, Cambridge, and Brantford before emptying into Lake Erie. After a particularly severe instance in 1929, an engineering survey recommended up to five reservoirs be built to absorb floodwaters and regulate minimum flows. Pressure from rural and urban business interests led to the founding of the Grand River Conservation Commission in 1934 and the preparation of a remedial plan. Four years later, by the terms of a cost-sharing agreement, Ottawa and Ontario each assumed 37.5 per cent of approved costs while the municipalities (through the Grand River Conservation Commission) covered the final 25 per cent. This formula anticipated the shape of postwar flood work financing. The Shand Dam was the first to be completed in 1941 and was followed by the Luther and Conestoga reservoirs in 1954 and 1958 respectively (Shrubsole 1992).

The Grand River Commission presaged wider developments in southern Ontario in the postwar decades. It culminated in the *Ontario Conservation Authorities Act* of 1946. There were several precipitants here: the widespread evidence of physical degradation through deforestation, floods, and erosion; the political pressures brought by expert lobbies and knowledge networks of naturalists, farmers, and conservationists; the operating examples such as the Grand River Commission and the Tennessee Valley Authority; and the highly favourable policy window opened by reconstruction planning and finance (Richardson 1974).

With the act in place, administrative responsibility was conferred on the new Conservation Branch located in the Ontario Department of Planning and Development. But the central actors were the newly proposed Conservation

Authorities that required local government support and financial participation to be established as designated watershed management agents. The take-up was rapid, with 10 conservation authorities established in the first three years from 1946 to 1948 and another 30 to follow in subsequent decades.

First Generation Flood Policy: The "Structural" Focus

The federal government also began to assume a more prominent role in the postwar reconstruction period. As in so many areas of natural resource policy, Ottawa was constrained by the federal division of powers. Despite its leverage over navigable waters and interprovincial rivers, the provincial jurisdiction over water use licensing and riparian activities proved paramount. The federal government was stirred to action, however, in the late 1940s. Its chosen instrument was the Prairie Farm Rehabilitation Administration (discussed in chapter 6), through which Ottawa built the St. Mary dam in Alberta and the Gardiner dam in Saskatchewan (de Loe 1997a).

This, as it turned out, was only the beginning. A trio of extreme flood events underlined the special role that the federal government was expected to play in response to disaster. In 1948 the Fraser River overflowed its banks on a scale not seen since the nineteenth century. Farm and urban areas were inundated along a 95-km front and remained at flood stage for more than a month, cutting Vancouver's land links to the rest of the province (Evenden 2004). A federal-provincial board was struck to deal with damage and recovery and future preparedness. Two years later, Manitoba's Red River rose in the spring in a century flood that forced mass evacuations and brought extraordinary property damage to the city of Winnipeg. This event, which figures in the watershed case study that follows, led once again to an unprecedented structural investment to protect the city. Finally, in 1954, Hurricane Hazel struck Toronto with devastating effect. Sudden, shocking, and comprehensive in impact, Hazel forced Ontario's first city to confront the vulnerabilities of an urban landscape dominated by asphalt and concrete.

Such cases spurred Ottawa to invoke the federal spending power to encourage provincial flood control programming through the offer of cost-shared finance. This was formalized in the 1953 *Canada Water Conservation Assistance Act*. By its terms the national government could assist provinces in the construction of major water conservation works. Significantly, this was restricted to physical works, required matching contributions, and did not acknowledge the value of integrated planning. Projects were put forward by provincial authorities and were decided on a case-by-case basis but always with a requirement for positive cost-benefit assessments.

Structural strategies involve engineered defences against flood damage. In the nineteenth century these could be relatively simple structures. For example, a weir is a low-level barrier built across a river that allows water to pool on the upstream side while at the same time flow over the top of the barrier. The weir functions as a simple and virtually self-regulating flood control defence on a small river or stream. It slows the progress of a swollen stream. A step up from the weir is the flood control dam built on a major tributary river of a flood-prone watershed. This consists of a dam (often earth-filled) across the river with an inlet pipe installed on the upstream side. This pipe carries reservoir water under or around the dam and releases it into the stream below. In dry seasons the reservoir storage level will fall below the spillway pipe so that only a "base pool" remains, while in wet seasons the reservoir level can rise into a "flood storage" zone above the pipe. Pure flood control works were sometimes known as "dry" dams. As they were not designed to fulfill more than one function, there was no need to maintain a permanent level of "conservation storage," so the reservoir could dry up entirely or fall to the level of the baseline (below the pipe) pool. In the United States more than 11,000 such flood dams were supported by the Soil Conservation Service (now the Natural Resources Conservation Service) in the US Department of Agriculture. State governments also supported flood control dams on small and regional watersheds. Often this involved the introduction of a special-purpose authority—the flood control district (FCD)—with varying provisions to elect trustees, borrow money, and plan and install flood control works. Because many FCDs were organized on a county basis, this introduced a municipal scale of flood control design and defence.

So far the focus has been on single-project flood control works, as many early projects were installed on a local scale—sponsored, built, and designed to deal with local flooding. Such projects sprang from conditions on a particular reach of a particular river. Only on this basis could local social and political support be secured. What happens, then, when flood control systems shift from the simple (single project) to complex (multiple dams and diversions) within a watershed system? If flows on several tributaries, each with several first- and second-order streams of its own, are jointly responsible for flood prospects, should they not be coordinated if possible? And if so, how can such goals be achieved? This is a complicated terrain, where hydrology is enlisted to tackle flow modelling and hydraulic engineering handles design and construction. Projects range from single dams to multiple dams and diversions installed in a single watershed. There is a corresponding politics of flood control engineering, as varying state agencies claim jurisdiction while advancing separate mandates and doctrines of flood control (Pisani 2006).

These are the types of projects first advanced by the Army Corps of Engineers in the Mississippi basin—levees or dikes to raise the banks or rivers, dredged river channels to bolster flow capacity, artificial canals or floodways to divert excess flows, and dam and reservoir complexes to slow floodwater buildup and allow more orderly release. In Canada the list of federally supported structural works included diking along the Fraser River, dams in the greater Toronto area, and of course the Red River floodway and associated works. The corollary to engineered protection is that once built, structures must be maintained to work over time. The latter are less politically visible but no less essential, and inattention to servicing existing works can be catastrophic. Depending on initial specifications and changing watershed flow characteristics, structural works may require enhancement. This involves a step change in many facilities. Widening a channel, for example, may require bridge replacements. The original Red River Floodway cost $63 million to build in 1958 while the recently completed upgrade cost $660 million.

Second Generation Flood Policy: The "Nonstructural" Approaches

In many respects the *Canada Water Act* of 1970 announced a new era in federal water policy. It repealed the 1953 statute and set out a broader vision of water planning that acknowledged the importance of watershed units, of public participation in planning processes, and of multiple use management. The principle of federal-provincial cooperation was clearly expressed in the new act. As far as flood control was concerned, there was recognition of the need for a wider range of policy tools and for a move beyond structural defences. The pace of urban migration was accelerating and with it an appetite for the sort of proximate development land offered by flood plains. Perhaps even more importantly, Ottawa's ongoing Disaster Assistance Program (DAP) was under severe financial pressure. By its terms, the federal government offered postflood damage relief, on a sliding per-capita scale. Major damages from recent floods meant rising outlays from this uncapped fund. In addition, there was reported concern in political circles for the "income transfer" effect, as real estate developers and flood plain property owners (not to mention property speculators) were being subsidized by general taxpayers (Watt 1995). In sum, the shift was driven in large part by the relentless rise in the DAP outlays by Ottawa and the sense that real estate development, if unregulated on flood-prone lands, would exacerbate the burden (Bruce 1976).

It was under this umbrella that the National Flood Damage Reduction Program (FDRP) was announced by the federal minister of environment in 1975. The centrepiece was preventive flood risk planning backed up with material incentives. Designated flood-prone areas would be studied, mapped, and integrated into local and regional land use plans. (Over 200 such areas figured in a preliminary estimate.) The maps would be based on 100-year (or greater) flood events and would be provided to municipalities and the public. The use of municipal zoning and permitting instruments would prevent new development on flood plains and limit development in the flood fringe areas. Perhaps most significantly, federal disaster relief would not apply to property development in designated flood risk areas nor would federal agencies support projects so located. An FDRP would begin with the negotiation of a 10-year General Agreement between Ottawa and a province affirming the goals just described (Page 1980). Beneath this umbrella a Mapping Agreement followed to identify the flood-prone areas for special attention. Once the data were generated, a variety of structural and nonstructural measures could be negotiated for particular settings. In the event that a federal-provincial agreement was not reached, Ottawa on its own would deny assistance for flood-prone land development. The results were tangible, with mapping studies completed in more than 900 communities across the country.

The capacity to recognize flood threats, and possible responses, marks a significant advance in policy capability. However, these administrative arrangements do not guarantee effective outcomes. The provincial-municipal link can still pose a weakness, particularly if a province is willing to grant exceptions from the general provisions on mapping, zoning, and licensing. The same applies to local authorities. Henstra and McBean note that "despite FDRP maps and flood-risk designations, numerous local policy exemptions allowed extensive development in floodplains in the Montreal area and elsewhere in Quebec" (Henstra and McBean 2005, 309). A major factor here is persistent commercial boosterism in local government combined with property interests, who together discount the prospects of risk in a particular community. Even in small-town Antigonish, Nova Scotia, a shopping mall was licensed on a known flood plain only a few years following Hurricane Beth. In such cases, there is no counterbalancing organizational lobby on behalf of vigorous enforcement on flood prevention.

In 1995 the federal government announced that the FDRP would be phased out over several years. This ran against the sentiment of almost the entire flood policy community outside of the senior bureaucratic ranks at Environment Canada. A 1993 workshop of federal and provincial officials judged the program "extremely successful" not only in the mapping and public awareness components but also in "redirecting damage-prone development away from flood-risk areas" (Watt 1995, 245). Unanimously the provincial delegates called for the FDRP to be maintained indefinitely but to no avail. By 2003 the last of the general agreements and mapping subagreements had lapsed.

The Disaster Financial Assistance Arrangements program continues, however. By its formula, federal assistance (to provinces that are paying out eligible compensation) increases as per-capita payouts exceed $1. Consequently, the greater the disaster, the greater the prospective federal share (Shrubsole et al. 2003). In the early 2000s, Ottawa sponsored an extended policy consultation on the subject of a new National Disaster Mitigation Strategy. This was unveiled in 2008 and reflects current thinking on mitigation (Public Safety Canada 2008). While it covers "all-hazard" causes, flood mitigation looms large and an elaborate federal-provincial network of ministers and officials drives the process.

CASE STUDY: RED RIVER BASIN, MANITOBA

The Red River basin covers parts of Minnesota, North Dakota, and Manitoba, along with a very small portion of South Dakota. The river rises at the southern extreme and flows northward to its mouth at Lake Winnipeg. The lake, in turn, empties into the Nelson River, which flows northward to Hudson's Bay. The axial length of the Red is 885 km of which 70 per cent is in the United States. The main stem is fed by a series of tributaries, making it a complex system with more than 30 sub-watersheds. Overall the watershed covers 116,000 km² (more than triple the area of the Oldman) with more than 85 per cent in the United States. Many of the tributaries flow intermittently throughout the year but all of them peak in the spring months and contribute to flood potential. Exacerbating the flood tendency is the south-to-north flow pattern, unusual on the North American plains. As a result, the headwaters and the upper sub-basins in the United States will melt and flow in the spring before breakup in the Manitoba reaches of the river. As the spring current builds, it encounters ice slab obstacles and frozen ground that enhance the flood effect. Map 7.1 illustrates the Red River basin.

The relief features are modest, as most of the area covers the flat bottom of the ancient glacial Lake Agassiz, resulting in an average slope along the river of less than one-tenth of a metre per kilometre. These features further explain the flood-prone character of the landscape, as there is little natural containment once the river overflows its banks. For the city of Winnipeg there is an added complication. The Assiniboine River basin is a drainage whose area rivals the Red. Sourced in Saskatchewan, it flows easterly and, augmented by the Souris basin discussed in chapter 4, delivers its own spring surge to downtown Winnipeg where it intersects with the Red.

Map 7.1 Red River Watershed, Manitoba

Residents of the Red River basin closely monitor three key variables as the flood season approaches. The first of these is soil moisture from the previous autumn, which will influence surface absorption in the spring. The second is the extent of the snowpack that comes with the prairie winter and will influence the volume of surface water flowing in the spring. A third is the spring weather trend, including both temperature and rainfall. The first two variables shape the emerging flood forecast, but the unpredictable third can be decisive. "Favourable" spring weather might be defined as generally dry and cool over the critical weeks and conducive to minor flood conditions. "Normal" weather involves mixed temperature and precipitation patterns that point toward more substantial floods. "Unfavourable" weather, not surprisingly, involves sudden but sustained high-temperature melts alongside spring rains and points toward major flooding.

The preponderance of land in the Red River basin is devoted to farming. Settlement began along the river and its tributaries, and advances in farm drainage in the 1880s triggered agricultural take-off. The goal here was to remove excess water from shallow soils around plant root structures in clay-based soils. It involved the removal of wetlands, bogs, and sloughs by means of ditches linked to waterways. In Manitoba, more than 2 million acres were drained between 1895 and 1930 and a new form of special-purpose government was devised in the form of the drainage district (Bower 2011). Following World War II, the US Soil Conservation Service promoted a new phase of water engineering that combined land drainage and flood control dams. The result was five large American flood dam and storage facilities plus almost 300 smaller water retention dams.

The Red River basin hosts a population of 1.3 million people, of whom more than half live in Manitoba and 90 per cent of these inhabit the city of Winnipeg. On the American side the rural and small town presence is more significant. The largest urban areas are Fargo-Moorhead at 145,000 and Grand Forks-East Grand Forks at 106,000. Together they amount to less than half of the US population share. In either case, there are two sides to flood control: one for the farm and small town population on the tributary basins and another for the cities exposed on the main stem.

In earlier chapters it was suggested that the sub-basins that make up a major drainage are potentially important planning units. Certainly there are a variety of circumstances at the tributary level. Consider, for example, the Traverse gap in the Bois des Sioux sub-basin. Stretching more than a kilometre along the continental divide, this valley separates the Bois des Sioux River (that flows into the Red) and the Little Minnesota River (that flows toward the Mississippi). Despite modest control structures at either end, there have been times when the river valley has flooded and waters have crossed the divide.

Another special set of circumstance is found in the Devil's Lake sub-basin in the west-central region. There is some debate on whether to even include Devil's Lake with the Red River, as it is by nature a shallow, saline, self-contained water body whose only natural release is by evaporation or seepage. In the wet-cycle of the 1990s, however, Devil's Lake doubled in size and farmers pressed for a remedy. The state of North Dakota opted for the cheapest option and constructed a diversion outlet to the Sheyenne River and thence to the Red River main stem. Despite Manitoba's objections over the possible introduction of invasive species, the International Joint Commission was unable to take up the issue when the American delegation withheld consent.

The Pembina River sub-basin offers a third variation. Rising in western Manitoba, it flows easterly for 513 km through rich farm country and crosses the border into North Dakota before joining the Red River. The Pembina flows throughout the year, supplemented by groundwater during the dry seasons. During the last quarter of the twentieth century, phosphorus loadings from septic systems and field treatments increased by more than 50 per cent, leading to algal blooms and fish kills in local lakes. In response to resident perceptions of basin overload, an integrated watershed management plan was prepared for the sub-basin (Pembina River Watershed Planning Authority 2011).

Despite the compositional complexity of the Red River basin, it is known in Manitoba principally for the spring flood phenomenon, where the river has produced some of the most intractable flood events in Canada. Over the past half-century, the need to deal with floods has become one of the most significant freshwater problems in Manitoba and has prompted some dramatic political interventions. In fact, the frequency of major floods has increased. A comparative ranking of flood years is difficult, since there are several standards of measurement. The high water mark can be compared at a specific point or the total damages can be computed. As well, the regional impacts can vary greatly by year. However, there is a general consensus on the all-time leaders.

The biggest flood ever recorded was in 1852 when the high water is estimated to have peaked at The Forks at 762 feet above sea level. This inflicted massive damage on Fort Garry and the surrounding homesteads. A generation earlier, in 1826, the flood peaked at an estimated 765 feet (Baker 1979). Analysis of oak tree ring cores has revealed two hitherto unrecorded floods in 1747 and 1762 (Manitoba n.d.). Three high-magnitude floods of the post-war era—1950, 1979, and 1997—have shaped contemporary state policy, and they figure in the discussion to follow. It is also telling that 5 of the top 10 flood events have occurred in the past two decades: in 1996, 1997, 2006, 2009, and 2011.

Perhaps the most politically crucial event was the great 1950 flood, in which waters crested 757 feet above sea level. This inflicted extraordinary destruction on the city of Winnipeg and proved, ultimately, to be a policy catalyst of the first order (Bumsted 1987). On May 8, 1950, eight dikes collapsed in Winnipeg and some 100,000 people were evacuated. The damage payouts by the federal and Manitoba governments, $26 million and $53 million respectively, were unprecedented. Not surprisingly, this prompted an engineering review of flood defences, and the first "boulevard dike" was built along the river bank in response.

An adequate political coalition backing a comprehensive structural flood protection plan was still not present. The rural-based Liberal-Progressive government of Premier Douglas Campbell harboured multiple doubts: the proposed schemes centred on the city but left the river valley and its communities exposed, the 1950 flood was the first in almost a century to match the level of the 1850s, and the scale of prospective remedies was deemed far too costly without substantial federal help (Bumsted 2002). These were continuing themes over the next half-century.

In 1953 federal engineers delivered a sweeping engineering study that anticipated the major structures ultimately put in place. Yet there was little political urgency to move forward on such plans. The winter of 1955–56 seemed to set the stage for a repeat flood, but this did not eventuate. In response, however, Premier Campbell appointed a royal commission to explore the costs and benefits of major new works, in the expectation (many suspected) that the case would fail. Reporting in the spring of 1958, the commission calculated a positive benefit/cost ratio of 2.7 to 1 (4 to 1 if city economic growth trends were taken into account).

The deliberations of the commission were critical in legitimating the new floodworks in socioeconomic terms. As Bumsted concludes, "its analysis shaped the flood mitigation agenda of Manitoba for more than a generation" (Bumsted 2002, 116). The commission endorsed three major projects with a total estimated cost of $72.5 million. This was, by any measure, a bold scheme. Its centrepiece was the Winnipeg Floodway, a 48-km concrete-lined channel to intercept the Red River flow south of the city and convey it east and north before rejoining the channel near Selkirk. Second, the Shellmouth dam and reservoir would hold up the flow at Russell on the Assiniboine River. Third, a gated diversionary channel at Portage la Prairie would carry Assiniboine floodwaters north to Lake Manitoba.

The executor of the new flood protection plan was new Premier Duff Roblin. His Conservative party made a comprehensive structural flood protection plan a centrepiece of the 1958 campaign and was rewarded by Winnipeg voters. Rural farmers correctly recognized that there was little in the scheme for them, and the Campbell Progressive-Liberals opposed the plan which was derided as "Duff's Ditch." Several years passed while financial negotiations took place with the Diefenbaker Conservatives in Ottawa, but in the spring of 1962 provincial legislation was enacted. Not surprisingly, the scale of the project was beyond the capacity of the province on its own. Excavations for the floodway moved more earth than either the St. Lawrence Seaway or Panama Canal projects (Bumsted 2002). The floodway was opened in 1969, the Portage diversion in 1970, and the Shellmouth dam in 1972. For rural communities in the flood zone south of Winnipeg, a series of ring dikes were installed around major rural towns including Ste. Agathe, Morris, Letellier, and Emerson. There was also aid to defend farm homes and outbuildings. Of the total $63 million spent on the floodway, the government of Canada covered 60 per cent, along with half the costs of the Portage and Shellmouth projects.

In the years since their openings, these works have proved sufficient to defend the city of Winnipeg against four decades of flood events. The floodway itself has been deployed in about three-quarters of the years since its opening. The most dangerous of these came with the so-called flood of the century in April 1997. In a very close call (prevailing winds shifted decisively at the last moment), the City was spared flood damage. The peak natural flow was 163,000 cubic feet per second (cfs) or just 6,000 cfs less than the floodway's designed capacity. By contrast, the exposed area of the Red River valley farm belt was devastated and more than 28,000 residents were evacuated. At its peak, some 2500 km^2 was inundated between the southern limits of the city and the US border.

While the flood diversion protocols were applied as authorized in 1997, the outcome highlighted a sharp contrast in protective impact between city and country. Indeed, the raising of the floodway gates served to exacerbate the rural damage. Shortly after, calls were made for significant infrastructure improvements (Red River Floodway Operations Review Committee 1999). Ultimately a federal-provincial agreement was struck to invest $665 million to increase the inlet, outlet, and channel flow capacity. This involved extensive bridge alterations and the raising of the 48-km-long West Dike. The result is designed to protect against a 1-in-700-year event.

A second post-1997 review was conducted by the International Joint Commission in reference to the entire Red River basin. This built on a 50-year history of basin collaboration, beginning with the International Souris-Red Rivers Engineering Board of 1948 and the International Red River Pollution Board of 1969. The IJC response was released in 2000. Entitled *Living with the Red*, it argued that the people of the basin would remain at risk until "comprehensive, integrated bi-national solutions to flood problems are developed" (IJC 2000). To this end it outlined a combined set of structural and nonstructural measures capable of handling an 1826-scale flood. It offered a panoramic survey of tools—added reservoir storage, wetland restoration, improved dikes and levees, floodwalls and bypasses, permanent evacuation of high-risk areas, flood-proofing of buildings, enhanced forecasts and warning systems, and a flood insurance scheme for Canada. The latter was viewed as a positive force insofar as it would provide an incentive for mitigation measures as well as encouraging landowner responsibility for personal preparedness. In conjunction with this review, arguments were advanced for the development of a computer-based "decision support system," drawing upon a wide range of stakeholders for data and providing comprehensive, real-time support for planning and response (Simonovic 1999).

Among the detailed discussions in *Living with the Red* was the choice between an expanded Winnipeg Floodway and a rural "detention structure" for waters at Ste. Agathe. The latter involved constructing a 40-km earth dike across the Red River valley south of the town, capable of discharging 70 per cent of the floodwaters in a 1:1,000 event. In effect, a massive plain south of Ste. Agathe would be transformed into a temporary reservoir (KGS Group 2001). This triggered a rural/urban political cleavage of major proportions. Public resistance surfaced immediately when the detention scheme was raised. Already small town and farm interests harboured bitter resentment over the Floodway operating rule of 1997, which was seen to have exacerbated rural flooding by applying an overly strict standard in closing the Winnipeg floodgates for the protection of the city.

Another telling section of the IJC report dealt with deficiencies in enforcing nonstructural rules, zones, and regulations. A close examination of enforcement revealed significant shortfalls, to the point that "lack of enforcement at the local, state and provincial levels of floodplain regulations, zoning bylaws and ordinances resulted in significantly higher damages than would have occurred with more effective enforcement" (IJC 2000, 43).

The shifting profile of the flood policy community is reminiscent of the changes to southern Alberta watershed management, captured in chapter 6. By the late 1990s the policy network for the Red River watershed extended well beyond government agencies and structural works operators. At least three civil society groups were operating. The Red River Basin Board, dominated by local authority interests, began in 1996 as a voice to influence water licensing and permitting processes. The International Coalition for Land and Water Stewardship in the Red River Basin was a grassroots citizens group that formed after the 1997 flood. And the Red River Water Resource Council was struck on the US side when the federal basin studies initiative finished in the 1970s. The merger of groups in 2002 created the Red River Basin Commission (RRBC), a broad-based constituency group led by 41 directors drawn from senior and local governments together with ENGOs, Native bands, and public members at large.

The Commission maintains dual offices in Manitoba and Minnesota, sponsors an annual conference, and disseminates studies and newsletters. It aspires to provide a "unified voice" for the entire basin. This is expressed through a "vision," a "mission statement," and "guiding principles." It also recognizes the idea of subsidiarity within the basin by affiliating and allying where possible with sub-watershed associations that are addressing more local issues in areas such as the Pembina valley or Devil's Lake. While flood damage reduction has been a longstanding concern, the mandate of the RRBC runs far wider. In 2005 it released a *Natural Resources Framework Plan* to guide integrated watershed management (Red River Basin Commission 2005).

While the RRBC's "voice and representation" function is important and perhaps unique in this setting, the championing of the *Framework Plan* is equally crucial as a means to overcome institutional fragmentation. The plan represents a set of preferences and priorities that were negotiated among the constituent interests. These are actively promoted and publicized within the region. However, the larger struggle is that of binding the relevant government authorities to support the plan in their own work. In this way the plan is an instrument to lever advances by means of external government actions.

An independent review of progress in implementing the recommendations of *Living with the Red* was released in 2009. It concluded that major efforts had been expended since 1997, with more than $1 billion spent on IJC agenda items. In Canada, the lion's share of funds went into increasing floodway capacity, scheduled to be completed by 2011. Outside of Winnipeg, it was estimated that almost all structures had been raised, diked, or relocated. In the United States, a major levee program was completed at Grand Forks. Across the watershed, tributary basins were getting increased attention (though still not enough), and there was significantly improved modelling and forecasting capacity, enabling greater public awareness during crisis periods. Overall, the study found increased "resiliency" in the Red River basin, with lessened effects in 2006 as compared to 1997 (Halliday and Associates 2009). At the same time there were shortcomings. Halliday reported little progress in grappling with environmental flood impacts such as invasive species transfer, hazardous material storage, and groundwater contamination. The problems that required inter-agency collaboration, as distinct from single-agency implementation, had also lagged, and there was some question of how far the public understanding of flood management had progressed beyond the "structural" level.

A second perspective on flood management progress comes from the RRBC 2011 report on long-term solutions. It cautioned that protection on the US side rarely exceeded 100-year events. Floodplain planning, it was argued, needed more determined enforcement. It also proposed that water retention projects aim for a 20 per cent flow reduction capability on the main stem of the Red. A major challenge is to weave together rural and urban concerns along with sub-basin needs, in a collective effort to slow the flow of water and hold it on the land for longer durations. To this end the RRBC advanced some new ideas for wetland "banking" and floodplain bills of rights (Red River Basin Commission 2011).

It should be noted that the Red River coordinating and planning groups described above account for a major, though not complete, part of southern Manitoba flood geography. For example, the Assiniboine River basin lies outside of the groups' jurisdiction. Thus when the Assiniboine experienced a 1:300 spring flood in 2011, it posed massive complications for the province of Manitoba, the city of Winnipeg, and points north.

Perhaps it was only a matter of time before environmental conditions at the lower end of the Red River system (north of Winnipeg) drew increased political attention. In 2008 the Lake Winnipeg Basin Initiative was announced by the federal and Manitoba governments. This was a belated recognition of the acute eutrophication problem that was evident in a massive blue-green algal bloom in the 2000s. Lake Winnipeg is the sixth largest freshwater lake in Canada and the tenth largest in the world, so its deterioration is a major issue within the province (Sandford 2013b). While the general causes were identified as nitrogen and phosphorus chemicals transported downstream by major floods as well as by normal drainage, possible responses were far from clear. Phase I of the Lake Winnipeg initiative covered a four-year period to 2012 and concentrated on science activities. A 2010 Canada-Manitoba memorandum of understanding signalled that Lake Winnipeg restoration would be a longer-term project, and a five-year Phase II commenced in 2012. Environment Canada again holds the lead federal role, and the focus will be on water quality improvement actions.

The efforts of the Red River Basin Commission and the International Joint Commission underline the recent transformations of the Manitoba flood policy network. In the 1960s the program was state-driven and depended crucially, on the Canadian side, on intergovernmental financing. It was engineering-based and politically had to overcome significant cultural drag to gain support for an expenditure equal to half of the Manitoba budget when Roblin took power. By the late 1990s water basin politics had evolved. It was approached in wider watershed frameworks that spanned the international border, it was partly grounded in ecological terms, and it admitted a far broader set of constituency interests (Hearne 2007). This was conditioned in part by more recent environmental sensitivities but was catalyzed in particular by the 1997 flood that, while sparing the city of Winnipeg, inflicted great damage across the basin. Such events partially fractured a generation-old political consensus and drove a new coalition-building process whose geographic, social, and intellectual context were wider. The rural–urban cleavage has lost none of its bite, though it is now joined by tensions between intellectual models. The annual spring breakup cycle also ensures a continuing preoccupation with handling each year's potential deluge.

The full-basin focus injected massive complexity, with federal and state authorities on both sides of the border now joined by energized cross-border institutions based in civil society interests. New issues have emerged to complement the flood focus, by tackling questions of drought management and even of formal basin-wide agreements on US and Canada water apportionment. Studies and actions are simultaneously advanced at both the basin and sub-basin levels, prompting tough questions about how to scale issues and interests. In sum, the new politics of the Red River basin illustrate the complicated character of multilevel water governance.

Conclusion

In the industrial age of western capitalism, the predominant political template for flood control was structural. This was deeply embedded in an engineering approach to waterways that overspilled their banks. The solutions pioneered in the nineteenth century by the Army Corps of Engineers focused on deepening channels, raising river banks, holding back the rate of flood flow by storage structures, and diverting rivers. This was acknowledged in legislative terms by acts of the US Congress, the Canadian Parliament, and state and provincial legislatures.

The structural approach to flood control remains integral to effective state strategies, but it is generally recognized to be insufficient in itself. An effective contemporary approach seeks to meld structural and nonstructural elements. In this, the government of Canada played a major role. The *Canada Water Act* and the Flood Damage Reduction Program served to refocus flood policy in the 1970s and 1980s. Effective mapping and planning served to highlight the extent of flood threat in over 900 settings across the country. This made Environment Canada's sudden exit from the FDRP all the more shocking. Not only did this continue the long-term trend of diminishing federal freshwater management capacity, but it also shifted the political burden back toward an earlier era when programs of property damage compensation and protective structures were the main tools.

The postwar years were politically transitional in Canadian flood policy, as illustrated in Manitoba. A government dedicated to rural small farmers was averse to big infrastructure, on grounds both financial and cultural. In the face of a century flood like 1950, however, this was difficult to sustain. Accordingly, the five years following 1953 were driven by a series of key events: the federal engineering survey, the 1956 (unfulfilled) flood threat, the cost-benefit conclusions of the provincial royal commission, and the rise of the Roblin Conservatives. Through all of this the federal government played a backstopping role even as the province was confirmed as the lead actor. The result was a "two-rivers" strategy that acknowledged the complex hydraulic geography of southern Manitoba.

In the flood policy sector there are pressing and complex distributional and redistributional issues. Is the purpose of policy defensive, restorative, realigning, or otherwise? Is the principal beneficiary group the existing floodplain population, the future population, or the general public? Is flood policy inherently protective of urban communities? How far will an urban priority be pursued at the expense of rural dwellers? These questions will lose none of their relevance as the policy paradigm of "flood damage reduction" is replaced by one of "disaster mitigation."

8
Hydro-power

FEW NATIONS HAVE BEEN AS WIDELY influenced by hydro-power as Canada. Dam and reservoir and turbine projects are found on rivers in all provinces and territories. Of the 850 large dams in the country (with a height of 10 m or more), 70 per cent were designed principally for power generation. This chapter examines how such projects are organized—how they are licensed and operated and what political constituencies are part of the hydro sector. Traditionally, the list starts with project owners, constructors, and regulators. In recent decades, however, a wider set of interests has claimed a place in the debate, including sporting groups, environmentalists, Aboriginal peoples, and upstream and downstream communities. Partly in response to the new players, the political debate about power projects has shifted. No longer is it exclusively about project costs and benefits narrowly defined. In Canada as elsewhere, the new issues include questions of social consent to new projects, environmental impacts on a watershed scale, the relative merits of "big" and "small" hydro, and the prospects for dam removal when enterprise life expires.

In this chapter, the watershed case study is the La Grande River, flowing westerly and emptying into James Bay in northern Quebec. Built and operated by the provincial crown enterprise Hydro-Québec, the project leads the nation in terms of project size and electricity output. The La Grande is probably the most heavily engineered basin in the country. A wild river as recently as 1975, it is now segmented by eight major turbine stations and multiple reservoirs and river diversions. The flows of three adjacent watersheds have been redirected to augment storage capacity on the La Grande. Despite the relatively small social community in the basin, the project faced deep political resistance that led to historic settlements with Cree First Nations. By the time the next generation of James Bay projects were proposed for watersheds north and south of the La Grande, the political landscape had been transformed. The dam and reservoir industry now acknowledges the importance of the new hydro constituencies as well as the new challenges to securing both regulatory and social consent.

Hydro-power and River Regulation in Canada

In 1899 the prominent engineer T.C. Keefer predicted to the Royal Society of Canada that "Canadian water power and its electrical product" would underwrite a new industrial revolution in the coming century (Nelles 1974). This was true in ways that even Keefer might not have imagined. A series of scientific and technological breakthroughs combined to establish a new industry that rapidly became prevalent in much of Canada. At its root was the fashioning of a new water value—as kinetic energy that could be mechanically captured to generate electricity. The core elements were as simple to specify as they were complex to implement: divert a flow of water, conduct it from a higher to lower altitude, channel it through a wheel or turbine device, and link the kinetic energy to an electrical generator and distribution grid. The attractions of this "white coal" or "white gold" were straightforward (Froshauer 1997). Canada was well endowed with major river systems. Water flow was continual or renewable, and the huge fixed capital investments required to control it could be recovered over an extended project life. Even better, in some cases hydro generating works could be replicated at successive stages of a river system to multiply the electricity commodity output from a single stream.

Not surprisingly, a political coalition quickly formed behind this potential. Central to it were business interests—the engineers, financiers, and corporate customers who promoted the new water power enterprise. Significantly, however, the road to commercial success was not as simple as the boosters might have hoped. The incipient hydro industry represented a challenge to existing energy sectors, including coal gas producers and distributors, who defended their investments vigorously. Neither was it a simple task to marshal the necessary capital for an essentially unproven form of business. In addition, the prospective consumers of electricity showed political ambivalence, intrigued by a possible new source of power but suspicious of possible monopoly features and costs of the new product. These contradictions played out over the formative decades from 1890 to 1920 (Armstrong and Nelles 1986).

The support of state agencies was equally critical. Provincial governments held prime constitutional jurisdiction and fortified their crown title to river flows and beds by statutory means. This meant that in seeking optimal development sites along watercourses, prospective developers would be subject to licensing and permitting controls. Key among these are the "storage rights" required for a dam and reservoir set-up. Consequently the hydro investor was destined for early and prolonged encounters with crown water administrators. As seen in chapter 6, both federal and provincial jurisdictions moved, around the turn of the twentieth century, to fortify their legal standing over flowing water. In fact, Nova Scotia passed its 1919 Water Act to smooth the path for dispensing hydro-power licenses.

At the same time, Keefer's insight about the growth-leveraging effect of abundant electricity was not lost on the political class. Provincial governments developed their own alliances with the industry, particularly once hydro-power had demonstrated its long-term commerciality. This extended to the point that, if private hydro capital proved hesitant to enter the smaller and rural provincial markets, governments resorted to state-owned enterprise to fill the gaps (Vining 1981). In particular, the relationship between provincial governments and their electric utilities became self-reinforcing in the decades following World War II. The alignment of hydro-electric projects with provincial economic development strategies meant that the crown would be supportive on land and water rights licensing. In addition, their respective assets could secure investment capital through long-term bond issues.

Hydro-power also needs to be approached from the perspective of its environmental footprint. How does the "store and release" design principle impact on rivers and watersheds? Rivers are inherently variable in their flow rates. The hydrograph measures fluctuations by site and season. Every river is distinct, but in Canada's northern climate this generally means high flows in the spring and autumn and lower flows in summer and winter. Yet electricity generation is a continuing need, and the huge amounts of capital sunk into any major project calls for the plant to operate as close to full capacity as possible. Thus the more steady release of water from a dam departs strikingly from the natural pulses of a wild river. The hydrograph of a regulated river is far more flat over time.

Altered flow regimes carry multiple implications for river ecology. Among the shifting variables are water depth, temperature, sediment load, velocity and deposition, and riparian vegetation. There is also the phenomenon of reservoirs as artificial lakes. Indeed, reservoir ecology has emerged as a distinct field of study (Richter and Thomas 2007). Furthermore, the segmentation of a river by virtue of barrier dams poses pressing questions of maintaining minimum stream flows and providing fishways for migrating species (Postel and Richter 2003). In the case of the Bennett dam on the Peace River in British Columbia, the downstream effects on the Peace-Athabasca delta were profound (Canada 1972). These effects fell principally in the province of Alberta, and, as mentioned in chapter 4, this project went virtually unchallenged by jurisdictions outside of British Columbia (Howell 1978).

For hydrologic engineers charged with project design, flow rate above the dam site is a key parameter. Natural flow is the starting point, but flow can be adjusted. In extreme cases, rivers in adjacent watersheds can be diverted as a supplement. As already seen in chapter 6, the province of Alberta entertained massive basin diversion possibilities during the PRIME years (1965–71). More recently, the province of Manitoba diverted a significant share of the Churchill River southward into the Nelson River, where multiple hydro-power projects were being planned and built (Loxley 1981). In the case study below, several large-scale diversions within Quebec's La Grande basin will be reviewed.

Such factors imposed a somewhat restricted "enterprise" mindset on provincial authorities when it came to hydro policy. They tended to define priorities and allocate resources largely from a perspective of commercial investment and return. Until the 1960s, the social and environmental consequences of major development projects had not yet registered politically and were virtually ignored. Civil interests raising such concerns found themselves almost entirely marginalized. Then in the 1970s the parallel challenges of environmental assessment monitoring and Aboriginal rights litigation served to alter this equation quite abruptly. It is revealing that the final installation of the last hydro mega-project in Canada, the James Bay complex on Quebec's La Grande River, was completed in 1996. This has raised the intriguing question of whether Canada's era of "big hydro" is over. Have the political barriers to new mega-projects become insurmountable? This will be explored in the sections below, along with a survey of the industry's future prospects.

History

The hydro-power industry was an outgrowth of an earlier and more fundamental technological revolution involving electricity. The business of electricity production combines three stages: i) a mechanical power source, which ii) turns an turbine generator unit to produce electricity, which iii) feeds continuous current into a transmission and supply system. In 1831 Michael Farraday discovered the electrical charge by rotating a copper disk between the poles of a magnet. The result was a continuous though low-level voltage. Scientific improvements brought more durable and efficient designs in subsequent decades, in which coil-wrapped armatures replaced the disks and rotated at great speed within fixed frames. Thomas Edison's inventions of the incandescent bulb (1879) and central station electrical generation (1882) set the stage for commercial take-off. Initially generators were turned by steam-powered belts, but turbines driven directly by steam or water soon supplanted them and both of these mechanical power systems advanced rapidly in the 1890s. Given the high levels of resistance (and therefore power loss) on early distribution lines, the initial range of service was essentially local. However, as high-voltage alternating current emerged in the 1890s, longer distance transmission became possible.

It was at this point that Keefer sensed great possibilities for Canada. No industrial nation was better endowed with the dynamic energy of flowing water. Early hydro-power sites were determined by one of two imperatives. The first was the intersection of river and urban electricity market, in places such as Niagara, Ottawa, and Winnipeg, where a public demand for electricity was clear. One of the first such enterprises was the Ottawa Electric Light Co., which installed turbines at Chaudière Falls in 1881. The second imperative lay at the intersection of river and raw material supply, where mine and mill enterprises dotted the boreal hinterland and depended on electricity for processing. By 1900 almost every newly constructed mine or pulp mill in eastern Canada included a companion hydro-power facility. Initially, both urban and remote types were built and owned by private capital.

Historically, the harnessing of water power began with the mechanism of the water wheel—a circular design of paddles or buckets driven by waterflow to transfer power to an axle. From here a stone could be turned to "mill" grain. In more elaborate set-ups, the power could be transferred to a saw blade for cutting logs or a mechanical system for spinning fibres and carding fabric into cloth. The industrialization of New England, beginning in the early 1800s, was based on textile mills powered by such a system. On a major Massachusetts river like the Merrimack, factory towns sprang up along its 190-km length. One of these was Lowell, located on the river bank with multiple canals running through the town with a vertical water drop that could be sold to the mills.

Land that was purchased at canal-side came with mill privileges in the form of water supply, and pricing was by units of "mill power." Originally one unit was defined as the power required to run 3,584 spindles on looms. Later it was revalued as a 25 cfs flow at a 30-foot fall. Once mill power was severed from land rights and sold separately, a free-standing water power industry was at hand (Steinberg 1991).

In the first electrical-generating wave, hydro-power was often based on "run of the river" mills, which diverted flowing water through a mill run or penstock before returning it to the channel. The Ontario Power Company's Niagara gorge turbine hall, opened in 1905, was fed by giant take-off tunnels that began above the falls. Elsewhere, however, natural flow rates varied considerably by season, and hydro-power required a store of latent energy by means of water impound. Water stored behind a dam represented stored potential energy. The operative concept here is hydraulic "head"—the height that water will fall to turn a turbine, along with the characteristics of the conduit. Depending on site conditions, hydraulic head can vary from 3 m (in flat landscapes such as plains and lowlands) to 1,700 m (in alpine valleys). The obvious advantage of water storage is that of operating flexibility, since the flow can be turned on and off with little wastage. Today, in fact, many hydro-facilities serve as "peaking plants" within connected electrical systems. This means that the turbines could be started and stopped to meet peak demand as well as serving base needs.

While the impounded water supply is indispensable, the water turbine is equally important (Canadian Hydropower Association 2008). As early as the 1820s, improved designs emerged in Europe. One of these is known as the "inner flow" turbine, in which flowing water enters a casing and turns the blades before flowing out through the centre. This was improved by James B. Francis in 1849 to a 90 per cent efficiency level. The Francis turbine is still the most common in the world and is especially adapted to utilize medium to low head flows. Another design came from Victor Kaplan in 1913. The Kaplan turbine involves a propeller with adjustable blades that turns in a way similar to that of a ship screw, only within a closed casing. It revolutionized the potential of low head sites where the vertical drop could be less than 3–6 metres. For high head sites, such as are found in mountainous terrains, the Pelton wheel is most common. Harking back to pre-industrial schemes, it directs jets of water at high speeds through nozzles to turn a bucket wheel made of hardened alloys (United States 2005).

In Canada, an early turbine system was built in 1899 at Shawinigan, east of Montreal, and it soon became the standard. A Montreal-American firm, Shawinigan Water & Power Co., acquired a monopoly of power rights on the St. Maurice River. The first plant opened in 1901 and attracted paper, aluminum, and chemical industries to the valley. In 1903, the company built a 135 km line, at 50,000 volts, that brought electricity to Montreal. Hydro-electricity was well on its way to becoming *the* water industry of twentieth-century Canada. The Shawinigan 2 plant opened in 1911, and a third followed in 1948. Ultimately, the company was purchased by the provincial state-owned Hydro-Québec in 1963.

The years 1900–10 were a boom decade, as innovations in electricity genera-tion, transmission, and delivery came together. Service areas grew in size. Private developers vied with crown corporations for the rights to manufacture electricity and distribute it. In Ontario, the "public power" movement led by Sir Adam Beck made the case for a state-owned electric utility and small private manu-facturing businesses were strongly supportive (Nelles 1974). Elsewhere private capital held sway. Either way, licensing powers lay in state hands. As we saw in chapter 4, Nova Scotia brought in a new water act in 1919 that vested propri-etary and regulatory interests in the provincial crown. This was designed to make it easier to license private hydro generating projects and to shield the firms from riparian lawsuits.

A fascinating glimpse into the politics of hydro-power during these dec-ades involves Quebec's Saguenay River. Late in 1922, Premier Louis-Alexandre Taschereau announced that the province had licensed a major dam at the out-let of Lac St. Jean. It was heralded as the lynchpin of industrial prosperity in the poor, agrarian Saguenay region. It would fuel timber, pulp and paper, and aluminum manufacturing. As the premier put it, a million horsepower were "wasted" each day as water flowed, unused, downstream (Massell 2000, 4). The industrialist behind this scheme was J.B. Duke, the tobacco king of the Carolinas, who came to Quebec to enter the bauxite-aluminum industry. Dam construc-tion began early in 1923, and electricity began to flow three and a half years later. Located at the larger of the two outlets of Lac St. Jean, at Isle Maligne, it generated more than half a million horsepower; over the next four decades the regional population of the Saguenay grew fourfold.

Of special interest here is the political relationship between the corporate sponsor and the provincial government. It has long been assumed by many scholars that the commercial bias for economic growth, combined with weak administrative capacity, rendered provincial governments powerless to say no to corporate power. Yet the Quebec provincial state, and its Hydraulic Service in particular, proved far from passive in dealing with the Duke interests. The head of this agency, Arthur Amos, was a hydraulic engineer of uncommon vision. During the 1910–20 period he advised a government that vigorously defended the pub-lic interest in Quebec watersheds. The tradition of selling water storage rights was terminated in favour of a system of emphyteutic leases (i.e., rental arrange-ments with an obligation to improve the property to retain rights). In addition, a power tax of 15–30 cents per horsepower per year was instituted on private corporate users. This was hardly the sort of pliable subordination that might have been hypothesized (and indeed was practiced in other settings). Significantly, the more assertive phases of water development regulation ended with the election of Taschereau in 1920.

One final political feature of the Saguenay development deserves mention. The Isle Maligne dam had the effect of raising the lake level a full 6 metres. Not announced in advance, this imposed immediate and severe dislocation on hun-dreds of farms with riparian holdings, spread over 12,000 flooded acres around

Lac St. Jean. In a description that recalls the impacts on the New Hampshire Lakes in the textile years, David Massell reports a period of "violent agitation" among the rural classes (Massell 2000, 8). This highlights the sharp contrast between powerful and powerless interests when a major new river works overturns established relations.

The Post-war Hydro Boom

In the half century and more since 1950, both the geography and the scale of hydro-power enterprise have changed dramatically. Where once plants were located close to urban markets, the new sites are distant. Where once plant capacity was measured in tens or hundreds of megawatts, it is now scaled in thousands. Modern reservoir and turbine complexes are found deep in the boreal forest, on northerly flowing rivers, and in lands inhabited mainly by Aboriginal peoples. For the most part these projects are proposed, built, and operated by provincial state-owned power companies. While all provinces have some potential, five provinces stand out in terms of hydro-electric installations: Quebec, British Columbia, Ontario, Newfoundland, and Manitoba.

A prerequisite for this transformation was the growing appreciation of hydro-power on the part of state elites. Abundant and affordable power was part of the equation for economic growth. It found many expressions, ranging from the nationalist celebration of Hydro-Québec as a chosen economic instrument during the Quiet Revolution (Faucher and Bergeron 1986), to Premier Joey Smallwood's alliance with the British-Newfoundland Corporation (BRINCO) in exploiting wild rivers in Labrador (Smith 1975), to W.A.C. Bennett's electric development ambitions in British Columbia (Mitchell 1983). On the prairies, the Saskatchewan-Nelson basin was being sized up for hydro development by three provincial governments (Saskatchewan-Nelson Basin Board 1972), with Manitoba fulfilling it most aggressively (Loxley 1981).

The results, in terms of big projects, can be seen in Table 8.1. Notably, only 2 of the largest 11 hydro facilities in Canada were opened before 1970. This underlines how the geography of site development has broadened in recent decades. Nine of the top stations are in remote or northern locations and most of these are single-use (i.e., electricity producing only) complexes. In total there are about 500 hydro-power stations operating in Canada today, with a generating capacity of 73,000 MW. This includes about 360 small stations, generating under 50 MW apiece (collectively 1/20 of total capacity).

Dam and reservoir systems on northern rivers offer several advantages. First, the watersheds rest on bedrock that provides secure foundations for dams and underground turbine halls. Second, many of the leading rivers offered opportunities for multiple dam and turbine installations along their lengths. These drainages could be augmented, if necessary, by diverting the flows of adjacent watersheds into the desired channels. Finally, the technical barriers to long distance electrical transmission from hinterland stations were met by breakthroughs in high-voltage, direct current carriage. Thus, when the new third wave of hydro-power began

Table 8.1 Canada's Largest Hydro Stations

Rank	Name	Province	Rated Capacity (MW)	Initial Year
1	Churchill Falls	NF	5,428	1971
2	La Grande 2	QC	5,328	1979
3	Gordon M. Shrum	BC	2,730	1968
4	La Grande 4	QC	2,650	1984
5	La Grande 3	QC	2,304	1982
6	Revelstoke	BC	1,980	1984
7	Mica	BC	1,805	1976
8	Beauharnois	QC	1,656	1932
9	Manic 5	QC	1,528	1970
10	Sir Adam Beck 2	ON	1,418	1954
11	Limestone	MB	1,330	1990

Source: Statistics Canada, 2000. *Electric Power Generating Stations.* Catalogue 57–206-XIB.

in the late 1960s, it was based on mega-projects of unprecedented scale. If they generated electricity in excess of domestic needs, ready export markets were available in the US Pacific Northwest, the Great Lakes states, and New England. In provincial government eyes, hydro became *the* water-based industry of the twentieth century, the ultimate renewable resource providing an endless supply of "white coal." To explore the politics of big hydro at a fine-grained level, the next section explores Canada's "ultimate" power play.

CASE STUDY: LA GRANDE BASIN HYDRO PROJECTS, QUEBEC

Former Quebec Premier Robert Bourassa described James Bay hydro as "the project of the century" (Bourassa 1973). It was, by any measure, an extraordinary scheme. As first announced, it would involve five major northern watersheds that flowed westerly into James Bay. These were the Nottaway, Broadback, Rupert, Eastmain, and La Grande drainages. James Bay was the largest integrated hydro strategy in Canadian history, and it took two decades to complete. Even before the La Grande scheme was finished, attention turned to the more northerly Great Whale River watershed that drained into Hudson's Bay. But here the similarity ends. Much had changed in the business, political, and legal worlds between 1971 and 1989. The reasons for the ultimate cancellation of the Great Whale project will also be addressed in this section.

For the government, the scheme was timely. Quebec's economy had slowed in the early 1970s and Bourassa's Liberal party faced an epic challenge from the new sovereigntist party, the Parti Québecois. James Bay, Bourassa hoped, would place him squarely in the tradition of Quebec nation-building. Hydro-Québec acquired all private hydro developers in 1963 and became the flagship for a high technology, French-language business culture in the province. Already Hydro-Québec had tackled the Manicouagan River on the lower north shore of the St. Lawrence River, with a combination of run-of-the-river and reservoir-style power stations, totaling over 5000 MW of electricity. Even as work on the "Manic" system was leveling off, the next generation of planning was taking form in northern Quebec.

It often requires a convergence of facilitating forces to bring a mega-project to fruition, and these are evident in Quebec. As the planner/operator, Hydro-Québec benefited from a combined accumulation of technical prestige and nationalist pride. It was seen as one of the key developmental agents of modern Quebec and its reputation gave instant credibility to the James Bay idea. In addition, the Liberal government of Premier Bourassa was open to economic strategies with extended impacts. James Bay offered decades of sustained construction employment for provincial workers together with an economical electrical supply for the indefinite future. Equally significant, it opened the possibility of massive export earnings from power sold to New England utilities. The premier could be forgiven if he sensed a development coalition that could propel the province into the twenty-first century. Central to this coalition was the government's financial interdependence with Hydro-Québec when it came to backstopping government and Hydro bonds.

On April 30, 1971 the project was announced. It was initially intended for the three more southerly watersheds—the Nottaway, Broadback, and Rupert. But following the work of a Canada-Quebec working group, Phase One was redesigned (Hornig 1999). This took account of biological issues together with Aboriginal protests from four bands that stood to lose their traditional hunting and trapping grounds as the lands were flooded. In January 1972 the James Bay Development Corporation (JBDC) announced the shift to the more northerly La Grande River system. Four possible generating sites were identified, with LG2 designated first for construction and site work beginning in 1975. Completed a decade later and known as the Robert Bourassa Generating Station, it is the world's largest underground power complex with 16 turbines and a capacity of 5,328 MW. This exceeds the total output of Manitoba and almost equals that of Newfoundland. Perhaps the most famous photograph of LG2 is of the Giant's Staircase—the tiered spillway below the dam that stands three times the height of Niagara Falls.

Generating capacity is in large part a function of water supply, and so this meant damming rivers and building reservoirs on an epic scale. Even the flow of the mighty La Grande proved insufficient, so massive diversions were added from adjacent watersheds. Sakami Lake brings waters from Opinaca Lake (south of the La Grande). The Caniapiscau reservoir, the largest artificial "lake" in Quebec, brings waters from the east as well. This required many major dams, dikes, and canals, along with the massive impoundment of waters above LG2 and the upstream station known as LG3. When the works were complete, the average flow of the La Grande River almost doubled from 1,700 m³/sec to 3,300 m³/sec. The overall project is captured in Map 8.1.

It is important to underline the scale of this geography. The natural size of the La Grande watershed was 97,600 km², an area comparable to the Athabasca watershed and surpassing the province of New Brunswick in size. However, the diversions from the Eastmain and Rupert Rivers served to almost double the watershed size, to 175,000 km². This is the equivalent of adding Newfoundland island to New Brunswick. Also noteworthy is the total population of approximately 5,000 centred mainly around the Cree community of Chisasibi near the river mouth on James Bay. Although this may qualify as the lowest social density for any major watershed in Canada, we will see that the external political community claiming an interest in the La Grande extends far further.

By the time of its announcement in 1972, there seemed little possibility that the project could be derailed. A juggernaut of provincial authorities and private industries had coalesced behind a multi-decade development scheme. But the Cree bands of northern Quebec, led by Grand Chief Billy Diamond, were mobilizing to defend a homeland and a way of life (McGregor 1989). The Cree engaged legal counsel to advance a case for damages to traditional lands on which, they argued, Aboriginal title remained intact. This title is defined as a legal interest in land by virtue of traditional occupancy since time immemorial. The title had never been surrendered to any government, either by treaty or sale.

Map 8.1 La Grande Watershed, Quebec

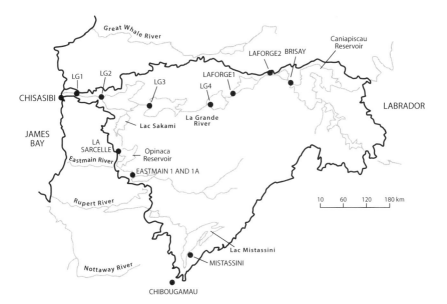

Indeed, the Indian title was acknowledged in the Royal Proclamation of 1763, directing colonial governors to protect Indian lands. In any case, the Quebec crown claim to the area was compromised by the fact that Ottawa possessed crown rights to northern Quebec from the time of Confederation until two huge land transfers of the James Bay drainage in 1898 and the Hudson's Bay drainage in 1912. Thus it was argued that Quebec lacked clear title to the lands in question, severely complicating its capacity to issue permits and licenses.

The legal action commenced in May 1972 and continued over the following 18 months, with a surprising result. Justice Albert Malouf of the Quebec Superior Court ruled in favour of the Cree in November 1973 and issued an interim injunction that stopped construction cold. One week later this was overturned on appeal. However, the Malouf decision was chastening to the Quebec government. Even before the reversal, Premier Bourassa announced his willingness to negotiate a comprehensive settlement for the extinguishment of Cree (and Inuit) title in all of northern Quebec. The Malouf ruling added massive political urgency for reaching a settlement with the Cree. With both sides under tremendous pressure, an agreement-in-principle was hammered out in less than a year. Twelve months after that, the final *James Bay and Northern Quebec Agreement* (JBNQA) was signed in 1975 (Quebec 1976). The "shotgun" quality of the talks was evident by the fact that LG2 was near completion in 1977 and site preparation had also begun for LG3 and LG4.

For Aboriginal Canada, the Cree and Inuit land claim negotiations were extremely controversial. Tribal groups in the Northwest Territories, Yukon, and British Columbia also claimed traditional title that had never been extinguished. Their ambitions for land and resource rights, as well as self-government, were often more expansive than those being addressed at the James Bay negotiating table. In fact some Aboriginal political leaders dismissed the James Bay agreement as a "beads and trinkets" settlement. From outside, there was genuine fear that a "weak" James Bay settlement (measured against other tribal and band political ambitions) would set an upper limit for negotiations elsewhere. At the same time, the James Bay Cree and northern Quebec Inuit faced imminent development that would permanently displace their way of life. Cree hunting and trapping lands stood to be inundated by the strings of reservoirs, canals, and diversions involved in the La Grande scheme. There was little awareness in southern Canada of just how intensively these watersheds were used by Aboriginal peoples, until documentary evidence was brought to the courtroom and the negotiating table.

In this light, the JBNQA is an impressive overall settlement package, achieved in only three years and in the face of full frontal resistance from corporations and state. Over 1 million km^2 of "traditional lands" were acknowledged for exclusive use, shared use (with industrial interests), and exclusive hunting and trapping use. A financial compensation package of $225 million was conveyed to Aboriginal development corporations. Regional governments were established for both Cree and Inuit territories, and various consultative and management boards followed. A guaranteed income scheme for hunters and trappers was also part of the mix.

In sum, although the La Grande project did proceed, the Cree gained new developmental resources in the form of land, capital, and institutions. In a pivotal decade, a "regional society" had begun to emerge in Cree country (Salisbury 1986). At the same time, the JBNQA was far from fulfilled as the 1980s opened. Aboriginal peoples discovered that a second struggle had to be waged to force state authorities to implement the provisions of the settlement (Vincent and Bowers 1988).

In less than two decades, however, the government of Quebec managed to transform the La Grande from a wild river, almost untouched by civilization, into one of the most heavily engineered and regulated watersheds in the country. Giant as it was, the La Grande complex was only the first phase of Quebec's northern hydro vision. The second involved the Great Whale River (Grande rivière de la Baleine), a watershed inhabited by both Cree and Inuit and situated immediately north of the La Grande watershed.

In 1988 the Quebec cabinet approved Hydro-Québec's strategic plan to 2002, including eight proposed diversion projects in the far north and on the lower North Shore of the St. Lawrence River. A year later, Bourassa, now in his second stint as premier, announced the beginning of the Great Whale project. The Great Whale River is some 720 km in length and the drainage area of 42,700 km^2 is less than half that of the neighbouring La Grande watershed. The Great Whale rises at Lac Bienville and flows westerly, emptying into Hudson's Bay near twin Cree and Inuit communities. The hydro project called for three generating stations with a combined output of 3160 MW.

There are several ways that the political context for hydro project licensing changed between 1971 and 1989. For one thing, the First Nations were far more organized for Great Whale and were able to draw on their experiences in the approval and implementation battles on the La Grande. Also, a far greater social awareness of big hydro impacts permeated the North American public. In Quebec and outside, Aboriginal groups, environmental NGOs, churches, diffuse public opinion, and even business interests were drawn into the Great Whale debates. There were also some new links in the political networks favouring hydro. Particularly important were the external (American) power buyers whose firm commitments were indispensable for raising capital for the project. Finally, the very existence of the La Grande project offered a standard against which future development schemes, and in particular the social and environmental dislocations that they entailed, could be measured.

For Great Whale, the process of environmental impact review would be different from that of the La Grande. In fact, multiple assessments were now legally mandated—several under the JBNQA, another under Quebec provincial law, and yet another by the government of Canada. (The Supreme Court of Canada ruled in 1991 that a federal environmental assessment was required.) As five separate proceedings would have been unworkable, a joint review process was negotiated. The result was to make the Great Whale project the first northern hydro development project to face a full public review.

In 1993 Hydro-Québec submitted a 5,000-page environmental impact statement. There were a wide range of issues to be addressed. Among the most important was methyl mercury entering the regional food chain. As vegetation and soils decomposed in the reservoirs of La Grande, they combined with natural, inorganic mercury to form a toxic organic mercury that concentrated in fish oil. Although fish in James Bay rivers already showed mercury levels above the Canadian safety standard, the levels were up to five times higher in the La Grande basin. Official opinions differed on the retention time for elevated mercury levels, with Hydro-Québec submitting that levels peaked two or three years after a reservoir was filled while the federal Department of Fisheries and Oceans suggested it might require up to a century to revert to natural levels. Either way, as Susan Williams puts it, fish moved from a staple to a poison for the Cree (Williams 1993).

This only began to document the environmental transformations. There were questions about changes to coastal marshes and lowlands, due to nutrient losses with reduced spring floods. Because the James Bay coast was a massive corridor for migrating waterfowl, changes to algae blooms or eel grass constituted potential threats. For inland caribou there were major questions about losses of feeding ranges and calving areas in newly flooded areas. This was an especially sensitive issue. In 1984 a devastating drowning of up to 10,000 caribou occurred on the Caniapiscau River, due either to torrential rains or water release from reservoirs (or both). In addition, there were issues of lost land use. The Great Whale plan called for the flooding of 11,400 km^2 in a watershed of 175,000 km^2. Cree leader Raymond Managoose put this in a holistic perspective by asking, "If they cut off your foot would you say that 5 per cent of your body was affected?" There were also urgent questions about the loss of spring and fall flow pulses and the commencement of a new winter pulse (Williams 1993).

The year 1994 was pivotal for the Great Whale project. The joint review began and with it an ongoing civic and media debate. There were many vectors to this process, including tactical splits among the environmental NGOs, campaigns by church groups, and investor-led initiatives to divest holdings in firms involved in the energy project. The signal event, however, came in March 1994 when the New York Power Authority announced the cancellation of its 800 MW purchase agreement for Great Whale electricity (almost one-third of the projected project capacity). Several forces converged to shape this decision. For several years, Hydro-Québec had resisted federal involvement in the environmental review, until a court order obliged a joint assessment. Large ENGOs were thus able to couple their ecological critiques of river disruption with charges of regulatory evasion. In addition, Inuit and Cree peoples in the Great Whale watershed demanded a new rights settlement, whereas Hydro-Québec took the view that the original James Bay settlement included blanket coverage. Finally, the New York Power Authority reviewed and scaled back its electricity demand in ways that made new deliveries less urgent. From this point forward the project was on life support, and months later the newly elected Parti Québécois government cancelled Great Whale. By any standard this was a shock to the provincial political system. It not only demonstrated the centrality of conservation politics, and especially of the EARP process, in the new age of sustainable development; it also highlighted a new form of environmental coalition building and campaigning in a globalized context.

If the Great Whale project constituted "James Bay II," then the third instalment arrived in the form of the Eastmain/La Sarcelle project (Quebec n.d.). Recall that the original plan for northern hydro targeted the Nottaway, Broadback, and Rupert rivers (the so-called NBR) for development. In the initial version, both of the latter rivers were slated for a half-dozen or more powerhouses. However, following its defeat on Great Whale, Hydro-Québec indicated a shift of development philosophy toward more "modest" projects. A severely scaled down version of NBR emerged in the late 1990s, calling for the partial diversion of Rupert River waters into the La Grande watershed. Three new powerhouses were constructed along the route—Eastmain 1 (480 MW) and Eastmain 1A (768 MW) at the Eastmain reservoir and La Sarcelle (125 MW) at the Opinaca reservoir. These can be seen on Map 8.1.

The most significant transformation in the Eastmain proposal was an altered approach to Aboriginal participation. Hydro-Québec put forward variants of the diversion plan along with impact assessments, and the choice was made jointly with the Cree. After extended negotiations between Quebec and the Grand Council of the Cree, a draft Agreement-in-Principle was put to a referendum of tribal members early in 2002. Over 60 per cent voted in favour. The package included some extremely innovative provisions, never seen in past proposals (Desbiens 2004). Perhaps the most striking was the recognition of Cree interests by means of a predevelopment consent to the project. Another involved state authorities sharing the revenues from the power business, with the Cree receiving $3.6 billion over 50 years. There were also provisions for the Cree to take over management of a series of social and economic programs. Detailed terms were negotiated to maintain the natural flows in key tributaries and for the Rupert River aquatic environment downstream of the "control structure" (Quebec n.d.). In return, the Cree agreed to the river diversion, containment works, and powerhouses, as well as agreeing to mineral and forest development leases in the future. Cree Grand Chief Ted Moses travelled to all nine communities for extensive meetings to explain the package that the Grand Council was recommending. The final agreement, known as La Paix des Braves, was endorsed in 2002 (Quebec and Grand Council of the Cree 2002).

Over three decades the James Bay Cree and Northern Quebec Inuit waged a persistent, inventive, and determined resistance to the water capitalism pursued by the provincial state. They drew on traditional knowledge to document Aboriginal land use and occupancy, used the courts to slow or block unilateral state actions that ignored and overrode those rights, and struck tactical alliances with a variety of groups pursuing congruent interests. The three phases of this struggle—La Grande, Great Whale, and Eastmain/La Sarcelle—illustrate both the tenacity of the hydro-power development coalition and the shifting contexts of public regulation and licensing.

Is the Era of Big Hydro Over?

Following the completion of the La Grande complex in the mid-1980s there was a hiatus in the big hydro field. This was not for want of potential projects (Martin and Hoffman 2008). Manitoba seemed poised to continue building on the Nelson River, with the Wuskwatim project set to follow the Limestone station that was commissioned in 1990. In Quebec, as just seen, the next phases of Hydro's northern strategy lay in the Great Whale River watershed and the Eastmain. And in British Columbia, the Bill Bennett government completed the Revelstoke dam project in 1985 and turned its attention north to the Peace River where a new project at Site C, downstream of the Bennett dam at a site near Fort St. John, was next in line.

Each was beset with complications, however (Netherton 2007). It was an era when all Canadian governments seemed locked in fiscal deficit and struggled to service their accumulated debts, making new borrowing problematical. In addition, northern Aboriginal groups had launched land claims that disputed the ownership to much of the northern hinterland where future projects would be built. Furthermore, Canadian jurisdictions had enacted environmental assessment laws that required more comprehensive review and public input before the necessary licenses could be issued. Finally, the markets for the next generation of projects required long-term export contracts to American distributors, since Canadian demand was largely met by existing capacity (Waldram 1988).

While each of these "next generation" projects had its own history, they were all ultimately deferred for at least 15–20 years. This prompted the question of whether the era of Big Hydro was finished in Canada. A variety of ENGOs certainly hoped so. With the newly emerging sustainability discourse, launched by the UN's Brundtland Commission Report of 1987, hydro-projects stood to be assessed by far more holistic criteria of costs and benefits (McCully 1996).

Moreover, Big Hydro was swept up in the 1990s' political challenge to dam and reservoir works worldwide. In 1997 the World Bank joined with the International Union for the Conservation of Nature (a longstanding NGO) to sponsor the World Commission on Dams (WCD). It singled out dams as stand-alone works and posed some blunt questions about costs and benefits. The background here was a growing number of indigenous protests against new projects around the world. The panel of inquiry was charged to explore the "developmental effectiveness" of dam projects and to generate international guidelines to project planning, construction, and management. The report *Dams and Development* conceded that dams can offer benefits but often with unacceptably high prices to displaced peoples, downstream communities, taxpayers, and the natural world (World Commission on Dams 2000).

Without question, the WCD report "infused debates about dams with new concepts" (International Rivers Network 2005, 3). It highlighted the neglected rights of affected communities, the failures of transparency in project decision-making, and the need to make "environmental flows" central to impact analysis. Since 2000, the World Bank has backed away somewhat from the Commission's findings. But the expanding civil society network on river conservation, led by the International Rivers Network (IRN), embraced the WCD perspective and has ensured that it will be integral to project deliberations in the future. Indicative of this is the IRN manifesto, "Twelve Reasons to Exclude Large Hydro from Renewables Initiatives" (2003). Another indication of alternative thinking on large dam viability is the growing movement for dam removal (Hawley 2011).

Despite World Bank ambivalence, several international development banks and private banks signed on to the WCD protocols for project analysis. This highlighted a critical link in the big hydro coalition—the terms of involvement by international capital. If project economics are framed more holistically, the dam critics argue, then the threshold of approval will be raised and projects will be better designed to win endorsement or will not be proposed at all. It should be recalled that even without the WCD benchmark, Aboriginal and environmental groups were able to successfully appeal to US financiers and corporate customers to re-evaluate the costs and benefits of Great Whale electricity. The new political narrative on dam development extends this even further.

On the other side of the balance sheet, the hydro-electric sector has gained a certain political advantage from the rise of the global climate change action movement and the international regime anchored in the 1992 UN Framework Convention and the Kyoto Protocol of 1997. The hydro industry can legitimately present itself as a relatively benevolent renewable energy source from a greenhouse gas perspective. Jurisdictions that rely principally on hydro-power enjoy significant advantages in the quest for low carbon futures.

For the Canadian hydro industry, the 1990s were a decade of political contradiction and uncertainty. The anti-dam movement gained strength on a global scale and demonstrated its ability to challenge big projects. In Canada, Aboriginal peoples successfully used the judicial system to defend traditional title and rights claims and oblige crown authorities to negotiate comprehensive settlements. Furthermore, environmental and social impact assessment procedures, both federal and provincial, would now apply to future hydro schemes. Indeed, the 1995 *Canadian Environmental Assessment Act* (CEAA) came with more rigorous federal criteria and processes. Recognizing these new political contexts, Canadian hydro producers acted to establish a new collective voice in the form of a national trade association. The Canadian Hydropower Association (CHA), founded in 1998, embraced not only the hydro-electric producers but their supplier sectors as well. The CHA faced "the necessity of rehabilitating hydropower as a clean and renewable source of electricity" that was "little known and underappreciated in Ottawa" (Fortin 2005). For instance, the CHA has argued that current environmental assessment regimes are tilted disproportionately toward "local" impacts such as river flows and reservoir displacement, while neglecting more comprehensive impacts such as air pollution and greenhouse gas emissions. As a result, the CEAA process "has the unintended effect of favouring the development of nonrenewable, more polluting forms of energy, specifically fossil-fuel generated electricity" (CHA 2002).

The CHA also argues that the industry has fashioned a new approach to collaborations with Aboriginal peoples. This involves partnerships, agreements, and joint ventures, as seen above in the case of La Paix des Braves and as extended to new projects in Manitoba, British Columbia, and elsewhere in Quebec (Fortin and Collu 2008). Hydro corporations in Quebec, Manitoba, and British Columbia have been forced, by the judicial cases mentioned earlier, to transform their political dealings with Aboriginal peoples. This is evident in the negotiations on the Rupert River, the Conawapa generating station, and the Peace River, respectively.

All of these initiatives are geared toward establishing the industry as a large-scale but low-impact enterprise. But perhaps the most graphic evidence of the new political narrative in the hydro-power sector involves the move toward explicit "sustainability standards" for company behaviour. Sponsored by the International Hydropower Association, the sustainability assessment protocol was released in 2010. It is designed to apply across the life cycle of a facility. Formal assessment criteria are to be applied on up to 23 topics in each life cycle stage, with third-party assessors handling the audits (IHA 2010). While it remains to be seen what degree of political legitimacy will be achieved, the IHA initiative constitutes a serious bid to redefine the sociopolitical standing of big hydro projects.

The situation at time of writing suggests that, in part at least, big hydro is recovering some developmental momentum. The Rupert River project (900 MW) is under construction in northern Quebec, just south of the La Grande. The La Romaine watershed on Quebec's North Shore is the proposed site of four generating stations (1,500 MW). Environmental reviews commenced in 2008 and construction work is underway. Newfoundland has advanced plans for the Muskrat Falls project as the opening phase of the Lower Churchill River scheme (totalling 2,800 MW). In Manitoba, the Conawapa and the Gull (Keeyask) projects (1,870 MW) are in the early planning stages. British Columbia has submitted the Peace River C project for environmental and social review.

What Role for Small Hydro?

Small hydro seems like an example of "back to the future." It involves scaling back on all dimensions—water use, mill capacity, and electrical output—to the levels before industrial hydro-power began. Small hydro relies on run-of-the-river or small impoundments formed by canals or locks. The generating facilities can be sited on shorelines or islands. In terms of power output, the mini projects may create less than 100 KW, the next level 100–1,000 KW, and the top-end 1–50 MW. The output may remain off the electrical grid, supplying homes or isolated projects, or it may feed into the main distribution network. One working formula for calculating electrical capacity in KW hours involves multiplying seven times the head (in metres) by the flow rate measured in cubic metres per second, or 7X head(m) x flow(m³/s).

One version is known as "low-head hydro," in which the vertical water drop is generally less than 5 metres (16 feet). Such projects possess a very light environmental footprint. Because they lack dams, there is no impediment to fish migration and no need for fish ladders. Suspended materials remain in the water and there is no silt accumulation behind an impound. Capital costs tend to be modest, as do maintenance costs. One highly publicized example is found on the upper Mississippi River near Hastings, Minnesota. Here the Army Corps of Engineers operate a lock and dam system that generates 4.4 MW of electricity. In addition, a smaller generating unit has been installed in the tail race of the Corps's installation. Owned privately by Hydro Green Energy, it can turn up to 250 KW.

It is clear that organizational attributes of small hydro are qualitatively different from the large industrial utilities, and it is difficult to reliably gauge its potential. In terms of physical sites, they are abundantly distributed around the country. By one calculation, if all available sites were exploited, combined electrical output would amount to one-half of the current annual US dam production. Obviously this theoretical capacity will never be reached. Going forward, however, there may be a significant role for small hydro in adding incrementally to electrical capacity. This will depend upon many variables: site licensing, capital access, technical capability, and the pricing terms of connection to electricity grids.

Conclusion

Hydro-power emerged as part of the industrial revolution, in all countries where watershed attributes were positive. The core elements are the dam, the storage reservoir, and the turbine hall. While the first two elements figure in other water sectors, such as irrigation, flood control, and drinking water supply, hydro-power accounts for the largest share of large dam and reservoir systems in Canada.

There is a distinct ecology associated with rivers segmented by dams. Natural processes are truncated. Seasonal pulses are severely moderated downstream. Sediment transport is confined. Migratory fish are blocked unless effective bypass works are installed. The conversion of a natural river into a segmented stream also alters the sociopolitical order in a watershed. New benefits can be conferred when hydro-power provides a fulcrum for attracting industry, or producing affordable electricity or recreational landscapes. However, burdens are also imposed, as reservoirs displace riparian dwellers and communities downstream of dams experience altered river conditions.

The policy networks associated with hydro-power in Canada coalesce around powerful proponents and supportive state agencies. In fact, these two elements anchored hydro-power networks for the first half century or more. During the early decades, water law was altered to confer hydro-power incentives. In the period from the 1950s to 1980s, industrial values were at an apex. Newly emergent interests toward the end of this period began to alter the equilibrium, tentatively at first but decisively over time. Two critical new policy challenges illustrate the shift. First, with the rise of modern conservation advocates, the techniques of environmental assessment and project review were entrenched. Second, with the political mobilization of Aboriginal peoples and a series of landmark judicial victories on Aboriginal rights, the hydro-politics of Canada's mid-north was fundamentally transformed. These are two emerging political polarities of extraordinary consequence that have reshaped the terms and prospects for future power projects. The distance travelled can be seen by contrasting the power relations of James Bay in the eras of the La Grande, Great Whale, and Eastmain projects.

The international anti-dam movement of the 1990s involved more than hydro-power, but in Canada, hydro-power was squarely in the cross-hairs. For a time it seemed that the era of big hydro was over, and this may yet prove to be the case. Either way, the patterns of preparing, approving, and implementing power projects has changed forever. If the industry is to survive, both corporate enterprise and state authorities must adapt to new policy network relations. Resident Aboriginal groups are now treated as potential partners in major decisions at every stage of the project development cycle. Quebec's Eastmain 1-A project and Manitoba's Wuskwatim project involve First Nations in design, ownership, and licensing decisions. British Columbia's Peace River C project seems to be following this as well. In any event, it may be that future hydro-power projects are destined to be smaller in scale than the giants of 1965–1990.

9
Groundwater Politics

IT IS SOMETIMES SAID THAT GROUNDWATER is a socially invisible resource since it cannot be directly observed. It resides in layers of porous rock well below the surface that are not open to observable impression. Social invisibility, however, does not prevent political contestability. People sink wells and draw upon the resource for varying purposes. Priority claims are asserted and adjudicated. Sustainability has become, belatedly, a central issue.

Periodically the veil of obscurity is shattered by a sudden and damaging event that reminds us about the need to husband and protect this crucial resource. Aquifers are vulnerable to pollution. In Canada, the May 2000 events at Walkerton, Ontario, where a municipal water supply well was contaminated to devastating effect, remain a powerful point of reference. Several days of heavy rains fell shortly after the application of manure to farm fields adjacent to one of three Walkerton water supply wells. Fractured rock formations allowed the contamination to travel quickly to the groundwater. This is certainly not an unknown risk to shallow water aquifers, and it would have been detected and neutralized if standard monitoring provisions had been followed by the staff of the Walkerton utilities commission (Burke 2001; Perkel 2002).

But a series of irregularities combined with fraudulent reporting to create a "perfect storm." Despite the requirement to make daily checks of the chlorine residuals that would have signalled the jump in *E. coli*, the staff opted (routinely as it turned out) to enter fictitious entries in the logs. Thus there was no way to discover the pollution in well no. 5. A second regulatory defence was to send well water samples for laboratory analysis. Here, however, a utilities staffer sent tap water rather than field samples to the regional lab. More than a week elapsed before the contamination was discovered, and by then a local epidemic was underway, leading ultimately to seven deaths and thousands of serious illnesses. Among the lessons here are that government oversight must be vigorous and mounted at multiple levels. Not only must staff be properly trained and responsible but they must understand groundwater dynamics and possible risks. In addition, provincial inspectors cannot turn blind eyes to operational failings at the local level. A combination of local and provincial arrangements caused the system failure (O'Connor 2002; Snider 2004).

The Walkerton case is only one example of many where users, host communities, and governments take decisions affecting groundwater without a full appreciation of its origins or its availability. This means that groundwater politics are fraught with conflicts among owners, producers, consumers, and public actors. A range of organized interests and state authorities interact in the groundwater sector, where decisions about allocation and conservation are made. It is also important to consider possible link-ups between groundwater conditions and other political fields such as irrigation, flood control, and power dam reservoirs. Across Canada, some 9 million people rely on groundwater in varying degrees. In aggregate, the groundwater endowment exceeds surface water in total volume, but it is distributed unevenly. It is also important to note that the limits of our knowledge of groundwater are far greater than is the case for surface watersheds. The characterization of fisheries in chapter 5—a national resource on a local scale—applies also to groundwater but with far lower certainty of basic information.

The sections below explore the nature of groundwater, physically and socially, and the role of state authorities in regulating its appropriation. Special attention is given to the political controversies surrounding shale gas fracturing and its impact on groundwater. The chapter concludes with a case study of groundwater politics in Prince Edward Island, the Canadian province that draws most heavily on this resource.

Groundwater and Rival Knowledge Domains

As a concealed resource, groundwater has lagged behind surface waters and has not been addressed at the same intensity for either research or management. It has been described as "the poor cousin" of the water cycle—overused, understudied, and rarely sustainably managed (Kendall 2009). This is ironic, as groundwater is closely related to surface flows in many cases. For shallow aquifers, surface watershed features can directly shape the flows below. Indeed, it has been said that in some cases a stream can be a visual manifestation of groundwater, if properly interpreted. Certainly there can be interaction between surface flows and groundwater reserves, as will be seen below. But the surface-subsurface parallel has definite limits and, for deeper confined aquifers, groundwater can follow quite different patterns.

For millennia there has been an elaborate practical knowledge of groundwater, held in particular by peoples in water-challenged areas. This is reflected, for example, in awareness of the locations of permanent and seasonal springs. It is manifest also in the reading of dryland and desert surfaces for shallow water tables and the ability to trap water in dugouts. Another application is techniques of well building and water storage. However, a striking feature of groundwater knowledge is its local nature. Each site is distinct. and local knowledge is, by its nature, not portable or generalizable.

During the pioneer period in the American west, "water holes" were strategic in the layout of settlement sites and cattle drive routes. The classic television western *Rawhide* was scripted around a succession of rivers and springs along driving routes between Texas and Kansas, and the social complications that they generated. When river beds were dry or water holes were blocked off by rival drovers, conflicts followed. When wells on pioneer homesteads failed, lands were abandoned. When Indian bands discovered cattlemen taking "their" ancestral waters, there was resistance (Robertson 1986).

Technology is another significant variable that co-determines patterns of groundwater use. On pioneer farms in America, windmills were first used to lift well water by Daniel Hallady in the 1850s. The early energy-capturing devices were wooden sails. These were followed later in the 1880s by steel-bladed windmills. The classic design involved a 2- to 3-m diameter wheel on a 10-m steel tower, with a set of gears activating the vertical pump pole.

But a critical prior question was where to site the wells, or put another way, where to dig? There were several answers. One was provided by water witchers, also known as dowsers or diviners. These practitioners claimed the skill of "divining" subsurface features such as metals or water. This was reported in Europe as early as the 1550s, used initially for mineral searches and favoured by alchemists. The key instrument here was the witching rod—a wand or a forked stick. But the crucial talent lay with the user who could sense or channel the "vital force" beneath the soil. Crucially, water witchers were local figures who were embedded in their communities, a factor that went some distance to legitimizing their work and rationalizing the inevitable failures when they came (Krautwurst 1998).

An alternate knowledge domain lay in the emerging modern science of hydrogeology. Here the initial studies came in the decades following the turn of the nineteenth century. In France, Darcy developed his law on the flow of groundwater. Other breakthroughs included calculating hydraulic properties of an aquifer by pumping a well and observing the resulting decline in water table in adjacent wells. According to John Mather (n.d.), early studies in the period 1790 to 1830 addressed artesian spring flows, fluctuating groundwater levels, and the impact of well withdrawals in creating cones of depression in groundwater.

Contamination research developed along a parallel track in the nineteenth century. Perhaps the key figure was Dr. John Snow, an English physician whose fame derives from his investigations of the causes of cholera in the 1850s. The city of London was wracked by cholera epidemics in the mid-nineteenth century, with 14,000 people killed in 1848 alone. Snow became aware of the very high death rate in his neighbourhood of Soho, and commenced investigations. This led him in the opposite direction from the prevailing theory that cholera was an airborne germ and the best solution was to empty cesspools into the River Thames. Snow mapped the location of the dead in Soho over a two-week period and found an anomaly—there were no reported deaths in an area immediately surrounding a brewery. At the same time, the incidence of deaths in the area adjacent to the neighbourhood pump was higher than the norm. Snow arranged for the handle of that pump to be removed, after which the rate of infection declined. On further investigation it was discovered that, 9 metres below the pump, the well lay only 2 metres away from the closest cesspool. Although it took several decades before there was wholesale construction of a city-wide sewage disposal system, Snow had unlocked a key insight for groundwater protection and urban public health (Johnson 2006).

If the science of groundwater systems and groundwater contamination originated in Europe, how did it evolve in the New World? North America presented different problems. In the United States, Chamberlin published the first hydrogeologic report by the US Geological Survey in 1885. Also notable was King's 1880 monograph on "Principles and Conditions of Groundwater Movement" (Anderson 2005; Fetter 2004). This captured the configuration of a water table by means of water level contour mapping along with the horizontal directions of groundwater flows. The University of Wisconsin was a key site for early groundwater science, as was the federal Geological Survey. The early twentieth century saw the expansion of the US Geological Survey's field exploration for groundwater supplies, fanning out across the country. The USGS also tackled industrial contamination issues in the early twentieth century, though there was little political action on any of this before the 1950s and 1960s. For academic training purposes, the central text was compiled by C.F. Tolman of Stanford, whose *Groundwater* (1937) remained the standard for the initial postwar generation.

The epistemological and cultural dichotomy between water witching and hydrogeology assumed an epic scale after the 1880s. As in other fields, the advocates of the new "science" pressed their case against what was regarded as folk-wisdom or "quackery." In turn, the champions of "local knowledge" launched their riposte against "idiot experts." Ultimately what mattered was more than documented results, it was the incorporation of respective knowledge domains into state policy and practice.

In fact, the results were anything but categorical. In a study of the "underground water rush" in Cape Colony, South Africa, between 1891 and 1910, van Sittert (2004) demonstrates how the struggles over control of the resource, the resistance of communities to state encroachment, and cultural tension between "indigenous" and "foreign" practices played out in knowledge wars. Despite this polarity, the battle lines were far from fixed. At times, colonial engineers compromised their adversarial stance on water witchers simply to get wells drilled, especially after the colonial state dropped its well-digging subsidies. There is a telling lesson here: the political forces favouring economic and social expansion can be pragmatic in sorting out doctrinal disputes. It is not pure science that drives policy, but science that offers policy-relevant knowledge. Furthermore it may be useful to distinguish between conceptual knowledge and field knowledge, science-based knowledge and local or popular knowledge. These categories frequently compete for political influence, and different permutations will influence policy making.

Some Groundwater Basics

The best starting point is with the integral connection between surface water and groundwater flows. Surface water can infiltrate the ground and enter into storage where it can reside for periods ranging from months and years to millennia. Equally, groundwater can return to the surface by feeding rivers, streams, and lakes and by spring waters. In earlier times it was common to think of underground lakes and rivers in terms similar to surface waters. It has long been clear, however, that most subsurface water resides in the spaces permitted by gravels, sands, and rock. Because some sediments provide better "reservoir rocks" than others, an aquifer can be spatially delineated in three-dimensional terms. Aquifers range in size from the gigantic—such as the Great Artesian Basin in Australia and the High Plains or Ogallala Aquifer in the US midwest—to the modest. In Canada the largest are the so-called regional aquifers, some 30 of which have been identified by the Geological Survey of Canada for basic survey (Rivera et al. 2003).

It is useful to think of subsurface lands in cross-sectional profile, where they reveal a series of sedimentary layers. There is normally a surface layer of topsoil that varies in depth. Below this is some arrangement of fine aggregates (sands and clays) and coarse aggregates (pebbles and stones). Below these aggregates, or in their place, there can be strata of solid rock. Some, like sandstone, are highly porous and hold high volumes of water while others are harder rocks but may have cracks and crevices.

Groundwater travels depending on the degree of porosity and permeability or fracture of the host rock. Two distinct physical processes interact here. On the one hand, gravity will draw water downward according to available channels. On the other, surface tension between water and rock will retard the flow. At the upper levels the ground may be dry or moist, a condition known as the unsaturated zone since air and water are mixed, while lower down is the saturated (water only) zone. The frontier between them is the water table, not a classic table with a flat top but a sloping and uneven profile that changes horizontally and vertically over time.

The particular forms, volumes, and channels for groundwater depend largely upon subsurface rock formations in which water resides and travels. For example it is common to distinguish between unconfined and confined aquifers. The former are constituted out of gravels and sands that lie below the topsoil and are easily permeated by surface waters. The latter are overlaid by impermeable rocks that act as a cap on the porous sandstones below. Confined aquifers are generally under pressure. Thus where the cap rock fractures and provides channels for escape, groundwater forces itself toward the surface as springs. Or where a hole is drilled down through the cap rock, the groundwater can rise within the well.

One of the key dimensions in understanding and managing an aquifer is establishing the direction and rate of natural flow. Once test wells are drilled, instruments can log water table levels, directions of flow, and other pertinent data. The piezometer, a water pressure measurement device, has become a key instrument of groundwater study. In coastal regions another factor is the boundary between fresh- and salt-groundwater reservoirs. Excessive withdrawals of fresh groundwater can intensify saltwater intrusion that can ruin groundwater supplies to coastal communities unless it is remedied by injecting freshwater and rebalancing the interface.

Another key variable is the water table, the dividing point between water-saturated rock and the unsaturated layers above it. This can vary according to the rates of infiltration and withdrawal. High seasonal precipitation can raise the water table while dry seasonal conditions work oppositely. Extraction can have a similar effect in drawing the water table downward. In extreme conditions the removal of vast quantities of water from host sediments leads to the subsidence of surface lands below their natural levels. Some of the most dramatic examples here involve central California. In the San Joaquin valley, the epicentre of groundwater withdrawal for irrigated farming, the subsidence was measured at more than 9 metres across the twentieth century. There are no dramatic cases of subsidence in Canada, as most of the larger aquifers are bedrock rather than unconsolidated materials.

Where a shallow water table intersects with streams and rivers, a declining water table can drain waters from the surface and reduce or even eliminate a surface flow. In one well-known case in southern Ontario, Spencer Creek dried up temporarily in the summer of 2000 at a time when groundwater withdrawal was high. After the provincial regulator imposed limits on groundwater takings, the creek flow returned. Even without significant extraction, water tables fluctuate naturally across the seasons. The spring melt is usually an important recharge period in Canada, when lower temperatures mean less evaporation, so water tables rise. In typical summer conditions, little precipitation passes through the upper level and water tables decline until autumn when another recharge can begin. Under conditions of rising water tables, in-stream flows tend to increase as well. It is important to note, however, that the surface-to-groundwater frontier remains one of the most complex of management questions.

Processes of extraction also influence patterns of flow. As a well withdraws water it "empties" groundwater from the immediate vicinity of the drill hole. This creates what is known as a cone of depression in the water table. Depending on flow rates, adjacent waters will travel to occupy the local "vacuum" and restore the equilibrium in the water table. Although single or widely spaced wells are unlikely to affect the water table dramatically over time, high-volume well fields are a different matter. Here the level of the water table can fall, seasonally or permanently. Under such circumstances it is possible for the subsurface to compact and subside, lowering the surface land elevation as mentioned earlier.

While the conceptual fundamentals of groundwater are now well understood, the practical knowledge and its applications remain inherently "local." As each physical setting is distinctive, it is necessary to understand both site geology and water dynamics before groundwater can be effectively managed. Once a political commitment is made to "manage" in such terms, applied hydrogeology becomes a central source of practical data. It becomes integral to modern groundwater regulation and planning. It enables aquifers to be mapped, either before exploitation (for planning purposes) or retroactively (to address problems).

As noted earlier, groundwater data vary greatly. While some reserves are intensively studied, others have yet to attract even preliminary examination. This turns partly on the expense of comprehensive studies and partly on a sociopolitical trade-off in judging urgency or need. Cases of water contamination, evidence of changing recharge and discharge with surface waters, or plans for significant new extraction works tend to trigger attention. Concerns over the cumulative impact of tens of thousands of rural household wells do not.

It should be evident how science expertise and sustainable water management planning are politically related. At all levels of government, officials will rely on hydrogeologists to analyze particular formations. While departments of natural resources and environment will maintain a level of in-house capability, this can vary widely. More commonly the survey work associated with withdrawal or remediation plans is contracted out to commercial consultants. It is estimated that the great majority of the 700–1,000 groundwater professionals practicing in Canada today are employed in private firms (Council of Canadian Academies 2009). The process of generating basic groundwater data is expensive. As a result, decisions are made based on varying degrees of certainty or uncertainty—itself a policy variable. This may also help explain why baseline research into Canada's 30 regional aquifers only became a high priority in the early 2000s.

Groundwater and the State Apparatus

If water below ground was a mysterious and elusive resource to social communities, the same has been true in law and policy. When groundwater disputes began to arise in English law in the eighteenth and early nineteenth centuries, judges concluded that groundwater was an unknown and unowned resource. A landmark case was that of *Acton v. Blundell*, which went before the English Exchequer Court in 1843. Acton's groundwater flow from a spring beneath his property had been seriously depleted by two nearby coal pits dug by Blundell. When Acton sought damages, the court faced the question of whether an underground spring is covered by the same legal rule as a surface watershed. Chief Justice Tindal ruled against Acton. The common law of riparian rights could hardly apply if the flow patterns of subterranean water could not be known. Instead the principle of absolute capture was advanced—surface landowners enjoyed the right to extract from wells on their property, regardless of consequent injury to others. This was extended to North America and taken up by Canadian and American courts (Drummond 2011).

Perhaps the boldest application appeared in the state of Texas in 1904 in the case of *Houston and Central Texas Central Railway v. East*. Mr. East brought a suit after high-volume pumping on the adjacent railway property caused his well to dry up. The court found a right to pump without liability, since groundwater movements were essentially unknowable. As Linda Nowlan (2005) points out, the wider political bias here was in favour of commercial development, since any rule that allocated or prioritized water among co-users risked alienating commercial investment.

In time, however, Canadian authorities asserted a crown title over groundwater that began to alter the political balance. Under the Constitution the lead role fell to the provinces, which had the benefit of several constitutional powers discussed earlier, including property and civil rights, natural resources, and surface lands (Coté 2006). Out of this came a power to regulate access to groundwater (through well-drilling regulations) and terms of use (rights of withdrawal and pollution control). Today all provinces except Ontario and Prince Edward Island have legislated to claim crown title to groundwater.

It was one thing to claim jurisdiction but another thing to legislate groundwater rules. The accumulated threads of common law were increasingly anachronistic as the industrial age played out. Statutory law could supplant common law to the extent that it enunciated new rules and procedures, but the pace was slow and cautious. The early twentieth-century legislation that dealt with surface water rights and administration remained largely silent on groundwater. Tellingly, the question of groundwater conservation hardly arose. Surface owners sank wells as desired or required. There seemed little evidence of excessive depletion. Not until the 1950s and 1960s did provinces begin to extend their surface water regimes and begin to license groundwater withdrawals.

This is especially curious given the contrasting history of oil and gas, an analogous underground resource but one with a very different political history. Here conservation emerged as a policy concern, in both the United States and Alberta, in the years following World War I. The change was provoked by the petroleum industry's wasteful rush for spoils under the traditional law of capture. In part to husband the resource and in part to increase their royalty takes, states and provinces began to regulate well spacing and extractive practices and to prorate (define the shares of) competitive extraction from multi-licensed reservoirs. In principle this could have been carried over to groundwater. Why was it not? Considerations of supply play a role—unlike oil, groundwater had a surface alternative so the resource was less scarce. Also unlike oil, groundwater lacked a ready commercial market value that might have accentuated its pursuit for corporate profit and required regulation for orderly development. A revealing exception that confirms the rule was the effort in 1860s' France to develop an alternative to the rule of capture in apportioning mineral water rights. Like crude oil, mineral water had a confirmed commercial value, and pressure from private interests gave rise to early regulatory schemes (Daintith 2010).

In general, however, groundwater remained rooted in the common law principles described above, as the established beneficiaries blocked the fashioning of new conservation practices. As Nowlan puts it, "the common law systems share the same central defects: they do not promote the optimum use of water and are too rigid to adapt to changing societal priorities. Neither system [riparian or capture] encourages conservation or recognizes public values like ecological functioning, neither provides a means to compel a transfer from a lower priority use to a higher use, and neither allows new users access to water rights if there is no riparian land or extra water capacity left" (Nowlan 2005, 15). Maintaining common law rules for groundwater appropriation and resisting statutory conservation fit well for established interests.

Today, all jurisdictions have established policy frameworks for groundwater administration. However, most of these only emerged after 1960. Prior to this time groundwater was handled, if at all, under surface water statutes. Provincial licensing provisions were extended to groundwater on the prairies in the 1950s and in Ontario in 1961. The underlying policy principles and the enabling provisions vary by jurisdiction.

What, in general, do the provinces do? To begin with, they hold the statutory power to license groundwater withdrawals. This is generally exercised for withdrawals that exceed a designated volume, often set to cover industrial as opposed to single-household levels. Provinces can also license well drillers and pump system installers, and enforce training standards and field practice regulations. In fact, in many jurisdictions the regulation of groundwater extraction systems is the main policy tool to influence rural farm and domestic groundwater use. Provinces also play an important role in regulating municipal government practices in using groundwater as part of drinking water delivery systems. (This is the area that failed in the Walkerton tragedy described earlier.)

Finally, provinces hold important roles in remediating groundwater contamination. In 1985, for example, it was discovered that polychlorinated biphenyls (PCBs) had leaked from an electrical transformer handling and storage facility at Smithville, in Ontario's Niagara Peninsula. The PCBs found their way from the plant's storage lagoon into soils and a shallow, fractured rock aquifer. Over the next three decades the government of Ontario spent some $70 million to secure the site, incinerate contaminated soils, build a replacement water pipe system for the town, and deal with the dissolved chemical plume underground through a pump and treat containment system.

More generally, provincial authorities face the inherently political question of how much emphasis to devote to groundwater management as opposed to competing priorities, and what degree of regulation and programming is required. This may be influenced in part by the extent of groundwater dependence as distinct from surface waters, or it may turn on the perceived level of threat or stress to groundwater supplies. As discussed in chapter 2, power can be exercised by non-decision-making as much as decision-making. A province may decide that commercial growth priorities—urban housing in southern Ontario or hydro-power facilities in northern Quebec—are worth pursuing without explicit reference to groundwater impacts. In southern Manitoba, for example, a massive expansion of hog production started in the 1970s. Although new water policies were proposed to deal with the impacts of manure disposal on farm fields, the provincial government opted not to act. Twenty years passed before the first dedicated livestock manure regulation came into force, by which time the politics of groundwater protection pitted urban environmentalists against a vastly enhanced rural livestock lobby (Manitoba 2007).

In conclusion, it can be said that provincial authorities play the lead role. They can respond collectively, if so desired, to major groundwater controversies such as the Walkerton events, which led to the development of model drinking water protection schemes. They also reserve the right to frame groundwater policies that reflect the regional importance of the resource and the perceived urgency of public management.

The federal position on groundwater might be described as a belated extension of its postwar approach to surface water. The Geological Survey of Canada assumed the science research lead. As little was known about the conditions of major aquifers, the interjurisdictional dimension to groundwater management was not yet significant. Only in 1992 did the Prairie Provinces Water Board assume responsibility for groundwater. The Federal Water Policy of 1987 had very little to say about groundwater issues. Data deficiencies were acknowledged and new groundwater quality assessment tools were promised. However, as seen in chapter 4, federal water initiatives languished over the subsequent 15 years due to program cuts imposed for deficit reduction. Only in the new millennium did momentum revive, with the 2003 release of the *Canadian Framework for Collaboration on Groundwater*. As the title implied, this was a joint federal-provincial plan that centred around improving the knowledge base for the 30 major regional aquifers that had been identified across Canada (Rivera et al. 2003). The Framework acknowledged that groundwater was "under significant stress due to increasing demand, contamination from intensified land-use activities, and potential variations in recharge patterns due to climate change impacts" (Geological Survey of Canada 2003, 1). By 2010, half of these regional aquifers had been mapped, with the remainder still to come.

The broader politics of groundwater management extends beyond intergovernmental relations. Each jurisdiction has forged a groundwater policy subsector, revolving around rival interests and coalitions of interest. Groundwater users, particularly those early entrants who enjoy "first in time, first in right" advantages, are an obvious group. Not surprisingly, they can be expected to defend the allocative status quo. Late arriving groundwater users may share those interests up to the point that caps are proposed on total withdrawals. From this point forward, an incipient cleavage within the groundwater-using community may emerge. This may take different forms, as farm users assert claims against urban users, or debates emerge over the state of the groundwater resource—the withdrawal/recharge balance or the aggregate level of supply.

In many jurisdictions, state authorities have opted to regulate extraction on an indirect basis. Rather than licensing the volumes of extraction, state and provincial authorities have developed clientelistic policy networks with the commercial service component of the groundwater sector. This includes well drillers and diggers, pump installers, and equipment manufacturers and suppliers. In each province a groundwater association serves as the institutional link between these interests and water management authorities (Canadian Groundwater Association n.d.). The value of concentrating on the commercial intermediaries is easily seen. If the hundreds or thousands of well drillers can be held to high professional standards, then landowner behaviour will largely follow. The relationship between state and drillers extends to professional training, installation practices, and well documentation.

Although the groundwater installation clientele network remains central to policy, a new coalition has emerged since the 1970s in the form of environmental conservationists. Here the questions of groundwater reserves, rates of extraction, and long-term sustainable use are squarely posed. A justification for continuing withdrawal, based on "first in time" rights, is no longer sufficient. In the American states, public concern about groundwater management rose in the 1980s (Blomquist 1991). One response was the establishment of local management units, which enabled local stakeholders to focus attention on local district conditions (Peck 1980). This opens new channels for data gathering and assessment. And as continuing institutions they offer opportunities to judge impacts and to frame adaptive responses.

The above discussion indicates that Canada has seen a belated recognition that groundwater management needs improvement. This is a multifaceted challenge, involving baseline studies, new training and staffing in public agencies, and a re-pointing of policy frameworks. On the last point, a new political narrative has emerged around the sustainable management of groundwater. What might this mean? The basic impulse derives from the Brundtland Report, to meet "the needs and aspirations of the present without compromising the ability to meet those of the future" (World Commission on Environment and Development 1987, 40). But what in particular does this imply for the groundwater resource? In a comprehensive 2009 review, the Council of Canadian Academies Panel put it this way. The goals were to protect groundwater supplies from depletion and from degradation of a chemical or biological sort, to protect ecosystem viability at the surface-to-groundwater interface, to maximize groundwater's contribution to social well-being, and to make groundwater decisions in transparent ways that include informed public participation and accountability (Council of Canadian Academies 2009, 16–17). This represents a worthy, but at present still aspirational, political program. The measure of its success will be the outcomes in actual groundwater management settings. In the next section, we look at one of the most pressing current problems.

Shale Fracturing and Groundwater: A New Political Frontier

In the early 2000s, a new political frontier opened up for groundwater management in response to the booming new petroleum industry based on shale gas fracturing. There is much that is controversial about shale gas production, with pressing questions being raised about the scale of the potential resource, the integrity of the extraction technology, and the effectiveness of state regulation. Here the focus is on the potential for shale fracturing operations to contaminate groundwater in the process of extracting gas. Across North America, at locations ranging from Texas to Pennsylvania and British Columbia to New Brunswick, the threat to groundwater has propelled local communities to join with environmental and water conservation advocates in opposition to this industry.

"Shale" gas is a relatively new form of unconventional natural gas that is extracted from shale rock as distinct from the more conventional sandstone. Whereas sandstone is both porous (with tiny spaces that can trap gas) and permeable (with channels that connect the pores and allow the gas to move under pressure), shale is porous without permeability. However if the shale, which is brittle, can be fractured by a combination of underground explosions and high-pressure fluid injection, the gas can be released and will flow under pressure to the surface. Recent technical advances facilitated industrial fractionation. Of particular significance is horizontal well drilling, or the ability to turn a drill hole 90 degrees from vertical to horizontal so that it passes through the heart of the shale deposit

(Parfitt 2010). The industrial rush into shale gas production began in the 1990s in the shale basins of Texas, Arkansas, and Louisiana. It has since expanded into the Marcellus shale of Pennsylvania and into Canada. Tens of thousands of wells have been drilled and gas production has soared to the point that more than 20 per cent of American natural gas came from shale in 2011.

Note the speed at which this subindustry has moved from basin to basin and the intensive footprint of gas facilities. Every well hole is drilled from a surface pad that contains a derrick, a well head, gas storage facilities, water injection supplies and chemicals, and the pressure-generating equipment for underground fracking. Because the horizontal casings radiate outward from the drill hole up to a kilometre in length, a new production pad may be required every several kilometres on the surface.

The rise of shale gas production is a complex story, but some of the key features are clear. First, state regulation has lagged well behind the frenetic expansion on the business side. Second, drilling, fracking, and production practices can vary greatly, by contractor or subcontractor or local conditions. Third, until very recently (in 2011), the chemicals used in the fracturing process have not been disclosed by operators. In many cases, groundwater has been infiltrated and contaminated in the drill-frack-gas-gathering process, by production chemicals or escaped gas or both. Finally, the industry position has been to deny that groundwater has been or can be affected. This leaves concerned residents with little remedy short of lobbying and litigation (Horne 2011; Conservation Council of New Brunswick 2010).

Reports of contaminated groundwater did not begin with shale exploration, and "natural" contamination has been long acknowledged. However the arrival of broad-scale shale fracking represents a significant geological disturbance and has coincided with reports of contaminated well water in the affected regions. A critical factor here was the beginning of mass media interest in the possibility of generic groundwater risks. Here a pivotal event was the release of Josh Fox's documentary/advocacy film *Gaslands* in 2009. Perhaps the most iconic image was the demonstration of how tap water could catch fire from gas imbrications. However, the range of crossover contaminants extends further, as detailed below.

There seems little doubt that some level of contamination is taking place at some sites (Osborn et al. 2011). How extensive it is remains to be determined, but it is unlikely to be rare. There are several possible migratory mechanisms. One involves flaws in the well casings, which are intended to seal frackwater and gas flows within the well and prevent the escape of production materials into the drill hole outside of the casing. Another mechanism involves the shale fracturing process, in which explosive charges and pressurized frackwater open new underground channels for gas to move within the shale formation, including contact with shallow groundwater reserves. A third mechanism involves surface spillage of chemicals or treated water, from well head or piping or storage pond leaks. These sequences are captured in Figure 9.1 below.

Figure 9.1 Possible Sources of Shale Fracturing Contamination

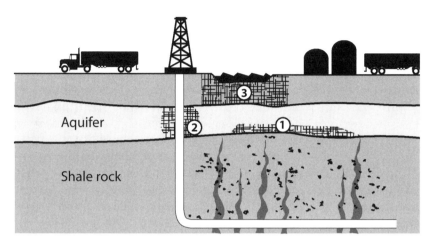

1 - Migration via fractured rock
2 - Faulty well casing
3 - Frackwater leaching from surface

At present, the policy and regulatory debate on groundwater pollution is beset by opposing forces. Industry advocates contend that standard practices are well tested and safe, and that there is no conclusive proof of groundwater contamination. Water/gas mixtures at the domestic tap are attributed to natural gas unrelated to fracking. Chemical contamination by fracking has never been legally established. And, it is said, shale formations are secured by overlying cap rock that prevents the upward migration of drill fluids and gas. On the other hand, a broad coalition of environmental NGOs and community groups have joined together to oppose shale fracking and to demand rigorous regulatory regimes or moratoria on shale exploration.

This volatility can be explained, in good part, as a product of a collision between policy subsectors. While questions of groundwater contamination by upstream oil and gas operations are far from unknown, to date they have been handled in petroleum-producing provinces by energy rather than environmental authorities. Thus, when questions arose about injecting water into depleted reservoirs for enhanced oil and gas recovery or about disposal of "process water" that returns from the shale fracturing zone, operators contend that these are well-established processes that were developed in conventional oil and gas. It is revealing that the US Environmental Protection Agency (EPA) was blocked from comprehensive shale fracking research during the George W. Bush administrations. Only in 2011 did the EPA announce a major program of inquiry.

For the foreseeable future, the patterns of political conflict seem evident. The shale-fracturing industry will press for self-regulation based on best practice codes and for the extension of conventional petroleum policies wherever possible. Rural landowners and local communities will press for a new, generic regulatory regime for shale operations, one that leans heavily on precautionary norms. Also, until environmental impact studies and state rule-setting have filled the present gaps, moratoria on shale operations will be demanded (CCNB 2010). There will be battles of rival studies, particular litigation on land and water damage, and cross-jurisdictional policy reviews. Given the relatively embryonic pattern of advocacy politics that prevails today, both "sides" will face challenges of further organizing. Perhaps most important in future shale gas management will be the fight to define the public interest (Jackson et al. 2011). Will the drive for a major new energy supply trump the unknown risks to human and environmental health? At the time of writing, British Columbia and Alberta (the traditional oil and gas producing jurisdictions) along with New Brunswick are proceeding with shale exploration. By contrast the "greenfield" jurisdictions of Quebec and Nova Scotia have announced interim moratoria on shale licensing and exploration, pending policy reviews.

CASE STUDY: GROUNDWATER POLITICS IN PRINCE EDWARD ISLAND

To find a highly groundwater-sensitive jurisdiction, we need look no further than the Maritime province of Prince Edward Island. Canada's smallest province encompasses 5,660 km^2 of land and includes 140,000 people. By comparison, the Greater Toronto Area (GTA) occupies 7,000 km^2 with 5.5 million people. Overall numbers do not tell the entire story, however, as groundwater provides the only source of drinking water for Islanders, whether they are connected to municipal delivery systems or rely on private rural wells.

Prince Edward Island features a gently rolling topography. The highest elevation is about 135 m above sea level, and three-quarters of the island rests less than 45 m above the sea. This is conducive to short, shallow, and slow-flowing rivers and streams, draining small watersheds. The largest is about 150 km^2, or one-sixth the area of the West River drainage discussed in chapter 1. Map 9.1 illustrates some of the 240 identified watersheds on the island. There is little potential for storage reservoirs, though small instream impoundments create ponds along the flows. Many of the rivers empty into brackish estuaries and bays where shellfish aquaculture has expanded rapidly since the 1970s.

When it comes to groundwater, PEI is underlain by sandstone ("red-bed") sediments arranged in stacks and interbedded with siltstone and claystone layers (Rice-Snow 2012). Fractures in the sandstone, along with layers of high-permeability sediment, offer pathways for groundwater flow within the aquifer. A combination of high porosity (averaging 15 per cent) and permeability means that groundwater flow can be relatively rapid. The sedimentary rocks are overlaid by glacial drift that is generally less than 8 metres thick. Not surprisingly, there

Map 9.1 Prince Edward Island Watersheds

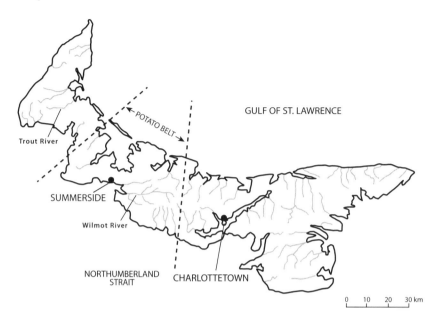

is a strong relationship between surface and groundwater in PEI. Groundwater base flow accounts for 55 to 65 per cent of the average annual surface stream flows. A typical water budget for a small Island watershed has annual precipitation of 1,100 mm. Of this, 440 mm goes to evaporation or plant transpiration, 300 mm runs off directly into surface streams and rivers, and 360 mm will recharge into aquifers, contributing in the process to stream base flows (Prince Edward Island n.d.).

The quality of Island groundwater is traditionally high, and almost all classes of users depend on it to meet their needs. There are several social and technical differences in the modes of demand and supply. PEI is the most rural of Canadian provinces, and 57 per cent of residents depend on private wells. In the small cities, high-pressure wells and well fields supply piped utilities. Water consumption for household needs is modest and unlikely to ever threaten sustainable supply. Commercial users include farms and factories and water utilities.

However, a series of contamination issues has developed in recent decades, arising mainly from farming practices but including sewage waste treatment as well. In nonagricultural settings, contamination has occurred at sites ranging from petroleum storage tanks (most famously at Kensington in 1977), faulty septic tanks, road salt runoff, and landfills. There are also issues of saltwater intrusion into groundwater that have drawn increased attention at coastal sites where municipal water systems are located. In terms of groundwater quantity, there has been little concern with long-term depletion from pumping, as total PEI groundwater withdrawals are estimated to average only 2 per cent of recharge rates. However, some crucial local variations where high-volume extraction poses concerns will be noted below.

Politically as well as culturally, Prince Edward Island remains a rural society. It is the only province in which rural dwellers still outnumber urbanites. And ever since European settlement began, the rural economy has been overwhelmingly agricultural. As rural small businesspeople, farmers are simultaneously landowners, cultivators, and self-employed workers. PEI politics has always revolved around issues of the farm sector, and the farm vote was a necessary part of a winning electoral coalition. Walter Jones, the premier from 1943 to 1953, was proudly known as "Farmer Jones," and he sided openly with small farm producers in conflicts with food processors or labour unions. Public policies that stabilized farm commodity prices, facilitated group marketing of products, and protected local land ownership found favour in rural communities. Policies that threatened to regulate what was raised on farms and how it was raised did not. For farmers, efforts to regulate chemical fertilizer and manure use or tillage patterns on private property were no more acceptable than directives on what machinery to use or what crops to sow. Furthermore, the political predominance of the rural farm class posed complications for provincial water policy. Despite the existence of crown title to flowing water and groundwater, the exercise of this jurisdiction was hesitant and cautious.

This structure of group representation was perpetuated late into the twentieth century, by virtue of several mechanisms. One was the PEI provincial electoral system that heavily overrepresented rural areas until a court-mandated boundary redistribution in 1996. Another was the transformation of the farm constituency from a predominantly small-scale and mixed family farm segment to a more industrial pattern of larger mechanized operations relying on chemical inputs and more specialized crops, particularly potatoes. A new political alliance between farmers and agribusiness shares an interest in self-regulation on issues of farm management, particularly on crop choice and field treatments (Shott 2012).

It would be wrong, however, to see the policy network for the rural environment as monolithic and one-sided. The family farm segment has not entirely disappeared, and many farmers see land stewardship in terms that extend beyond cultivated fields and maximum outputs. Thus debates have developed within the farm sector on the appropriate scale of "environmental farming." Other rural interest groups have also come to play expanded roles in recent decades, including shellfish aquaculture producers, recreational fishers, and tourist operators. By the 1990s the frequent fish kills linked to chemical contaminants were a fixture of every Island summer. In response to this and other concerns, community-centred water protection groups began to form in local watersheds. In time, the provincial department of the environment offered financial and technical support for group formation, and in 2009 an umbrella PEI Watershed Alliance came together and now numbers more than two dozen local groups.

The effect has been to widen the terms of discussion on water protection issues since the 1990s and to heighten public awareness of the links between surface water and groundwater management. While the "productivist" lobby remains highly influential, particularly in concert with the department of agriculture and farm marketing agencies, the "environmental" lobby has a presence across the province in the watershed citizen groups. The latter's connection to the PEI department of environment may be less firmly clientelist than the agriculturalists, but the ENGOs are now a fixture on water policy issues ranging from farm chemicals to fish habitat to fish kills and watershed planning. So far as groundwater is concerned, policy questions have arisen on both the quantitative and qualitative sides. Each is discussed below.

The central challenge of groundwater quantity policy is how to regulate for a sustainable future and, in particular, how to avoid excess depletion. Traditionally the accepted standard was to ensure that the rate of depletion not exceed the rate of recharge. Here the maximum depletion was 50 per cent of recharge. As mentioned above, PEI has fared well by this standard, though there are certain districts, in the vicinity of municipal water storage facilities, where withdrawals approach this level. Another concern involves applications for high capacity irrigation withdrawals. In 1995, PEI encouraged the agricultural use of groundwater, subject to the 50 per cent standard. Eight years later the provincial government declared a moratorium on irrigation permitting and recalled all existing permits to impose reporting terms. This was in the face of an abrupt rise in new applications in consecutive dry years, such that irrigation withdrawals would have doubled or even tripled if all were granted (Nowlan 2005, 48). The moratorium was justified by the absence of the necessary data and flow models to make appropriate determinations on sustainable volumes. It has been suggested that the moratorium on irrigation permits was an instance of the precautionary principle in action. That is, although the evidence was not conclusive, the risk of overcommitment was deemed greater than the claims of need by applicants. In 2013 the moratorium remained in effect, though farm spokespeople have called for it to be lifted.

The conceptual framework for assessing sustainable groundwater withdrawal volumes has also evolved over time. In place of the recharge standard, the new measure is tied to instream flow needs. This was announced in a new permitting policy in 2013. Because base flows into streams occur in the shallower portion of the aquifer, they are especially sensitive to groundwater extraction (PEI 2013). The new calculation sets maximum groundwater extraction levels at 15–35 per cent of the natural seasonal flows. As this policy is implemented, the regulation of surface and subsurface water withdrawals will be closely coordinated.

Turning to groundwater quality, the chief concern is with contamination insofar as it threatens either human and ecological health. In PEI there have been two dominant public policy concerns, both related to farming—nitrate deposits in watercourses from fertilizer runoff and other chemicals from pesticide use. While each polluting sequence has distinct symptoms and consequences, the two are increasingly seen as ecological threats. As one commentator put it, "pesticides and fertilizers are not just issues for the farm community—they affect the recreational fishing industry, shellfish harvesting, tourist operations and anyone who lives in the environment or is simply concerned about human health" (Water Alliance of Prince Edward Island 2013).

Although nitrogen and nitrous oxide (N-NO$_3$) levels vary by watershed, they tend to peak in highly cultivated farm areas. Concern for field runoff resulting in stream nitrate loading was expressed as far back as the 1980s. One approach was to call for limits on chemical applications, as was done by the Land Use Committee of 1997. But this ran against the prevailing thinking in the agricultural power bloc, which warned against the loss of crop production and a consequential farm profit crisis. These were decades in which the potato industry was expanding and with it a heightened use of fertilizer treatments. The Canadian Drinking Water Quality Guidelines set a maximum level for dissolved nitrates of 10 milligrams per litre (mg/L). Tests of private wells revealed that the share of noncomplying wells was increasing over time, from 3.5 per cent in 2000 to 5.2 per cent in 2002. By 2007 the figure was 6 per cent, with another 11 per cent in the range immediately below the limit at 8–10 mg/L (PEI 2008). In the early 2000s, the scientific understanding of the nitrate cycle changed, with more accurate data on soil absorption and the discovery that winter nitrate loading continued as well (Natural Resources Canada 2007; Somers et al. 2011). This led to renewed interest in longer crop rotation cycles and rules for permissible slopes for furrow crops.

Mounting public concern led Premier Robert Ghiz to strike a Commission on Nitrates in Groundwater, with representation from the farm, science, health, and First Nations interests. The Commission stressed the multiple sources of nitrate loadings and the long-term nature of remediation, and its basic message was blunt, asserting that "further delays in implementing sound farm practices could be catastrophic" (PEI 2008). Of the six most essential recommendations, three challenged the agricultural status quo: a mandatory three-year crop rotation to reduce nitrate applications; specific nutrient management plans to lessen excess nitrates; and the identification of high nitrate areas for mandatory nutrient management and compulsory well testing. The PEI government accepted all of the recommendations, but implementation has lacked urgency. Two years after the report, only one point was fully adopted, and a biologist observed that "the pace on the nitrate issue itself has been fairly glacial." One factor that served to dampen nitrate application, unrelated to the policy process, was the slump in the potato market that reduced planted acreage in recent years.

The political concern with nitrates involves more than drinking water. Although nitrates in field runoff are not directly toxic to fish, there is concern that absorption into groundwater may return to streams through baseflow. Although fish are threatened only by extremely high nitrate concentrations, the Canadian guideline for long-term aquatic wildlife health (including more sensitive aquatic species) is 3 mg/L. The consequences of nitrate loadings contributing to eutrophication in ponds and estuaries, as distinct from flowing waters, remains serious, particularly for shellfish acquaculture operations.

The second agricultural pollution concern involves pesticide contamination of waterways. Here the field runoff impact is manifest in fish kills in polluted streams. Once again the problem was far from new. Official statistics have recorded 48 episodes since 1960, in all parts of the island, and unreported episodes are certainly more numerous. Several variables are bundled together here, including the role of buffer zones between cultivated fields and streams, the proximity of pesticide-sprayed land to streams, the chemical concentrations applied, the possibility of leaks from the spray apparatus, and the coincidence of intense rainfall and pesticide applications.

Mandatory buffer zones were established in 1998, and the width of the buffer from row crops such as potatoes was expanded from 10 to 15 metres in 2008. "Headland" areas are created at the end of fields to enable machinery to turn. Headlands near watercourses are required to be planted in grass, but this is not always observed and potatoes are sometimes planted in riparian headlands. Another important factor is the choice of chemical pesticide or fungicide, given that a typical potato crop is subject to 15–20 distinct treatments during the season (PEI 2012). The choice of product is important here, as highly soluble products have a greater likelihood of being transported during rainfall, while high soil absorption products are less prone to this risk but more likely to enter streams if the soil itself runs into streams.

Following a 2012 fish kill in Barclay Brook, a part of the Trout River system in western PEI, the provincial government struck an Action Committee to investigate the incident. Once again it was a multi-stakeholder panel that combined site analysis with a broader review of farm practice and policy. In a wide-ranging report, no single cause of or single solution to the problem could be identified. The Committee underlined the need for full compliance with buffer and headland rules. But it stressed the need to remove high-risk lands permanently from production, and proposed that an "environmental impact fund" be created by the province to purchase such farmlands for management by watershed groups. There are also mechanical techniques that can increase water retention in rows on sloped fields and make spray applications more precise. In sum, the Committee argued that progressive changes in farm practice since 2000 had reduced fish kill risks but that targeted changes for row crop cultivation near streams, through a suite of concrete measures, is essential (PEI 2012).

Clearly the high level of groundwater dependence on the Island makes it a critical policy subsector. Administrative authority rests in the Water Resources Division of the Department of Environment, Labour and Justice. The key legislative instruments are sections of the *Environmental Protection Act* and the *Water Well Regulations*. However, the overlaps with agriculture, fisheries, municipal affairs, and tourism are evident. Water resource officials have a range of executive tools at their disposal, including environmental protection orders, emergency field orders, written warnings, and formal charges. Since 2000 there has been increased reliance on public reporting, and a telephone hotline is in place. It is estimated that 40 per cent of investigations arise from public complaint and that two-thirds of them are resolved by measures short of formal enforcement (PEI 2011). Overall, there is a marked preference for soft enforcement techniques grounded where possible in nonlegal measures. This begins with public awareness campaigns, continues by enlisting clientele groups such as the Federation of Agriculture as intermediaries, and emphasizes mediation in dealing with field disputes. This stress on education and persuasion for consensual best practice is undoubtedly linked to the fact that 90 per cent of the land base is privately owned.

The reliance of soft instruments carries a cost, however. It delays a direct confrontation with groundwater (and surfacestream) contamination. Prince Edward Island has seen a series of high profile incidents and inquiries since 1995, but delay is also a political tool. All incidents point to deficiencies in farm practices near watersheds. Despite calls for more decisive action in each case, the provincial government responds with cautious appeals for collective responsibility. Political scapegoating is avoided and official discourse declares that "all of us must be part of the solution." On matters of water contamination, the government of Prince Edward Island typically declares an acceptance of recommendations by inquiries. Implementation, however, tends to lag or evaporate. The Nitrate Commission is a classic example.

If there is a "retail" (i.e., street-level) political dimension to the groundwater resource, on the Island as elsewhere in the country, it concerns drinking water. In common with most provinces, PEI reviewed its drinking water protection measures in the wake of the Walkerton crisis. Given the source patterns noted above and the emerging evidence of contaminants, the provincial government offered the public a groundwater management update. In the 2001 statement, *Clear from the Ground to the Glass*, the regime was described. For private wells, the focus was on educating homeowners and working through well drilling and service providers to improve design and maintenance standards. Over half of Island consumers rely on private domestic wells, which are exempt from water quality permitting if they pump at a rate of less than 4 litres/sec (almost always the case for residential users). This arrangement was reconfirmed in the 2001 statement. For municipal supply systems, monitoring and reporting procedures and staff training and lab certifications would be upgraded. A strategy for municipal wellfield protection was also pledged within three years. The 2001 plan sought to reassure that Island groundwater was "generally of good quality" by referencing a recent study of samples from municipal water supplies. There is little reason to doubt the general accuracy of this claim. However, as seen above, it was during these years that evidence accumulated about multiple source water contamination.

The competing vectors converged in 2007. Issues of watershed management gained a higher public profile when, late in the electoral term, Premier Pat Binns asked the Environmental Advisory Council to consult with Islanders on the question of managing resources on a watershed basis. The EAC's extensive report began with the statement that "there is a feeling of urgency" in the need to address water quantity and quality issues. Several dozen watershed groups appeared before the panel to make a consensus case that agricultural practices and municipal sewage were core threats; provincial government policy was too passive and reactive; and community-base watershed management was the necessary vehicle for meaningful change, before aquatic degradation became irreversible (EAC 2007).

It is striking, however, that the focus of discussion and recommendations tilted heavily toward surface water conditions. In part this reflected the traditional concerns of local communities with observable and accessible waterflows. It may also underline the greater technical resources required to appraise and respond to groundwater conditions. In the words of one government official, the "circularity" of the water cycle had not yet been adequately grasped.

Given the emerging recognition of the watershed as the unit for management, however, an agenda centred on revised farm practices, more comprehensive testing and modelling, coordinated provincial government action and an enhanced role for watershed NGOs would embrace groundwater issues as a matter of course. Notable among the findings of the 2007 consultation was the critical role of provincial agencies beyond the department of the environment. For example, Agriculture was expected to take the lead in environmental farm planning and nutrient management. Finally, it is telling that the public discussions explicitly questioned the accuracy of the "Clear from Ground to Glass" premise, asserting that it "is not the current state of water on PEI" (EAC 2007, 33).

This public consultation lifted awareness of watershed management to a new political level and launched a new phase in society-state relations. Since the report's release, the provincial government has produced an organizing "manual" for community groups (PEI, 2007). In addition, the government announced a budget increase of $750,000 in the watershed conservation envelope for 2007–08, the majority of which was directed to supporting the organizing efforts of community groups. By 2008 the government could point to four groups having completed "full" watershed plans and seven others on their way to "watershed lite" plans (Raymond 2008). A survey the following year identified 31 watershed groups on the Island.

Early in 2010 a cross-section of these NGOs gathered to formulate bylaws for the new PEI Watershed Alliance, with which the government committed to work on a province-wide watershed "strategy." By this time the Commission on Nitrates was on record with its 2007 report. In fact the Commission was responsible for a well test clinic in 2007 where concerned citizens could bring domestic samples. A glance at the issues being tracked by the Watershed Alliance confirms that the nitrates question, along with herbicides, fish kills, irrigation, shale gas, and riparian forestry remain front and centre. Indeed, the community group in Clyde River ran its own water testing program for well water in 2009 and mapped the results according to concentrations.

Overall there is a pattern of cautious transformation in groundwater management in PEI. Government action is still incremental, driven by field controversies or new science findings. In addition, there is a marked preference for policy tools that aim at soft compliance rather than aggressive legal enforcement. There are, however, a series of decisions that point toward a more holistic grasp on provincial water management. Among these are the linkage of surface and groundwater withdrawal policies, the multifaceted approaches to fertilizer and herbicide management, and the policy support for community watershed groups as both catalysts and partners for government programming. Perhaps this should not be surprising, given the centrality of groundwater in Island life. Yet the province has evolved significantly since 1995, from an ingrained alliance with commercial farm interests to a more diversified policy network with multiple coalitions. Despite the political pivot described above, agriculture still functions as a privileged policy subsector. Its priorities remain firmly entrenched, and the pressures for further transformation point to the continuing fault-line of Island freshwater politics.

Conclusions

It seems evident that groundwater politics is as "territorial" in character as its counterpart on the surface. There is also an irreducible local dimension, reflected in the shape of aquifers and in the pattern of bore holes, well fields, and watersheds. Because groundwater is an essential source for so many Canadians, and the level of physical knowledge lags dramatically behind the level of use, there is considerable room for political difference and conflict.

A striking feature of the groundwater resource is the variation in its physical and social conditions. In Canada, there are many sites and aquifers under serious stress, many "steady-state" areas where the recharge-discharge cycle is in approximate balance, and many areas where it is basically in "predevelopment" condition. The overall condition of the groundwater is considered to be positive although, as Alfonso Rivera observes, "the lack of detailed data and information severely hinder the application of best water management practices, in particular practices for water takings and interactions between surface water, groundwater and aquatic and terrestrial habitats" (Rivera et al. 2003, 12).

Groundwater "hot spots" appear for various reasons. Perhaps the most obvious is overdepletion and all that this entails, from declining water tables to loss of base flow in surface streams and rivers. Of parallel concern is the degradation of groundwater quality. It is striking how many of the environmental externalities of commercial capitalism impinge on groundwater. These include farm chemical leaching, leaking storage tanks and landfills, and excessive groundwater takings.

At the same time, groundwater management faces a distinct set of challenges. Its relative social invisibility and the difficulty of precise delineation complicates the process of building coalitions in support. The reality of crown property is not widely appreciated. And the traditional "free" status of groundwater poses obstacles to the use of pricing as a management tool.

Equally confounding are the range of eligible responses. In governance terms, groundwater is a complex resource. The provincial crown holds title and enjoys the lead role. Private surface landowners exploit groundwater—under license when volume thresholds are exceeded and without license at lower volumes. Municipal utilities are involved as major groundwater users for municipal distribution, and are regulated for both quantity and quality. The government of Canada has a restricted mandate, with a direct role in groundwater research and an indirect role by means of cost-shared projects.

In political terms, the prime contradiction seems likely to involve the tension between surface land use and groundwater source contamination. Farming remains at the forefront, as the Prince Edward Island case attests. However, point-source industrial pollution will also remain prominent. Though the problems are generic, the political style is one of fashioning local responses. PEI shows signs of transforming this political narrative. In little more than a decade the thematic focus has shifted from one of assurance—our water is good, our vigilance sound—to one of problem recognition—the nitrates situation is an expanding threat—to one of active intervention, through public engagement and institutional reform. Such dynamics can be expected to emerge with increasing frequency in other parts of Canada.

10
Emerging Trends in Canadian Freshwater Politics

THIS CHAPTER STEPS BACK FROM THE study of particular subsectors to pose a different question. In the twenty-first century, are we entering a new era of freshwater politics in Canada? If so, what are some of its distinguishing features? There are no simple answers here. Freshwater politics is contested terrain, and we should not be surprised that emerging trends point in contrasting directions. Nevertheless, what trends are evident? Consider some of the findings in earlier chapters.

First, civil society actors are proliferating in the water sector, though the associational landscape is uneven. Groups appear at varying scales in response to community concerns, in cases ranging from Boat Harbour to the Athabasca to the Miramichi. Acting on their own and in coalition, groups have used a variety of tactics—field studies, lobbying, and litigation among them—to influence key decisions. Sometimes state authorities are proactive in encouraging group formation, offering finance, technical support, and participative channels through stakeholder bodies. The federal Atlantic Coastal Action Program and the Alberta watershed council structures come to mind here.

Second, within state circles, commitments to freshwater programming wax and wane. The early 2000s were a period when provincial governments acknowledged shortcomings in their crown water roles. Often this was driven by controversy and crisis, as with drinking water contamination, failure of flood defences, or overcommitments in licensing water withdrawals. Provincial governments responded with public inquiries, legislation, and administrative adaptations. Some jurisdictions—Quebec, Alberta, and Saskatchewan among them—added watershed planning structures to their toolkits. In Ottawa, however, the opposite trend is evident. Federal freshwater programming may have been in retreat since 1986 but the trend seems to have accelerated in recent years. The Harper government's pruning of key environmental statutes, evident in Bills C-33 and C-45, signals a clear intent to lighten the regulatory oversight of major commercial projects in both aquatic and terrestrial settings. Expansion and retreat may be opposite sides of the same coin in an era of neoliberal politics, when deficit finance, civil service cuts, and contracting out of program delivery have become standard features. Here the provinces as well as the federal government will be affected. Furthermore, it is possible that the reverberations of the 2008 financial crisis and economic slump continue to echo through the corridors of the state and freshwater mandates in particular.

Third, water policy subsectors centred on single uses remain strong in Canada, as the chapters above attest. There has, however, been a shift of perspective in recent decades in the growing awareness of ecological frameworks. In the simplest sense, ecology argues that "everything is connected." If this is taken seriously, then the hydrologic cycle and the watershed scale become central points of reference. One manifestation of this new thinking is the legislative and policy recognition of environmental flows or ecological services. Once merely afterthoughts in river engineering, they are now increasingly central to freshwater management—assessed for commercial value and embedded in regulatory criteria. The increasing reliance on state of the river reporting as a measure of watershed health and vulnerability speaks further to the ecological impulse. But it is important to recognize that political rhetoric and reality are frequently discordant. The experimental lakes program, a world-class research facility, was shuttered by the Harper government before the Ontario government offered a lifeline. Rigorous water monitoring on the Athabasca River was delayed or blocked for more than a decade into the current oil sands boom. Across North America, research on the environmental impacts of shale gas extraction has been either delayed or suppressed while the industry has been positively encouraged.

Fourth, the effects of climate change are increasingly impinging on water regimes and challenging the suitability of conventional hydrologic models and management frameworks. If the decade after 1995 introduced the global public to climate science and mitigation strategies, the decade after 2005 added the challenge of climate adaptation. Both dimensions are evident in freshwater politics. Perhaps the most obvious is flood management. One aspect of changing atmospheric circulation patterns is an increase in the sort of high-intensity precipitation events that beset Calgary and Toronto in 2013. Challenges for groundwater management are no less severe. Recharge rates to aquifers can be reduced as higher surface temperatures accelerate water evaporation and reduced stream flows in summer and autumn can draw increased groundwater into surface flows. In coastal settings like PEI, sea level rise will increase the chances for saltwater intrusion into freshwater storage. Many fish stocks will be vulnerable to the combination of warmer water temperatures and higher evaporation. Salmon, for example, prefer cool water during their river residency, and mortality of both juveniles and adults will increase as watersheds like the Miramichi warm up. Because the fish will seek out cool water refuges, their range of viable habitat will narrow, particularly if main stem rivers warm while smaller upland tributaries remain cool. Finally, the underlying conditions for hydro-power projects will be altered by shifting temperature and precipitation regimes. Historical rainfall and water flow data, on which projects were designed, may cease to be accurate, and evaporation from reservoirs will alter management practice. Overall, climate change has injected new levels of uncertainty into freshwater programming, with more sudden and acute disturbances and a disruption of traditional data streams.

Fifth, while decisions about freshwater politics are taken at all levels of the state, there is increasing concern about the institutional match between issues and responses. This is evident in a variety of experiments in intermediate or "meso" authorities. The term "meso" refers to a middle range that is located between the extremes of "macro" and "micro." In the present context, meso-authorities are governing arrangements that are located between the senior federal and provincial governments and the municipal authorities. Some aspects of institutional power—representation and mandate—are discussed elsewhere in this chapter. But organizationally, two forms of meso-authorities are especially relevant in Canada. One is the interjurisdictional board in which delegates from multiple state authorities address issues that arise in transboundary watersheds. This is reflected in the Prairie Provinces Water Board and in the various Canada–US boards sponsored by the International Joint Commission. The other is the district stakeholder council structure that brings together interest-holders at the watershed or subwatershed level in any basin. In earlier chapters we have seen such structures established on the Athabasca, the Oldman, the Souris, and the Red Rivers.

Sixth and finally is the question of water citizenship. This raises questions about whether power relations can be structurally altered by fashioning new participative roles. Already the world of freshwater politics has been altered by the emergence of a panoply of group interests. In this study we have seen cases ranging from Riverkeeper to the Pembina Institute, the Miramichi Salmon Association to the Friends of the Oldman, the Cree First Nations to the PEI Watershed Alliance, and the Red River Basin Commission to the Scrap Rafferty movement. Nonetheless, there remain new directions for water citizenship including new ideologies, rights declarations, and field roles.

Of the many potential factors, the discussion below will concentrate on three. None of them is entirely new or unique to the twenty-first century. But each can be detected with increasing frequency in the years since 2000. Furthermore it can be argued that these trends are, to an extent, mutually reinforcing. To be clear, this is not an argument that earlier practices have been, or will be, fully displaced. We have seen that established perspectives, instruments, and coalitions are deeply embedded and they can be self-renewing. However, they are not immune to challenge from pressures like the ones discussed below. The first is the new appreciation of what is often called "environmental flows" or "ecological services." The second is the extension of watershed-based meso-authorities that operate below the federal and provincial level but above the municipal. The third involves deeper and richer patterns of "freshwater citizenship," where civil society and state actors are engaging on resource management issues. These trends are reflected, in varying degrees, in the case study of the Mackenzie River basin. As an example of twenty-first-century management challenges, the Mackenzie has the potential to generate new perspectives for other Canadian watersheds as well.

The Rise of Ecological Paradigms

Given that ecology, as a body of thought, originated in the nineteenth century, it should not be surprising that it has been reflected periodically in freshwater policy (Bocking 1997). This has been episodic and incremental, however, rather than continuous and comprehensive. Moreover, the principal policy tools were fashioned and applied in a decidedly non-ecological context. Consider, for example, the federal Pulp and Paper Effluent Regulations, issued in 1972 under the *Fisheries Act*. This declared a series of water quality standards related to suspended solids, biological oxygen demand, and toxic chemicals entering watercourses from mill discharge. These were hard-fought political battles, but the impact was limited by a grandfathered exemption for existing mills (Sinclair 1990). As well, a more ecological approach to effluent regulation, in terms of the assimilative capacity of receiving waters, was discussed but rejected at that time. In short, first-generation tools to fight water pollution were defined partially and incrementally rather than holistically.

Another policy innovation came in the early 1970s, with the first environmental impact assessments for major new commercial projects. This new policy tool was the Environmental Assessment Review Process (EARP). As seen in earlier chapters, however, there were definite limits to environmental review. The trigger for review was often exercised by ministerial discretion. Also, as projects were assessed on a stand-alone basis, the critical question of cumulative impacts within a watershed (as in the Athabasca basin) was not addressed until the past decade.

Another notable step in watershed regulation took place in 1986 when the federal Department of Fisheries and Oceans released a new fish habitat protection policy. Here habitat is defined as "parts of the environment on which fish depend to carry out their life processes" (Canada Department of Fisheries and Oceans 1986, 1). This brought the recognition that fish habitat should be managed on a par with fish stocks. Central to this policy was the principle of "no net loss," which meant that where habitat damage was unavoidable, replacements would be required. This marked a major boost in DFO and Environment Canada involvement in aquatic environmental management along several fronts including water pollution, acid rain, biological pollutants, and physical disruptions to habitat. It was thus a significant extension of the water pollution concerns declared earlier in the pulp and paper effluent regulations.

Also in the 1980s, governments were pressed to set aside select natural areas for more stringent levels of protection. These so-called protected area or special place programs aimed to preserve natural areas for their inherent physical attributes (Marsh and Hodgins 1998). Protected area programs emerged as a counterweight to concerns about wilderness loss (Beazeley and Boardman 2001). The rigorous defence of unspoiled areas was, in some respects, a quid pro quo to the environmental movement by governments, acknowledging the relentless modification of physical nature. There were, of course, inevitable questions about the necessary scope of protected areas. Should 5 per cent of jurisdictional area be set aside or was 10 per cent or more required? As a guide to land selection, the notion of biophysical "representative areas" became influential. By the 1990s, aquatic areas joined terrestrial sites on the protected areas agenda.

The policy logic of protected spaces brought the potential for alternate ecological classifications. An example is endangered species regulation, which opens complex questions about ecosystem structures. In Canada, nominated species were subject to scientific assessment and classified according to severity of risk.

Once again, the Canadian species at risk regime was mediated by ministerial discretion. Only in 2001 did it achieve statutory standing. The key responses, as seen in the chapters above, involved remedial plans geared to countering the systemic threats. Not only did endangered species policies assert the inherent value of all global species, but they also acknowledged the value of preventing extinction and remediating endangerment.

In sum, then, ecological perspectives have in the past influenced water conservation schemes in limited degrees. However, the contemporary wrinkle in ecological management puts the biophysical needs of watersheds at the centre—indeed the forefront—of aquatic resource use, planning, and management. Such innovative thinking and policy applications began not in Europe or North America but in South Africa and Australia, two notably water-stressed areas. At the core is the belief that "a river's natural flow regime—its variable pattern of high and low flows throughout the year as well as across many years— exerts a great influence on river health" (Postel and Richter 2003, 3). The radical twentieth-century modifications of river flow regimes often obscured this fundamental insight. Consequently a determined effort to restore in-stream services to a central role has the potential to overturn the accumulated conventions of watershed management. It is no longer a matter of establishing riparian reserves but a challenge of re-regulating whole watersheds.

The new ecological thinking began with a focus to guarantee minimum instream flows, particularly at choke points such as dams and reservoirs and canals. Later, the conceptual approach shifted to natural flow regimes. Here stream flows are managed to mimic seasonal and cyclical fluctuations that, by emulating the pulses of wild rivers, can support a wide variety of species coexisting in a watershed. In South Africa, the difficulty of applying pure natural flow models led to a four-part classification of ecological watershed health. Management strategies could be selected according to the degree of ecological health being sought (Postel and Richter 2003). Significantly, this opens the way for public political debate and deliberate choice on the level of watershed health that is desired. Put another way, choices that were once settled by nondecisions can be transformed into visible decisions, and management prescriptions can follow rather than precede public choice.

During the 1990s another tool that attracted increasing attention was "state of the river" (SOR) analysis. Here the target was the river system, both in-stream and riparian and from source to mouth. As a result it reinforced the awareness of the whole watershed as a key unit of analysis. SOR reporting is a potentially powerful tool. It seeks to highlight the key issues, problems, and priorities that are embedded in a river system. Such studies are based at points in time, offering snapshots of watershed conditions. The SOR can also provide a baseline for gauging subsequent change or a point of comparison for capturing trends. SOR studies can have many sponsors. Whole basins may be the prime targets, although most of the analyses mentioned in this study—of the Oldman, the South Saskatchewan, the Athabasca, and the Miramichi, for instance—were more closely associated with the regional and local scale. State of the river reporting need not necessarily originate with senior state authorities. The prime movers may be NGOs or water basin bodies. It is worth remembering that the Oldman Watershed Council, the Miramichi River Committee, and the Keepers of the Athabasca were instrumental in launching watershed studies. Once complete, SOR reports can be a fulcrum for public education and for gathering essential local knowledge.

A final contribution to watershed ecology takes the form of the evaluative underpinnings for state of the river reporting. This has seen the introduction of new criteria of assessment around concepts such as "stress" and "health." One Saskatchewan scheme offers 25 criteria, accompanied by scale thresholds, for comparing levels of stress, condition, and response across provincial watersheds (SWA 2006). Another approach is to prepare a "league table" of rivers according to the condition of natural flows. A case in point is the 10-river comparison offered by the World Wildlife Federation–Canada in 2009 (WWF-C 2009).

The Role of Meso-authorities at the Watershed Level

This points to a zone between the senior (national and provincial) governments and the local. In the freshwater field, the watershed is an obvious candidate for intermediate governance. The roles may be advisory or executive, technical or representational. Participation may be limited to governmental delegates or may be designed for social constituencies. In earlier chapters we saw examples of two primary types: the interjurisdictional board that deals with assigned issues in transboundary watersheds and the district stakeholder council that can aggregate interest-holders at the sub-watershed level.

Neither type of meso-authority is entirely new in North America. There have been some notable innovations in the twentieth century, particularly in cases where political conflicts escalated to a point that required shared resolution. Thus when rival governments threatened to face off for control of transboundary water flows, new mechanisms could be fashioned. While they are little known, inter-jurisdictional boards function in several major watersheds while district stake-holder bodies have been authorized by provincial policy. What are new in recent decades are the shifting constituency base, the expanded range of responsibility, and the heightened policy-making influence associated with such structures.

Inter-jurisdictional Boards

The geography of Canadian watersheds pays little attention to political boundaries, so it is hardly surprising that interjurisdictional issues arise. Some of the nation's most illustrious rivers defy sovereign boundaries, including the Peace-Athabasca-Mackenzie system, the Saskatchewan, the Churchill, the Winnipeg, the Ottawa, and the Churchill in Labrador. On the surface, the constitutional heads of powers would seem to point to national government primacy. But rivers consist of legal "dimensions." So while the interprovincial flow certainly offers Ottawa a foothold, the crown water title aspect does the same for the provinces.

One of the first such cases arose shortly after World War I. The Canadian Lake of the Woods Control Board (LWCB) was established in 1919 by a federal order-in-council, out of concern for high and low water level fluctuations that followed the installation of multiple hydro dams in northwest Ontario. The purpose of this new body was to "secure … the most dependable flow and the most advantageous beneficial use of the Winnipeg River and the English River" (Canada 1921, s.3). In other words, it sought to regulate the rivers for commercial development by stabilizing water levels across the watershed. Several drainages are involved here. The LWCB regulates the flow from Ontario's Lac Seul running west through the English River into the Winnipeg River and on to Lake Winnipeg. A second set of more southerly sub-basins link Rainy Lake and Lake of the Woods to the Winnipeg River. Since the latter two sub-basins span the Canada-US border, the International Joint Commission took up the matter of coordinated control, leading to a 1925 deal that established a water operating range for Lake of the Woods (LWCB 2002). The tripartite Canadian agreement provides for capital cost sharing for hydraulic works and operations required to manage flows throughout the watershed on the Canadian side.

The LWCB has always concentrated on volumes of flow. When necessary, water release can be coordinated at a series of lake and reservoir outlets, to maintain levels within the designated range. Not surprisingly, an elaborate hydrological model lies at the core of this scheme. While all of the participating jurisdictions send delegates to the Board, the operational practice is driven principally at the engineering level, and civil society involvement in decision-making is limited.

The Lake of the Woods Board is not unlike the Prairie Provinces Water Board discussed in earlier chapters. The latter was established in 1948, when growing water appropriations in southern Alberta triggered downstream concerns over the security of future access in Saskatchewan and Manitoba. The PPWB began tentatively, as an advisory body to sponsoring governments. Then in 1968 the endorsement of apportioning rules to guarantee ongoing flows across the three provinces marked a major change. Since then, the PPWB has also expanded its monitoring work into water quality issues and groundwater.

The classic interjurisdictional structure, as sketched above, may prove to be resistant to change. Its origins were inherently statist, as provincial and federal authorities were forced to collaborate to deal with looming problems of proportional allocation. Is it possible that this institutional mechanism is frozen in time, a product of an earlier age of engineering solutions? Perhaps, but not inevitably. Reformist trends are visible elsewhere. These include research mobilization, shifting terms of reference, the establishment of stakeholder bodies, and the development of downward links to the sub-watershed level. Such properties bring the potential to make interjurisdictional boards stronger institutions.

Not all boards will necessarily move in this direction. However there are signs of experimentation at two levels; the cross-border and the subprovincial. The former is evident in the changes since the late 1990s associated with the Canada-US International Joint Commission (IJC). Part of this story was noted in chapter 7, in the IJC response to the 1997 flood event. The IJC's new International Red River Board (IRRB) was established in 2001, as a consolidated body to implement the vision articulated in *Living with the Red* (IJC 2000). Here the IJC asserted the need for a holistic grasp of the watershed and its ecosystem, marking a symbolic break with the more traditional engineering and regulatory focus. The mandate transmitted to the IRRB in 2001 is illustrative of the changing orientation. Where IJC activities were traditionally centred on adjudicating boundary water disputes, the IRRB now pursues a proactive mandate involving research, assessment, and consultation on an ongoing basis. Specifically it is directed to promote public awareness, provide a continuing forum for Red River matters, recommend to the IJC on basin management, mount inspections and assessments of flood control plans, and involve the public in its deliberations (IJC 2001). Several other IJC river boards preside over transboundary watersheds from the Yukon to New Brunswick (Norman, Cohen, and Bakker 2013).

Water Basin Councils

Following World War II, the province of Ontario took an innovative step in the direction of watershed management, with the enactment of the *Conservation Authorities Act* of 1946. This established a new level of water resource management to be delineated on the basis of watershed geography. One of the innovative features was the set of core partners that were prescribed in the act. The new conservation authorities (CAs) could only be established with the prior consent of affected municipalities to formally associate with, support, and help finance the new bodies.

This political initiative sprang from a convergence of separate forces (Richardson 1974). In southern Ontario where land is densely used by farms and cities, a variety of resource degradations were evident by the 1930s, including soil erosion, deforestation, and flood damage. Several expert lobbies and knowledge networks grasped the issue, including the Ontario Federation of Naturalists, the Ontario Conservation and Reforestation Association, and the *Farmers' Advocate* press. They shared a conviction that progress was only possible through resource management.

Several prototype organizations were closely scrutinized for guidance on the road to the CA model, ranging from the Tennessee Valley Authority to the Grand River Commission in Ontario to the Muskingum Watershed Conservancy District. in Ohio. The Ontario government had also begun reconstruction planning in 1944, and land–water rehabilitation was identified as a priority field. A key insight was the need to secure the participation of local governments to achieve results. Municipalities wielded many key powers over zoning and land use, and they also had a fiscal capacity through the property tax. However, a watershed initiative required a higher spatial focus and this is where the conservation authority came in.

Under the *Conservation Authorities Act*, the originating initiative had to come from local governments within a watershed area in the form of an application to the Ontario government. This committed municipalities to cooperate in financing and implementing CA programs and projects while at the same time providing representation at the Board level to ensure direct input. Once a formal agreement was signed between the two levels of government, an authority could be organized, staffed, and commence operations. Ten authorities began during the first three years to 1948, in urban and rural drainages across southern Ontario. During this period the driving pressure was flood abatement, and early works often centred on storage (dam and reservoir) facilities. A related concern lay with land rehabilitation, which meant reforestation and wetland protection. The Ganaraska authority plan led to 20,000 acres being reforested after 1947 in the upper half of that watershed (Richardson 1974).

A second wave of CAs appeared in the 1950s and a third a decade later. The Canadian *Water Conservation Assistance Act* of 1953 made federal funds available for river regulation and contributed to seven large dams and more than 80 smaller dam projects. By 1970 there were 38 conservation authorities in total. In a predominantly crown lands resource bureaucracy, the CA program stood out for its private land and water orientation and its municipal co-sponsorship.

Significantly, a multiple-use philosophy took hold in the 1960s (Mitchell and Gardiner 1983). The classic mandates of flood control and river restoration remained strong, but there were also programs ranging from recreation works to water quality monitoring and protection. Water storage reservoirs provided beach and boating opportunities. In addition, by creating conservation areas, authorities were able to offer tangible "services" to the public, enhance their profiles, and extend their educational work. Authorities are also involved in local building and assessment issues, aspiring to serve as a first line of defence, as it were, against inappropriate development.

The rise of environmental groups has registered with most conservation authorities since the 1970s. Fish and wildlife organizations are potential allies, as are naturalist and outdoors groups in favour of protected spaces and trails. Historical associations may also get involved if a conservation authority opts to take over a heritage site. Local citizen groups can also play important roles by participating in authority work and in lobbying senior governments.

The provincial CA network had a near-death experience during the neo-liberal years of Premier Mike Harris after 1995. As part of draconian across-the-board cuts to public programs, the conservation authorities were deemed to be an expendable luxury. Funding arrangements were shifted 90 per cent to municipal partners and, ultimately, provincial funding ceased altogether. Ironically, Harris was driven from office in part by the Walkerton water scandal, to which his government contributed by cuts to inspection services in the provincial environment ministry. Also ironically, the provincial drinking water safety regime installed since that time has opened new programming opportunities for conservation authorities.

Overall, conservation authorities have served as institutional champions for watershed planning, for land-water linkages, and for networking municipalities and advocacy groups within a watershed context. All of these roles are unique, as no other provincial program is explicitly designed to perform watershed planning. At the same time, each authority is distinct and reflects indigenous conditions and priorities. This facilitates experiment, learning, and adaptation.

The first generation of water basin councils was state-centred. That is, the institutional focus was in a designated public authority, established within government and equipped with some combination of legal, advisory, and fiscal attributes. The first wave design has not disappeared. Many such councils persist today, but alongside a new type of representative social council for water. The new generation is more diverse in inspiration and more experimental in structure.

One feature is a greater sensitivity to the need for scaling to regional communities. It is no longer sufficient to rely on municipal representatives alone to inject "public" input. In fact, the cumulative impact of new environmental activism is to encourage a supply of groups and committees that have been formed from the ground up. One of the new indicators of watershed council vitality is the number of nongovernmental partners.

Another feature is the partial dissolution of the line that distinguishes special interest from public interest voices. The former normally begins by advancing restricted benefit claims—to build or appropriate or sell. The latter can assert wider claims as personal claims. The most expressive of these is the health of the watershed as an integrated system. It is not coincidental that the state of the river or watershed report has become a popular focus in contemporary times. Not only does it assert the connectivity of the flow system, but it also underlines the mutual dependencies within a watershed community. It renders particular use-claims secondary to the health of the overall system.

The SOR/W has the potential to provide an organizing agenda for a water council. The report can speak to the new politics in several ways: reconceptualizing the freshwater resource; aggregating richer and more diverse knowledge forms; identifying and prioritizing areas of concern; building consensus behind interventions; and "testing" the plan through the experience of component groups. These are the very features in which traditional water authorities have been limited. There is now an active subdiscipline for evaluative appraisals of rivers according to stress levels that can be measured by key criteria.

Another feature of new water councils is the potential clash between old and new processes. Even without formal structures for political deliberation, sovereign authorities continue to possess the legal and fiscal resources that regulate watershed use. When the state is unresponsive to community concerns, either in efforts to maintain established political relations or through the inertia of institutional persistence, challenges will rise from below. The Athabasca Keepers movement is an expressive case in point.

In sum, whether the new institutional processes are designated a river council, a stakeholder forum, or a water parliament, the signature features reflect a new political complexity. The core qualities are representation, deliberation, framework-setting, ongoing investigation, and review. Instruments that assist in renegotiating relationships with more flexibility than the state offers will flourish.

If one term captures the shift in watershed council dynamics, it is "stewardship." The older generation councils were bureaucratic in composition, technocratic in outlook, and commercial-development oriented. Ecology was considered too complex a framework, involving too many variables and constraints to positive programming. The central meaning of stewardship is to service the needs of the waterway. This may involve passive attendance until an intervention is needed. But when stress is detected or remediation is warranted, the stewardship approach draws upon its familiarity with the natural or default processes to generate appropriate responses.

Water Citizenship

The notion of citizenship is a formal part of both classical and modern politics. It emerges partly out of the foundational debates about political association or, put another way, the purposes for which people agree to deal with collective affairs. The status of citizen denotes a basic role for people as self-directed actors in a political context, and is often distinguished from "subject," which implies a more passive and subordinate status. Citizens may be formative agents, in the sense of providing their consent for the establishment of political arrangements and thereby bestowing legitimacy. They may also, or alternately, be considered as participative agents, in the sense of holding basic interests and rights that can be asserted as part of group deliberations. Although the popular understanding of citizenship may assume that it is a comprehensive or even universal status, this is not necessarily the case. To be sure, there have been profound debates and struggles about the appropriate scope of citizenship, and the frontiers remain in flux.

The rise of water consciousness in today's public is clear. It is illustrated by many of the issues in this book: the allocative issues arising from overuse and short supply; the power of wild waters in extreme situations; the vulnerability of aquatic species to human disturbances; the importance of secure drinking water systems; and the consequences of watershed regulation. In this light it should not be surprising that new citizen roles have also emerged. This section looks at three examples: expanding spheres of democratic action, water rights as an instance of citizenship, and citizen science as a new dimension of governance.

In an influential study, Vandana Shiva (2002) argues that *water democracy* has emerged as a central field of politics, particularly in the global south. She points out that social claims on water can be seen as a basic element of life itself. This means that all people have an ongoing interest in issues of water supply, water use, and water management. Moreover, water democracy marks freshwater out from other natural materials which, while still necessary in some combination and proportions, are qualitatively different. Shiva points out the central role of water imagery in the religions and belief systems of many peoples. Historically, the relative lapse of water awareness is a recent phenomenon that is most evident in the West. It may have something to do with the technical and scientific establishment of water knowledge as a dominant framework. Equally, the reinsertion of popular concerns may have to do with the perceived limits of that expertise in practice.

There is certainly a growing sense that freshwater resource stewardship is too important a matter to leave to experts, much less businesspeople and politicians. An invigorated water democracy can take several forms. One is through citizen mobilization via freshwater interest groups. We have seen in the chapters above how groups ranging from local watersheds (Hudson Riverkeeper, Friends of the Oldman) to province- or region-wide actors (New Brunswick Salmon Council, Grand Council of the Cree, Alberta Water Matters) to national advocacy groups (WWF, Pembina Institute, Canadian Water Resources Association) are embedded in water decision-making. Groups can play an advocacy role in campaigning for issue awareness and policy adoption. Groups can also play a program delivery role by working in concert with state authorities as partners in water management.

A line of political discourse that both parallels and intersects with water democracy is that of *water rights.* This usually refers to the enactment of a legal right of all people to adequate drinking and sanitary water. It may be advanced as part of a broader environmental rights package or it may stand on its own. To date such proposals have faced significant resistance from sitting governments. However, campaigns are presently underway in various jurisdictions. Among them is the initiative to secure a water right provision in federal Canadian law (a private member's bill has been advanced without passage in recent parliamentary sessions). At the international level, the Article 31 campaign maintains an online petition to add a right to drinkable water to the United Nations Declaration of Human Rights of 1948 (Article 31 n.d.).

In Canada, a water right could take several possible forms. One of these could focus on strengthened procedural guarantees for citizen access to essential information regarding water licensing applications and review proceedings. This would serve to open such transactions, which have traditionally been conducted with a restricted range of participants, to wider public engagement. This potentially transformative measure could go a long way in levelling the playing field in water allocation and water withdrawal matters. Such provisions could also broaden the rules of judicial standing to enable third parties to bring challenges on water use rulings.

A different line of action would involve the passage of a water rights bill that specified social rights on water entitlements. For example, this could offer higher standards of water quality and quantity protection in river and lake systems, as in the European Union's 2000 Water Framework Directive (WFD). Not only does it oblige member states to meet such standards by 2015, but it also enumerates the necessary ecological and chemical indicators (EU 2000). Significantly, the WFD also calls for governments to encourage interested parties to collaborate in compliance efforts, and it endorses River Basin Districts as the units of planning and programming.

In the Parliament of Canada, a private member's bill on an Environmental Bill of Rights was advanced in 2009 by New Democratic MP Linda Duncan. Bill C-469 advanced to the committee stage but no further. The central provision was a "right to a healthy and ecologically balanced environment" (House of

Commons 2009). To this end, the bill included provisions for access to information and enhanced public participation, as well as a federal public trust duty to meet the commitments. Remedies included judicial review and civil action provisions for citizen challenge. The 2009 bill could offer a template for future activities.

Another avenue of citizen water action is available through municipal government. Given the division of powers at senior levels, local authorities are not generally considered key actors for resource management. However, in its Spraytech decision of 2001, the Supreme Court of Canada found that a pesticide ban could be upheld, in certain circumstances, under the general welfare provision that is normally a part of provincial legislation that authorizes municipalities (*114957 Canada Ltée v. Hudson [Town] 2001*). The local bylaw must be framed to address local concerns, it must not encroach on provincial or federal jurisdiction, and the subject matter must not be ruled out by explicit provincial exemption. (In Ontario, municipalities are prevented from regulating renewable energy facilities within their boundaries, and in Alberta a similar constraint applies to oil and gas facilities.)

Still another political venue is through the activities of *citizen science*. At the root of this movement is a determination to break down the barriers separating expert information and popular understanding. It is hard to overestimate the political significance of professionalizing the domain of water knowledge. It has enabled authorities to depreciate the inputs of fishers, Aboriginal users, local residents, and observers while affording privileged status to inputs from certified professionals and employees of accredited businesses.

Because water politics is spatially grounded and data about local conditions are often indispensible prerequisites, the status of knowledge becomes politically pivotal. Watershed residents are often considered compromised, on grounds of training or placement that render them vested interests, or anecdotal informants when it comes to regulatory or judicial proceedings. By contrast, commercial consultants or academic specialists do not suffer these limitations.

Citizen science seeks to break down the distinction by equipping individuals and organizations with the tools to gain entry into political circles (Conrad and Hilchey 2011). In part the tools are technical: scanning and observational techniques; documentary conventions; and sampling, storage, and custody procedures. In another part the tools are organizational. This involves tapping the capacity of social networks to extend observational reach while maintaining consistent standards. Citizen science remains a work in progress, but it speaks to the extension of participative roles that form part of water politics. In addition, citizen science has the potential to contribute meaningfully to a plurality of water knowledge domains and explorations of their interplay. It signifies an openness to alternative perspectives as well as a deeper questioning of entrenched and established policy discourse.

Drawing together these several threads of water citizenship, it might be said that today's freshwater citizens can express political concerns in many forms. They can engage in a local river cleanup, observe and report possible disturbances, join in a political campaign for new programs or regulations, mount a court challenge, attend watershed community meetings, and more. The institutions that serve as targets for such collective action include not just legislatures, bureaucracies, and judicial panels. There are also a variety of intermediary channels at the community and watershed levels. Such campaigns feature rich veins of information and complicated solidarity patterns that are as much ground-up as top-down. The potential for issue-based campaigning is greater than ever before, and this poses new challenges for aggregating and mobilizing winning coalitions.

CASE STUDY: WATER POLITICS IN THE MACKENZIE BASIN

Innovation often occurs on the so-called fringes—the spaces that are different from the perceived mainstream. Recent developments in the Mackenzie basin reinforce this when it comes to freshwater. As noted earlier, the Mackenzie River is one of the longest unobstructed systems in the country, flowing northerly through the Northwest Territories and emptying into the Arctic Ocean. Most of the towns and settlements in the NWT are situated on the banks of the river or associated tributaries. To the Dene people it is known as the Deh Cho, or the Great River. Europeans named it after Alexander Mackenzie, the explorer and fur trader of the late 1700s. The river has been a highway that links frontier society while providing sustenance for northern residents. Few in the NWT are untouched by river culture.

Important as it is, the Mackenzie River is but one part of a more extensive watershed. Several of its tributary basins rise in the provinces to the south. The best known of these are the Peace and the Athabasca systems. The Peace River originates in north-central British Columbia and flows easterly through the mountains, continuing across northern Alberta to its mouth at Lake Athabasca. Earlier in the book we noted the construction by BC Hydro of two major hydro-electric works on the upper reaches of the river—the Bennett/Schrum facility and the Peace Canyon. The closing of the river flow at the Bennett dam in the late 1960s had profound effects on the downstream flow regime, most particularly in the delta region of Lake Athabasca. British Columbia now proposes a third hydro-power project on the Peace, downstream of existing facilities at Site C, and environmental and social impact reviews are underway at time of writing. The Athabasca River rises in the Rocky Mountains in Alberta and flows northeasterly through the boreal forest before emptying into the Peace–Athabasca delta. It was described in detail in chapter 3, where the key water-using industries of pulp and paper and oil sands processing were explored.

Other significant Mackenzie River tributaries should be noted as well. Lake Athabasca, a key connecting water body, is situated mainly in northwestern Saskatchewan and is fed by several provincial rivers as well as the two mentioned above. Also, the Liard River rises in northern British Columbia and flows through the NWT to reach the Mackenzie at Fort Simpson. Further north again, the Peel River rises in Yukon and flows easterly to meet the Mackenzie at Fort MacPherson.

Map 10.1 captures the vast scale of these interconnecting basins, together with the geopolitical grid that overlays the Mackenzie drainage. It includes three provinces and two territories as well as the Government of Canada as crown title holder north of the 60th parallel. The basins are also home to Aboriginal tribal groups who, following the conclusion of land claim settlement agreements, are the largest private landholders as well as holders of preferential resource harvesting rights.

This watershed first became a target for conservation management in the 1970s. The Peace-Athabasca delta in northern Alberta suffered drastic disturbance after British Columbia's Bennett dam commenced power generation. Downstream at the delta—the largest inland freshwater delta in the world— seasonal floods were reduced, wetlands were drying out, wildlife was lost, and the Aboriginal economy came under pressure. It was, by one description, an

Map 10.1 Mackenzie Basin Watersheds

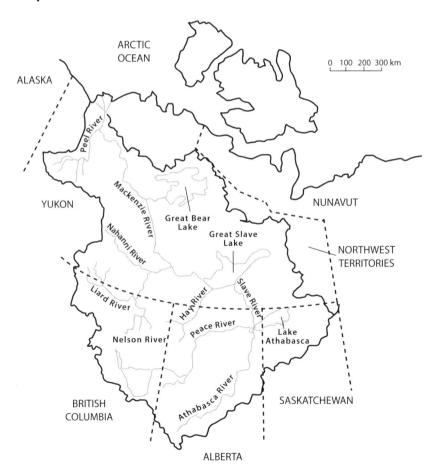

"ecological disaster" in the making (Canada 1972). The delta water cover had declined by almost 40 per cent by 1971. Two decades of dry conditions followed, with negative impacts on bioproductivity and diversity.

In response, the affected governments struck a study group in 1971, involving 30 federal and provincial agencies as well as NGOs. Reporting a year later, it proposed several new installations—a dam, a diversionary channel, and several rock weirs. Not until the damage to the delta was undeniable did whole-basin awareness begin to spread.

In 1972 an intergovernmental liaison committee was struck by the six jurisdictions, to meet on a continuing basis to address issues within the watershed. Given the absence of accurate data, a series of studies were commissioned over the next several decades. For example, a three-year study program took place between 1978 and 1981. The final report recommended that an agreement be reached on minimum flow levels, flow regulation, and water quality, and ministers endorsed this proposal. A further field monitoring program was authorized for the 1980s. The federally funded science efforts of the 1970s and 1980s offered a potential bridge to more formal organization. By 1991 some terms of potential agreement were beginning to emerge. After a series of public consultative workshops between 1991 and 1993, drafts began to circulate among the participating governments. In 1997 the Mackenzie River Basin Master Agreement was signed by the six governments.

The net result was to put the Mackenzie River Basin Board (MRBB) in a similar position to the Prairie Provinces Water Board in 1968. Considering the advances in freshwater science since that time, this was a relatively modest step forward over 30 years. Indeed, it could be argued that the participating governments opted for a minimal structure for the Mackenzie basin to perpetuate the status quo.

In what sense, then, does the MRBB relate to a "new" water politics? Events in the 2000s, most notably in the Northwest Territories, have set out a new policy agenda to challenge the 1997 settlement. Described in more detail below, this agenda insists on the importance of the whole basin as a hydrologic and political system. It demonstrates keen awareness of the upstream/downstream consequences of development decisions by partner governments, as well as an appreciation of the links of water flows to both land and atmosphere. It also asserts the need to mobilize the public and the necessity to grasp new policy instruments for water management.

As the twenty-first century opened, it was the government of the Northwest Territories (GNWT) that took the political lead. For this there were many reasons. One was the resource management priorities of Aboriginal land claims beneficiaries. Another was the shifting NWT political context following the west-east division that created Nunavut Territory, a shift that made the Mackenzie basin far more central to the NWT experience. A third was the mounting anxiety about negative potential impacts of the upstream industrial projects that were being assessed and approved by government authorities. In addition, and underlying all resource management discussions in the far north, was the striking evidence of arctic climate change.

Beginning in 2002, for example, the Sahtu Dene First Nation launched discussions on a water strategy for the Great Bear Lake basin. This led to the innovative "water heart" management plan document of 2005, a proposal for tri-government cooperation with stakeholder groups for managing the Sahtu portion of the subbasin (Great Bear Lake Working Group 2005). The "water heart" strategy envisaged a water use plan that nested within both land claim and statutory systems.

Over the next several years, a series of follow-up initiatives occurred at a territorial scale. These included successive Keepers of the Water conferences beginning in 2006. In addition, the Legislative Assembly of the NWT unanimously passed a Right To Water motion in March 2007, asserting a right of "access to water bodies for purposes of harvesting, travel and navigation" that "must take precedence over the use of water for industrial and commercial purposes" (Northwest Territories Legislative Assembly 2007).

Building on this momentum, the GNWT released a discussion paper in June 2008, proposing a collaborative approach to freshwater management. After a year of workshops and consultations, a draft water stewardship strategy followed late in 2009 and a final version titled *Northern Voices, Northern Waters* appeared in 2010 (Northwest Territories 2010). The thrust here was for a "made in the north" strategy, driven by a combination of public, Aboriginal, and government interests. Notably, the strategy was endorsed by both territorial and federal ministers. The discourse of the strategy emphasized a partner-use-manager constituency of interests. It acknowledged the scaling challenges entailed in an ecosystem approach, and the need to elevate freshwater above its traditional status in management and programming. Multiple knowledge streams (science, indigenous, and local) were recognized. A telling clue to the NWT approach could be found in the "goals" section of *Northern Voices*. It began with the need to ensure that "waters that flow into, within or through the NWT are substantially unaltered in quality, quantity and rates of flow" (Northwest Territories 2010, 11). What made these statements more than rhetorical gestures was the emergence of a ministerial champion in the person of Michael Miltenberger, who held the environment and resources portfolio. This executive political pressure maintained the momentum toward the water reform agenda (Northwest Territories 2011).

The spirit of adaptive water management was soon evident when Miltenberger invited the Rosenberg International Forum on Water Policy to appraise the 2009 strategy. This involved an expert panel meeting NWT stakeholders and examining the *Northern Voices* document. The Rosenberg report provided an early benchmark for the NWT strategy. The panel praised the innovative and forward-looking thrust of the strategy and underlined the critical importance of holistic management of such a massive arctic basin. It echoed the case for whole-basin action while also emphasizing the changing character of "eco-hydrographic" dynamics under the force of arctic climate change. A corollary here was the recognition of hydrologic "non-stationarity" (a loss of equilibrium in existing models) and the need to factor this into watershed plans. The panel expressed concern about the limited implementation capacities of northern governments, given the scale of the challenge. It also worried about signs of federal government passivity and disengagement from northern water management. The Mackenzie River Basin Board was recognized as a potential instrument for whole-basin action, but the panel argued the need to move far beyond the apportionment terms of the 1997 master agreement. It also questioned the reliance on bilateral deals as the principal connecting tool (Rosenberg International Forum on Water Policy 2009).

Overall, the panel offered timely suggestions about how to enhance and lever insights from the NWT strategy. Not only did the panel affirm the innovative aspects of the process, it also highlighted a dual character to Mackenzie basin water management, distinguishing what actors in the NWT can do on their own and what requires a wider set of governmental and societal actors.

The Rosenberg report was not wrong in its concerns about the need to maintain political and administrative momentum across a broad front. Already in Ottawa the Harper minority government had launched a "rebalancing" initiative involving northern natural resource regulation schemes. This combined an ideological suspicion that existing state regulations were unwieldy and excessive with a discomfort concerning the particular form of federal-territorial-land claim management institutions that had emerged north of the 60th parallel. This view was sometimes expressed as a problem of "too many veto points" in decision-making processes having the effect of blocking commercial resource exploitation. In response, the Harper government appointed Neil McCrank to review the regulatory regime and advise on how to reduce its complexity. While this review extended well beyond freshwater management, it bore direct implications for the water agenda. In a 2008 report, McCrank concluded that northern regulatory structures fell short on criteria of neutrality, clarity, timeliness, and accountability. In response, he proposed that licensing powers be restructured to facilitate "responsible resource development" (McCrank 2008). This was widely contested in the north. The agency at the centre of land and water policy, the Mackenzie Valley Land and Water Board, declared that "we maintain that the regulatory process in the Mackenzie Valley is not complex" but it is, by virtue of land claims agreements, different (MVLWB 2011). The Board launched its own streamlining review by striking standard procedures and consistency working groups, while vigorously rejecting the suggestion that it amounted to regressive bureaucracy.

Although the federal critique was not specifically directed at the water resource, it bristled with implications. For its part, the GNWT has not wavered in its support of the *Northern Voices* strategy. In 2011, the NWT Department of Environment and Resource Protection (in association with Ottawa) prepared a five-year action plan outlining dozens of concrete actions (2011). The GNWT also began to frame an approach to using the Mackenzie River Basin Board for whole-watershed management.

As seen earlier, the MRBB is the most recent of Canada's interjurisdictional structures designed to manage transboundary water flows. Despite the decline in federal water engagement noted in chapter 4, the Mackenzie River Basin Board was established, and a master agreement (partly modelled on the Prairie

Provinces deal of 1968) entered effect in 1997. The six government parties were joined by five Aboriginal members (from the provinces and territories). The master agreement sets out policy principles, a board structure, a financial regime, and a dispute settlement procedure.

The principles include the goal of managing water "in a manner consistent with the maintenance of the Ecological Integrity of the Aquatic Ecosystem." There is also a "right of each [party] to use or manage the Water Resource within its jurisdiction provided such use does not unreasonably harm the Ecological Integrity of the Aquatic Ecosystem in any other jurisdiction" (MRBB 1997). Under this umbrella, however, the key working tools are bilateral deals negotiated among the provincial and territorial signatories. Over the ensuing 10 years, the provinces showed little sense of priority, and the only one of the seven potential bilateral deals to be agreed linked the Yukon and NWT. Perhaps in response to this failure of take-up, the MRBB issued a framework document setting out a process and timetable for bilateral discussions (MRBB 2006). Four "watersheds" were delineated and a process was stipulated for bilaterals to be tackled on a watershed-by-watershed basis. For example, the Peace-Athabasca-Slave watershed would require four bilaterals to complete the coverage. A proposed schedule called for the parties to begin with the Peace-Athabasca-Slave in the period 2009–12.

Talks between the NWT and Alberta progressed sufficiently for a draft agreement to be expected in 2013, though no result has been announced at time of writing. By one report, it included language to guarantee that waters entering the NWT will be substantially unaltered from past flows (Wahlberg 2013). More specifically, four "risk categories" would be identified for transboundary waters. Those at "limited risk" would not require management action, those "of concern" would elicit further studies, those "facing imminent development" would be evaluated for potential harm, and those where "undue harm had been done" must be remediated to level 3 status. Criteria of undue harm will be spelled out in the agreement.

What would this mean in practice? A new project, such as the oft-discussed Slave River hydro dam, would fit into level 3. But what about oil sands pollution into the Athabasca River? Would impacts from operating plants be grandfathered as category 1 cases or be classified as category 4? And before a case like the proposed Site C hydro project on the Peace River could be subject to review, a BC-Alberta bilateral agreement would have to be struck.

There are other potential challenges in the new NWT approach. The position called for an agreement that would ensure that Mackenzie River flow was "substantially unaltered in quality, quantity or rate of flow" (Wood 2010). This goes considerably further than the master agreement, whose language centres on the use or management of water so long as it did not impose "unreasonable harm" on the ecology of other jurisdictions.

Overall, the reliance on bilateral agreements has the effect of shifting focus from the basin as a whole to more limited tributaries and sub-basins. This was confirmed in the MRBB's 2006 framework document, which doubly segmented the negotiations, by tributary system and by pairs of government. In effect, the pacing of negotiations and the range of negotiable issues could be dictated by the most reluctant party. Even with high-level government commitments to an agreement, the primacy of bilateral relationships detracts from whole-basin integrity. Each jurisdiction concentrates on immediate borders. Saskatchewan, for example, negotiating with Alberta in 2013, has yet to open discussions with the NWT, and will have no direct involvement with British Columbia or the Yukon.

This coincided with the thrusts of a 2013 follow-up report by the Rosenberg regional panel (Rosenberg International Forum on Water Policy 2013). It presented new data and arguments for the criticality of basin-wide studies and regulation. The Mackenzie basin was portrayed as an epicentre of biophysical activity, with implications for continental climate patterns (Sandford 2013a). Ultimately, however, the outcomes of any efforts to expand the scope or restructure the terms of the MRBB regime will require more than research. Here we return to questions of power—of organization, coalition building, and decision-making.

In its fullest dimensions, the Mackenzie drainage is vast—the largest in the country. While it appears on first inspection to be wild and undeveloped, the reality is different. The Peace and Athabasca tributaries are deeply connected to the hydro-power and oil sands industries, respectively, businesses that predate efforts at whole-basin watershed management.

The NWT jurisdiction, where the most original and collaborative water strategy has emerged, covers only the lower third of the basin. North of 60, commitment to enhanced water management springs from a variety of concerns, ranging from guarantees of continuing flows to water quality protection to stabilizing climate dynamics. The catalysts for action are partly upstream threats and partly rooted in territorial waters. For the GNWT, there are two components—what the NWT can do on its own and what it requires interjurisdictional collaboration to accomplish. In the north, watershed management is seen as an integrative activity inviting the involvement of multiple levels.

Even though Mackenzie water politics are in flux, what conclusions can be drawn from events to date? First, the NWT process is notable for its scale and for the associational infrastructure and self-awareness reflected in the task. Not only does it align with emerging thinking on integrated management but it is leading the search for effective solutions. A federal role could still be constructive—some would say essential—here, providing that Ottawa reverses its three-decade-long trend of disengaging from freshwater issues. Second, the NWT thinking is a product of a particularly northern mix of interests, laws, and themes. This is expressed in the aspirations for multiple knowledge streams, a coordinate role for civil society interests, and the centrality of Aboriginal rights-holders in any watershed initiative.

Third, the *Northern Voices* strategy acknowledges the scaling challenges involved in effective water action and seeks an effective "fit" to NWT society. This ranges from the community to the tribal territory to the basin as a whole. At aggregate levels, the Mackenzie River Basin Board has the potential to play a crucial role, though the "weak" attributes of this institution to date (passive, bureaucratic, and fragmented) give cause for concern. Fourth, the launch of new freshwater management proposals faces considerable political counterpressures, which can be expected to resist an expanded governmental role. The counterpressures may spring from existing industrial water rights holders or from governments harbouring unilateral ambitions for new commercial development.

In this context, the key political choice is reflected in the contrasting policy goals expressed by the MRBB master agreement and the GNWT water strategy. "No unreasonable harm" and "substantially unaltered" represent distinct and colliding principles for freshwater management, and the outcome of this contest will be politically revealing. In the process, it will become clear whether an NWT-Alberta bilateral deal will provide a creative precedent or simply perpetuate the balance of political forces to date.

Conclusion

In the pages above, some key contemporary trends of a new freshwater politics are identified. Some argue for new ways of thinking about watersheds, others focus on science inquiry, and still others concentrate on decision-making processes and tools of policy intervention. Not surprisingly, the trends are not always consistent. Water politics has become increasingly pluralistic in its range of organized interests, and this has both enriched the freshwater debates and widened the range of alternatives. This highlights the broad repertoire of interests, agendas, and conflicts that are part of freshwater politics today. Clearly the "old" and "new" categories are relative rather than absolute descriptions. The real worlds of water politics involve both, and this will continue for the foreseeable future. Indeed, it could be argued that, depending on the substance and scale of a problem, traditional approaches will continue to offer valuable tools for meeting tomorrow's problems. Nonetheless, it is evident that the contours of freshwater politics are changing and that authorities ignore these new dimensions at their peril.

The Mackenzie basin will bear watching in particular. Will the government of the Northwest Territories and its stakeholder allies succeed in entrenching the desired new policy agenda? Can working relations among community governments, NGOs, and First Nation groups be further developed? Can the GNWT succeed in expanding not only the terms of political debate but also the institutional sites for action in the Mackenzie Basin as a whole? This experiment is unfolding in an especially challenging drainage basin. There are six participating jurisdictions. The major commercial interests and provincial development priorities are deeply entrenched. The Mackenzie River Basin Board, in its present form, has a modest record of achievement and may serve more as a blocking structure than an instigator of change. With the exception of the northern Territories, the MRBB members prefer to innovate inside their provincial water jurisdictions, at the major watershed level, while at the same time showing caution about strengthening the interjurisdictional machinery. The accumulating political pressures show no signs of slackening.

Conclusion

IN THE COURSE OF THIS BOOK we have examined a wide range of freshwater settings, issues, and decisions, with the accent on their inherently political character. Water is not always approached in this way. However, the increasing public interest in the resource—its physical attributes, social uses, and management—raises persistently political questions. Canadians are expressing growing awareness of the need for water stewardship. Over the past five years, the Canadian Water Attitudes Survey has found that freshwater ranks highest in importance among all natural resources and highest in terms of public concern. Hopefully the findings in this study can help clarify some of the issues.

Freshwater Politics and Power

The book began by asking what is "political" about the freshwater resource. Politics arises when interests, rooted in social and economic differences, come into conflict. Furthermore, politics offers ways of managing, containing, or resolving such water conflicts. In any dispute it is useful to ask about which interests and which processes are involved. The watershed scale is especially useful here, as it allows us to combine the biophysical and social dimensions of the resource, to highlight both their interdependencies and the cumulative layers of political involvement. Aldo Leopold makes the case for the long view—for thinking like a watershed. But water politics takes place both inside and outside the watershed. External political forces are constantly in play. Because states hold jurisdictions over broader territories, key constraints on community politics are imposed from outside. Many of the values, rules, and decision-making processes for freshwater management are defined non-locally. The challenge for watershed interests is to work within such parameters while at the same time struggling to transform them.

Power is integral to politics. When rival interests converge in efforts to control decision-making outputs, not all can prevail. Success in achieving preferred outcomes signifies power while failure points to powerlessness. Dahl, Bachrach, and Foucault all highlight relevant dimensions of power. Power can be exercised in observable contests, in the capacity to block or suppress issues, and in constituting the knowledge systems through which issues are perceived.

At the same time, power can be an elusive concept. In some situations it can be observed in the overt actions of key players. If a roster of observable group interests is compiled and then assessed against the outcomes of water policy decisions, hierarchies of power may be revealed. The "winners" in these struggles have power while the "losers" do not. However, the visible state of play tells only part of the story. Power can be embedded in established arrangements in ways that can prove difficult for challengers to overturn. This is how pollution politics was analyzed at Boat Harbour, where the pulp company, the First Nation, the provincial and federal governments, and the court system all played roles in shaping key decisions. The winning coalition of 1965, organized around a company-province axis, defined the basic arrangement. By 1995, however, the balance was shifting, and this resulted in significant realignments on the question of burden-sharing the mill effluent damages.

In other cases power can be exercised in more subtle ways. A second face of power involves the capacity to block an issue from reaching the public domain, or coopting and redefining an issue in terms more favourable to established interests. This was evident, for example, in the irrigated farm zone of southern Alberta, where a commercial investment coalition of farmers, irrigation districts, and municipal interests allied with provincial government agencies to sponsor the Oldman dam. Yet an equally significant part of this political struggle was the nondecision taken by the government of Canada in enforcing its environmental impact review policies. In this case, interest group forces that were initially on the losing side—environmentalists and First Nations—made a tactical decision to shift the political status quo by judicial action to enforce those environmental reviews. A parallel version of federal non-decision-making appeared in the case of the Rafferty dam in neighbouring Saskatchewan.

Knowledge systems can also convey power relations in the ways that they define physical and social practice. The role of hydraulic engineers in freshwater development is a case in point. From Johann Tulla to the Army Corps of Engineers, efforts at river "regulation" have been codified and applied to a constellation of problems. Rival knowledge streams, such as those devised by First Nations or ecologists, can be equally rich sources of pure or practical understanding. But they may lack institutional standing among decision-making elites.

How important are civil society groups in achieving an element of water democracy? Water groups can play a variety of roles. For one, they give voice to interests in political debates. Consider the impact of the Atlantic Salmon Federation and its regional affiliates in advocating for a key species under stress. Another role is to promote watershed research and planning on a holistic scale. The Athabasca Waterkeepers is a case in point with their state of the river reporting and their efforts to build bridges among civil society groups. Water groups can also serve as allies and extensions of state agencies when it comes to program delivery. Recall that Environment Canada founded the Atlantic Coastal Action Program to foster and interact with community stakeholders. In a similar impulse, the province of Alberta underwrote the irrigation districts to mobilize water infrastructure. That same province later designed a system for river boards in major basins such as the Oldman and the Athabasca.

Our case studies have also illustrated how group interests can evolve in form and function over time. A group once known as the Western Canada Irrigation Association, formed as the national voice of watered farming, became the Canadian Water Resources Association and an advocate for freshwater conservation, education, and management. But the most dramatic instance of civil society transformation must surely involve Aboriginal peoples. First Nations' interests figured frequently in the case study profiles in the chapters above, from Nova Scotia and New Brunswick to Quebec and Alberta. At the beginnings of these episodes, Indian bands were often the vulnerable parties in development projects that they did little to provoke. Yet over time they demonstrated tenacity in the face of politically antagonistic coalitions. They also showed a shrewd sense of tactics by combining direct protest action, coalition building, and judicial litigation. These tactics brought results in resisting pulp mill pollution, hydro-electric displacement, and irrigation diversions.

Water democracy can also be advanced by the creation of new deliberative and decision-making venues. It is notable that a variety of local and regional water interest communities have been fostered by state authorities to provide a focal point for collective action. These include groundwater management units, land drainage units, floodplain management units, conservation authorities, and watershed management units as well as the irrigation districts just mentioned. While such units may not meet the classic definition of civil society groups, they do provide potential nodes where citizen interests can gather and act.

The Freshwater State Structure: Strong or Weak?

A continuing theme in the chapters above is the varied capabilities of Canadian state authorities to deal with the freshwater resource. There is no simple and categorical answer here. In liberal democracies, the state is usefully conceived as an ensemble of distinct parts or subsystems. Each part offers a potential point of political contact on key decisions. At executive levels, ministers separately and the cabinet collectively may have the final word on water policy matters. Alternatively, if legislation is required or desired, the consent of elected assemblies will be sought. For the implementation of approved programs, the bureaucracy can be expected to play a lead role and a specialized civil service offers multiple points of contact. Should adversely affected interests wish to challenge policy decisions after the fact, the judicial system offers an avenue for review that may block or delay implementation. In a federal system like Canada's, the existence of federal and provincial governments multiplies the points at which political pressure may be applied. In addition, an intermediate level of district or watershed authorities may function as forums for political debate and choice.

There seems nothing in the freshwater sector that suggests the state is inherently weak, that is, easily captured by outside interests or ineffective in achieving desired results. Neither do any traits point to an inherently strong freshwater state, which enjoys sufficient autonomy that it can deflect group pressures and pursue strategies of its own choice. We have seen examples where organized interests have effectively enlisted state power to achieve their objectives. Colonial anglers succeeded in marginalizing Aboriginal fishers in the late 1800s by lobbying for gear, bag limit, and seasonal restrictions. Land development companies extracted licences for prairie irrigation schemes, and farmer-owned irrigation districts perpetuated this prerogative. Established pulp and paper mills achieved an initial exemption from the federal water pollution regulations of the 1970s. Hydroelectric companies won approval for dam and reservoir schemes that refashioned the shapes of the designated basins.

What about situations where rival developmental agencies collide in common space or encroach on one another's mandates? This can happen within a single jurisdiction, where federal fisheries and navigable waters and environmental assessment functions are grounded in separate departments. It can also happen between jurisdictions, where federal and provincial fisheries, or federal and provincial environmental assessment agencies, bid for primacy. This is increasingly common in recent times as the number of water policy paradigms has proliferated.

One trend that is difficult to deny is the longitudinal decline of the national freshwater mandate and the expansion of provincial domains. In the postwar decades, the government of Canada mounted a series of new measures for flood management, irrigated agriculture, water research, and watershed planning. There were also new programs in environmental impact assessment, fish habitat protection, and pulp and paper effluent regulation. Although these initiatives were restricted in scope and not always implemented with full rigour, they were vital catalysts for freshwater management. However, this 45-year trend was slowed and reversed in the decades that followed Ottawa's National Water Strategy of 1987. Evidence can be seen in the deep program cuts that accompanied the Chrétien-Martin fiscal program review and the deregulatory measures enacted by the Harper government in recent years.

By comparison, certain provincial governments have shown an increased willingness to acknowledge and confront freshwater imperatives. This is far from a uniform trend, of course, and provincial action often requires a catalyst in the form of an apprehended crisis. Acute flood events, drinking water contaminations, fish kills, and lake eutrophication are cases in point. Alternatively, civil society campaigns have triggered policy reversals and reforms in the cases of northern hydro plans (Great Whale), dirty oil sands boycotts (Athabasca), grassroots litigation to force comprehensive environmental review (Souris), and unsustainable water allocations (Oldman). In responding to such cases, provincial governments have fashioned several innovative practices. Water management branches within departments of environment have been bolstered. Watershed councils and river boards have been established with stakeholder representation. Monitoring networks have been installed and data streams made publicly available. It remains to be seen whether the 2010 water charter, ratified by provincial premiers at the Council of the Federation, signifies a new level of joint provincial resolve. In any event, provincial authorities have not been reluctant to expand their freshwater parameters.

Similarly, when the focus shifts from project management to water basin management, different issues arise. The watershed scale, which is increasingly recognized as an appropriate unit for integrated management, does not match up readily with standard jurisdictional boundaries. Consequently basin authorities have been established in different shapes and sizes. In Ontario, more than 30 conservation authorities have been created to focus attention on local watershed needs. In Alberta, the environment department sponsors a dozen major watershed councils and boards to deal with in-stream use, and in neighbouring Saskatchewan the Water Security Agency promotes a similar process. For border waters, the International Joint Commission has embraced an integrated watershed initiative for its river boards. And for transboundary watersheds within Canada, there are examples ranging from the Saskatchewan River to the Mackenzie River and the Lake of the Woods.

Most of these display two striking features: they are composite authorities involving multiple interests and they are designed to fit "on top" of prior institutions. Lacking an independent fiscal base, they depend heavily on senior governments for program resources. In addition, coming relatively late to the water management table, they must deal with a crowded field of organizational rivals. In process terms, however, interjurisdictional deliberations have the potential to alter the prevailing balances of forces, introduce new policy narratives, and overcome deadlocks in traditional structures.

Policy Subsectors and Networks

One of the findings in this study is that the power structures shaping modern water politics were often forged in earlier times. Put another way, to understand the power relations in irrigated farming, flood control programs, or hydro-power production, we need to take account of key events in the 1920s, 1950s, and 1960s respectively. In such cases, a blend of technological, legal, and political forces were fused into developmental policies. Once established, sets of supportive interests provided reinforcement and validation. If sufficiently strong and durable, such coalitions ensured that government commitment remained strong.

There are many policy subsectors of this type in the freshwater domain and only a sampling has been explored here. Each subsector can be approached on its own terms. Yet at the same time, subsectors are not entirely self-contained and policy spill-overs are inevitable. This suggests that in some situations a hierarchy of policy fields can be identified. A critical subsector is one that is sufficiently autonomous that, in cases of overlap, it forces changes on adjacent subsectors rather than being forced to adjust itself.

In the chapters above we have seen many cases where subsectors function on a separate-but-equal basis. Think of postwar flood control or irrigation works for farming. A distinct set of social interests coalesced around each government agency, grounded in statutes and spending programs and technical cultures and operating essentially independent of one another. This pattern of multiple policy silos can be reinforced by the fact that separate departments guard their own water programs and measure their success in terms of specialized mandates. In some cases, collaboration between federal and provincial authorities makes for even deeper embeddedness, as reciprocal obligations can lock in a program against normal policy challenges. Equally, the sudden withdrawal of support at one of these levels can spark a crisis.

For a deeper understanding of subsectors, the notion of the policy network is useful. It suggests that organized groups and government agencies are connected in patterned relationships. Any subsector is likely to include a cluster of diverse groups and one or more state agencies. But it is the pattern of group–state relations that matters. Are there many groups within a subsector or few? Do some groups enjoy more influence than others? Do some groups enjoy authority within the sector? How does the state relate to its organized public? Are groups kept at arm's length or are select groups granted privileged access to closed consultation and partnership? Can groups migrate over time between the outer orbit of policy advocacy and the inner orbit of clientele connection, and vice versa?

Groups can take a variety of organizational forms, and they target government decision-makers for particular purposes. Some groups concentrate on campaigning for government action. These advocacy groups pressure public authorities for action. The Pictou Landing First Nation sought a remedy for the damage in Boat Harbour. The Friends of the Oldman demanded a comprehensive environmental review before licensing the dam. The Miramichi Salmon Association called for more aggressive fish conservation measures. The logic of effective advocacy campaigns is to build the widest possible coalition to secure the desired action. At the same time there are clientele groups. The government of Nova Scotia was so willing to collaborate with Scott Paper that the province assumed all responsibilities for waterborne effluent. The government of Alberta sponsored the Oldman dam out of its commitment to a quantum expansion of the southern irrigation districts.

In some respects, the politics of autonomous subsectors corresponds to the era of single-use water management. We have seen, however, that as early as the 1900s advocates of resource conservation called single-use into question. In its place emerged the doctrine of multiple-use. At the project level this suggested that multiple policy goals could be served simultaneously. The classic example is the dam and reservoir facility that could contain flood waters, store water for irrigation, drive a hydro turbine, and facilitate river transport.

Despite the intellectual persuasiveness of this doctrine, it proved difficult to implement in practice. This was in part due to resistance from prevailing powers—no one wished to surrender the hard-fought gains of previous battles. We should make no mistake: the call for multiple-use management involved overturning the single-use status quo. It is hardly surprising that it was resisted. Equally, once a designated set of multiple users were profitably linked, the defence of their shared benefits posed barriers to late-arriving political claimants.

The same applies to integrated use. Here the range of variables jumps again. Integrated use implies the controlled manipulation of more complex systems such as watersheds. To begin, this poses data and knowledge challenges of a high order. The field work and modelling needs are extensive and expensive, and very few watersheds or sub-watersheds have been studied to the necessary level. Then comes the question of whether multiple domains of watershed knowledge are required and, if so, whether they can interconnect. At the very least there will be a need for water budgets, watershed society profiles, and assessments of governmental structures.

None of this work comes cheap, and political elites are well aware of the expenditure costs of watershed planning. If comprehensive planning cannot be undertaken at a stroke (recall that the Ontario Conservation Authority network took decades to complete), then prioritization may be necessary. Rivers experiencing high stress, whether due to overwithdrawal, pollution, or engineering impacts, will be identified and tackled first.

Watersheds as Political Systems

Each chapter in the book has been accompanied by a watershed case study that captures some of the central themes. This is done for several reasons—to demonstrate how watersheds can be seen as a type of political system, to illustrate the power relations that policy networks create on the ground, and to sample the continuum of primary watersheds in Canada. We make no claims that these watershed cases are in any way representative. After all, there are 25 major basins, hundreds of tributary basins, and thousands of sub-watersheds to be found across the country. However, the 10 cases above do illustrate a range of variation.

We have seen drainages that are largely devoted to agriculture and others devoted to forestry or petroleum or hydro-power or hunting-trapping-fishing. Some of them are heavily populated, like the Red River, and others are sparsely populated, like the La Grande. Many watersheds combine a rural resource hinterland with a large urban centre like Miramichi City, Fort McMurray, or Lethbridge. First Nations peoples play leading roles in watersheds large (Mackenzie, La Grande), intermediate (Oldman, Miramichi, and Athabasca), and small (Boat Harbour, Prince Edward Island). Some of the river systems are heavily regulated in the engineering sense (Red, Oldman, and Boat Harbour), while others are natural flows. There are watersheds located at different geopolitical scales, some located within a single province (Quebec, New Brunswick, Nova Scotia), others that cross provincial or territorial boundaries (Alberta, Northwest Territories), and others that flow between Canada and the United States (Saskatchewan, Manitoba).

As a political unit, the watershed remains embryonic. Its early social significance in pre-industrial society declined with the advent of railway and highway transportation networks. Freshwater retained an economic importance wherever stored or flowing supplies offered commercial opportunities. Yet this was largely appropriated on a project basis, with little or no reference to cumulative impacts across the drainage basin. The modern appreciation of the watershed is linked to its potential as a resource planning unit. Part of this is driven by engineering considerations where watersheds are measured and modelled in physical terms, as in flood control and hydro-power applications. Another part is linked to the emergence of ecological perspectives and an appreciation of the hydrologic cycle.

Conservation lobbies became increasingly assertive in the era of aquatic environmental assessments.

In social terms, a watershed can be similarly approached as a multidimensional construct. This includes relations of interest-holders in upstream and downstream locations, relations of riparian and non-riparian holders, relations between surface water and groundwater interest holders, and the accumulation of interest holders in a fixed space over time. These are precisely the types of political claimants that are captured in watershed authorities. We have seen that the earliest prototypes appeared in the twentieth century. The International Joint Commission was established to adjudicate cross-border water tensions. A half-century later, the Ontario Conservation Authorities gathered municipal and rural resource users together to document and plan the management of district watersheds. Beginning in the 1990s a new set of mechanisms appeared with river planning boards, watershed commissions, and ENGO coalitions. The tools for this emerging watershed politics are diverse. They include field research programs that inform state of the river or state of the watershed reports (Oldman and Miramichi) as well as basin plans and strategies (Athabasca, Souris, and Red) and interjurisdictional agreements (Prairie Provinces, Mackenzie Basin, and IJC boards).

The result has been a marked redefinition of the boundaries of local or regional governments to include watershed and sub-watershed communities. In this way latent political interests can become manifest. As newly established forums, watershed institutions can offer a voice to new political interests or to existing interests that were hitherto ignored or suppressed. In contrast to conventional municipal authorities, where the usual range of political interests includes property owners, commercial developers, and public utility services, watershed authorities invite participants from a far wider freshwater constituency. Consequently the contrast between municipal self-government and watershed self-government is substantial. Although Canada is still at an early stage of this transition, grassroots awareness and mobilization seems likely to ensure that meso-institution building will continue.

Multilevel Water Governance

The discussion above underlines another feature of freshwater politics. It operates, by necessity, at multiple levels. This is how the problems of social watersheds are solved. Particular interests, once apprehended at the micro level, band together or confront one another. These interests may then percolate upward to broader spatial levels or to the legal institutions with the capacity to make choices. Such choices may be advisory or binding. They may be exercised within single institutions or shared among multiple institutions. Some of these institutions may enjoy political precedence over others, in the sense that they possess superior resources or exercise senior authority that can alter or supplant decisions made below.

But what we see today in Canada is a particular form of watershed governance. First there appears to be an expanding vacuum at senior levels. In Ottawa, a 20-year trend of federal disengagement is apparently being deepened by recent choices by the Harper majority government. This is evident in the curtailment and abolition of several aquatic resource and environmental programs, along with the elimination or modification of core regulations. Correspondingly, there is a greater awareness at the provincial and territorial levels that key constitutional powers and policy instruments lie there. Certainly there are differing degrees of urgency and capacity to act within the provincial and territorial subset. As the chapters above have shown, there are leaders and laggards depending on policy subsector. Looking beyond governmental structures, we see today more formal recognition of the role for local-regional mobilization, with special-purpose bodies emerging to facilitate these linkages. Many of these are rooted in water subsectors as mentioned above—for irrigation development, flood planning, drinking water protection, groundwater regulation, or water conservation. This includes extra-governmental initiatives such as waterkeeper groups, water basin councils, and river restoration movements.

Clearly it is not possible to roll back decades of institutional history in the freshwater field. The constitutional division of powers, the bureaucratic traditions, and the accumulations of water development interests are firmly, though not immutably, fixed. How then to respond? To operate at levels higher than has been achieved thus far, two possible pathways can be described as segmentation and coordination.

Segmentation suggests the existence of dedicated authorities and policy communities and governance arrangements, defined by geopolitical boundaries. If such a scheme helped to move watersheds to centre stage, it could be a positive force. Attention to boundaries is also critical, and traditional jurisdictional claims will not fade away quietly. In political circles, segmentation often carries pejorative overtones. It can imply balkanization—the breaking up of larger wholes into arbitrary or incoherent segments. But multiple spatial authorities, based upon efficient designs for clear purposes, can also be creative, experimental, and cross-fertilizing. They can be conducive to policy learning and elevated practice.

An alternative is the coordination of existing functional authorities to create a virtual water authority. In a newly emerging world of watershed-based politics, coordination may be more frequent and more easily achieved than it is among traditional legal authorities. For example, nesting arrangements can link local watersheds, tributary basins, and major watersheds. As issues move "up" a scaled watershed structure, the authority could be qualitatively transformed. Field interventions could be concentrated at the local or district levels while information gathering and modelling (and planning) could be lodged at higher levels. Senior governments could concentrate on the role of framework-setting. This is where policy goals could be formulated, and where financial and legal incentives (resource provisioning) could be arranged for consenting partners. In addition, senior governments could formulate a default system to apply to unorganized or non-participating areas. In any event, macro-level debates on policy and legislation are clearly appropriate here.

Pathways for Water Policy Renewal

Taken together, the narratives of water politics presented in this book suggest several broad patterns. First, the role of a political crisis should never be underestimated as a force for change. Even policy regimes that appear to be solidly entrenched are vulnerable to overthrow as a result of systems failure. Take for instance the Walkerton water tragedy of 2000 and its counterpart at North Battleford, Saskatchewan. The evident vulnerabilities of municipal and provincial water delivery systems led to public inquiries, administrative restructuring, and a new grand policy for ensuring secure drinking water supply. In the aftermath, new practices were disseminated across the country. Another aspect of crisis is the revelation of unrecognized complexity and dysfunction. Lessons were learned here about the need to weave together separate technical systems (e.g., water supply, water testing, and operator training). It was also evident that the integrity of a policy subsector is only as strong as its weakest link.

Second, the prospect of increasingly stressed rivers and watersheds is now acknowledged in all parts of Canada. More than half a century of intensive and expanding social appropriation has left many watersheds at or beyond their sustainable capacity. This highlights the insufficiency of traditional forms of crown regulation by way of incremental or project-based licensing. In Alberta such a predicament led the provincial government to fashion its forward-looking Water for Life framework. This involved the establishment of basin boards, sub-basin councils, and management frameworks for each major watershed. While statutory authority remains in the hands of ministers, a large degree of practical subsidiarity has been enabled by allowing basin water communities to commission studies and weigh potential licensing strategies. Parallel initiatives can be seen in other provinces.

Third is the repointing of water policy thinking by elevating the importance of natural system needs. Often described as ecological services, this includes the prioritization of in-stream flow patterns, aquatic animal health, and restoration programming. Fourth and finally, there are political and legal relationships that call out for clarity and for adjustment. This may include the recalibration of rights and obligations toward water. It may involve sunset rules for water allocations, formally stipulated triggers for reviews and consultations, novel methods of weighting social and personal claims, and enlisting price mechanisms to alter patterns of preference and choice. And, as already argued, a new water politics will confer elevated roles on watershed authorities and citizen stakeholders. Nongovernmental groups are increasingly welcomed as partners in management in recognition of their distinctive, even essential, contributions in local knowledge, community organization, and program delivery.

References

114957 Canada Ltée (Spraytech) v. Hudson (Town). 2001. 2 Supreme Court Reports: 241–80.

Adlam, Robert. 2002. "Fish Talk." *Anthropologica* 44 (1): 99–111. http://dx.doi.org/10.2307/25606063.

Alberta. 2012. *Lower Athabasca Regional Plan, 2012–2011*. Edmonton: Government of Alberta.

Alberta Agriculture and Irrigation. 2013. Alberta Irrigation Information, 2012. http://www1.agric.gov.ab.ca/$Department/deptdocs.nsf/all/irr7401/$FILE/altairriginfo2012.pdf.

Alberta Environment. 2003. *South Saskatchewan River Basin Water Management Plan. Phase Two: Background Studies*. Edmonton: Alberta Environment.

Alberta Environment. 2006. *Approved Water Management Plan for the South Saskatchewan River (Alberta)*. Edmonton: Alberta Environment.

Alberta Environment. 2007. *Athabasca River Water Management Framework*. Edmonton: Alberta Environment.

Alberta Irrigation Projects Association. n.d. http://www.aipa.ca/.

Allison, Graham. 1971. *The Essence of Decision: Explaining the Cuban Missile Crisis*. Boston: Little, Brown.

Anderson, Mary P. 2005. "The Wisconsin Roots of Ground Water Hydrology." *Ground Water* 43 (1): 142–45.

Armstrong, Christopher, and H.V. Nelles. 1986. *Monopoly's Moment: Organization and Regulation of Canadian Utilities, 1830–1930*. Toronto: University of Toronto Press.

Armstrong, Christopher, Matthew Evenden, and H.V. Nelles. 2009. *The River Returns: An Environmental History of the Bow*. Montreal: McGill-Queen's University Press.

Article 31. n.d. http://www.article31.org.

Athabasca Watershed Council. 2011. *State of the Watershed Report*. Hatfield Consultants.

Atlantic Coastal Action Program. n.d. Environment Canada, Atlantic Coastal Action Program, https://www.ec.gc.ca/iea-aei/default.asp?lang=En&n=AE53A7A0-.

Atlantic Development Board. 1969. *Water Resources in the Atlantic Provinces*. Ottawa: Atlantic Development Board.

Atlantic Salmon Federation. n.d. http://www.asf.ca/main.html.

Atlantic Salmon Federation and Environment Canada. 2007. *Proceedings of the 2006 Acid Rain Mitigation Workshop*, Bedford, NS.

Bachrach, Peter, and Morton Baratz. 1962. "Two Faces of Power." *American Political Science Review* 56 (04): 947–52. http://dx.doi.org/10.2307/1952796.

Bachrach, Peter, and Morton S. Baratz. 1970. *Power and Poverty: Theory and Practice*. New York: Oxford University Press.

Bai, Matt. 2007. *The Argument*. New York: Penguin Press.

Baker, Ralph C. 1979. "Historic Flood Profile—City of Winnipeg." *Manitoba Pageant* 24 (4).

Bakker, Karen. 2007. *Eau Canada: The Future of Canada's Water*. Vancouver: UBC Press.

Bartlett, Richard. 1988. *Aboriginal Water Rights in Canada: A Study of Aboriginal Title to Water and Indian Rights*. Calgary: Canadian Institute of Resources Law.

Beattie, Billie L., and Chul-Un Ro. 1998. *Trends in Acid Precipitation in the Atlantic Provinces, 1980–98.* Dartmouth: Meteorological Service of Canada, Environment Canada.

Beazeley, Karen, and Robert Boardman, eds. 2001. *Politics of the Wild: Canada and Endangered Species.* Toronto: Oxford University Press.

Beveridge, Meghan, and Danielle Droitsch. 2008. *Piping Water between Watersheds: An Analysis of Basin-to-Basin and Sub-basin-to-Sub-basin Diversions in Alberta.* Canmore: Water Matters Society of Alberta.

Blackbourn, David. 2006. *The Conquest of Nature: Water, Landscape and the Making of Modern Germany.* New York: Norton.

Blomquist, William. 1991. "Exploring State Differences in Groundwater Policy Adoptions, 1980–1989." *Publius* 21 (2): 101–15.

Bocking, Richard. 1972. *Canada's Water: For Sale?* Toronto: James Lewis and Samuel.

Bocking, Stephen. 1997. *Ecologists and Environmental Politics: A History of Contemporary Ecology.* New Haven: Yale University Press.

Bourassa, Robert. 1973. *James Bay.* Montreal: Harvest House.

Bower, Shannon Stunden. 2011. *Wet Prairie: People, Land and Water in Agricultural Manitoba.* Vancouver: UBC Press.

Boyle, Robert. 1969. *The Hudson River: A Natural and Unnatural History.* New York: Norton.

Brownsey, Keith. 2008. "Enough for Everyone: Policy Fragmentation and Water Institutions in Alberta." In *Canadian Water Politics: Conflicts and Institutions,* ed. Mark Sproule-Jones, Carolyn Johns, and B. Timothy Heinmiller, 133–55. Montreal: McGill-Queen's University Press.

Bruce, J.P. 1976. "The National Flood Damage Reduction Program." *Canadian Water Resources Journal* 1 (1): 5–14. http://dx.doi.org/10.4296/cwrj0101005.

Bumsted, J.M. 1987. "Developing a Canadian Disaster Relief Policy: The 1950 Manitoba Flood." *Canadian Historical Review* 68 (September): 347–73.

Bumsted, J.M. 2002. "The Manitoba Royal Commission on Flood Cost Benefit and the Origins of Cost Benefit Analysis in Canada." *American Review of Canadian Studies* 32 (1): 97–121. http://dx.doi.org/10.1080/02722010209481659.

Burke, Brenda Lee. 2001. *Don't Drink the Water: The Walkerton Water Tragedy.* Victoria: Trafford.

Burke, Monte. 2013. "Endangered Atlantic Salmon Are Facing a New and Potentially Devastating Threat." *Forbes* 14 (June). http://www.forbes.com/sites/monteburke/2013/06/14/endangered-atlantic-salmon-are-facing-a-new-and-potentially-devastating-threat/.

Canada. 1921. *An Act Respecting The Lake of the Woods Control Board.* Statutes of Canada 1921.

Canada. 1972. *Peace-Athabasca Delta—A Canadian Resource: A Report on Low Water Levels in Lake Athabasca.* Edmonton: Peace-Athabasca Delta Planning Group.

Canada. 1987. *Federal Water Policy.* Ottawa: Environment Canada. http://www.cwwa.ca/pdf_files/Federal%20Water%20Policy,%201987_e.pdf.

Canada. 1991. *Report of the Panel on Rafferty-Alameda Dams.* Ottawa: Supply and Services Canada.

Canada. 2005. *Water in the West: Under Pressure.* Ottawa: Parliament of Canada. Senate. Standing Committee on Energy, Environment and Natural Resources.

Canada. 2010a. *Assessment and Status Report on the Atlantic Salmon, Salmo salar, in Canada.* Ottawa: Committee on the Status of Endangered Wildlife in Canada.

Canada. 2010b. *Species at Risk: Recovery Strategy for the Atlantic Salmon, Inner Bay of Fundy Populations.* Ottawa: Fisheries and Oceans. https://www.registrelep-sararegistry.gc.ca/virtual_sara/files/plans/rs_atlantic_salmon_ibof_0510a_e.pdf.

Canada Department of Fisheries and Oceans. 1986. *Policy for the Management of Fish Habitat*. Ottawa: Department of Fisheries and Oceans. http://www.dfo-mpo.gc.ca/Library/23654.pdf.

Canada Department of Fisheries and Oceans. 2009. *Canada's Policy for Conservation of Wild Atlantic Salmon*. http://www.dfo-mpo.gc.ca/fm-gp/policies-politiques/wasp-pss/wasp-psas-2009-eng.htm.

Canada Department of Fisheries and Oceans. 2010a. *Freshwater Initiative: Issues and Future Directions*. Ottawa: Department of Fisheries and Oceans.

Canada Department of Fisheries and Oceans. 2010b. *Information on Atlantic Salmon (Salvo salar) from Fishing Area 16 (Gulf NB) of Relevance to the Development of a COSEWIC Status Report*. CSAS Research Document 2010/064. Ottawa: Department of Fisheries and Oceans.

Canada Department of Fisheries and Oceans. 2013. *Atlantic Salmon (Salmo salar) Returns to the Miramichi River New Brunswick for 2012*. Gulf Region Science Response 2013/009. Moncton: Canada Department of Fisheries and Oceans.

Canada and U.S.A. 1989. *Souris River Flood Control Agreement*. Ottawa and Washington, DC: International Souris River Board.

Canadian Dam Association. n.d. http://www.imis100ca1.ca/cda.

Canadian Groundwater Association. n.d. www.cgwa.org.

Canadian Hydropower Association. 2002. Presentation to House of Commons Standing Committee on Environment on CEAA. Ottawa: Canadian Hydropower Association.

Canadian Hydropower Association. 2008. *Hydropower in Canada: Past, Present and Future*. https://canadahydro.ca/reportsreference/cha-reports-and-publications.

Carolan, Michael S. 2007. "One Step Forward, Two Steps Back: Flood Management Policy in the United States." *Environmental Politics* 16 (1): 36–51. http://dx.doi.org/10.1080/09644010601073507.

Carson, Rachel. 1962. *Silent Spring*. New York: Houghton Mifflin.

CBCL Ltd. 2003. *Watershed Management Plan for James River Watershed*. Halifax: CBCL.

Cech, Thomas V. 2003. *Principles of Water Resources*. New York: John Wiley and Sons.

CEMA. 2012. *End Pit Lakes Guidance Document*. Fort McMurray: Cumulative Environmental Management Association.

Chadwick, E.M.P., ed. 1995. *Water, Science and the Public: The Miramichi Ecosystem*. Canadian Special Publication of Fisheries and Aquatic Sciences No. 123. Ottawa: National Research Council.

Clancy, Peter. 2004. *Micropolitics and Canadian Industry: Paper, Steel and the Airlines*. Toronto: University of Toronto Press.

Clarke, Jeanne N., and Daniel C. McCool. 1996. *Staking Out the Terrain: Power and Performance among Natural Resource Agencies*. Albany: SUNY Press.

Coates, Ken. 2000. *The Marshall Decision and Native Rights*. Montreal: McGill-Queen's University Press.

Colborn, Theo, Dianne Dumanoski, and John Peterson Myers. 1996. *Our Stolen Future*. London: Abacus.

Conrad, Cathy, and Krista Hilchey. 2011. "A Review of Citizen Science and Community-based Environmental Monitoring: Issues and Opportunities." *Environmental Monitoring and Assessment* 176 (1–4): 273–91.

Conservation Council of New Brunswick. 2010. *Fracking for Shale Gas in New Brunswick: What You Need to Know*. Fredericton: Conservation Council of New Brunswick.

Corkal, D.R., B. Inch, and P.E. Adkins. 2007. "The Case of Canada: Institutions and Water in the South Saskatchewan Basin." Working Paper, Institutional Adaptations to Climate Change, Regina, SK.

Costa, John E. 1978. "The Dilemma of Flood Control in the United States." *Environmental Management* 2 (4): 313–22. http://dx.doi.org/10.1007/BF01866671.

Coté, Francois. 2006. *Freshwater Management in Canada: IV. Groundwater.* Ottawa: Library of Parliament, Research Service.

Council of Canadian Academies. 2009. *The Sustainable Management of Groundwater in Canada.* Ottawa: Expert Panel.

Council of the Federation. 2010. *Water Charter.* http://www.councilofthefederation.ca.

Cronin, John. 1999. *The Riverkeepers.* New York: Simon and Schuster.

Dahl, Robert. 1961. *Who Governs? Democracy and Power in an American City.* New Haven: Yale University Press.

Daintith, Terrence. 2010. *Finders Keepers? How the Law of Capture Shaped the World Oil Industry.* Washington, DC: Resources for the Future Press.

d'Aliesio, Renata. 2011. "Alberta Water Project Hopes to Quench Parched Farms' Thirst." *Globe and Mail,* July 27.

de Loe, Rob. 1997a. "Return of the Feds, Part I: The St Mary Dam." *Canadian Water Resources Journal* 22 (1): 53–62.

de Loe, Rob. 1997b. "Return of the Feds, Part II: The Oldman River Dam." *Canadian Water Resources Journal* 22 (1): 63–72.

de Villiers, Marq. 1999. *Water.* Toronto: Stoddart Publishing.

den Otter, A.A. 1982. *Civilizing the West: The Galts and the Development of Western Canada.* Edmonton: University of Alberta Press.

den Otter, A.A. 1988. "Irrigation and Flood Control." In *Building Canada: A History of Public Works,* ed. Norman R. Ball, 142–68. Toronto: University of Toronto Press.

Desbiens, Caroline. 2004. "Producing North and South: A Political Geography of Hydro Development in Quebec." *Canadian Geographer* 48 (2): 101-18. http://dx.doi.org/10.1111/j.0008-3658.2004.00050.x.

Doern, G. Bruce, and Thomas Conway. 1994. *The Greening of Canada: Federal Institutions and Decisions.* Toronto: University of Toronto Press.

Drummond, Dylan O. 2011. "Texas Groundwater Rights and Immunities: From East to Sipriano and Beyond." Paper presented at the Annual Meeting of the Texas State Historical Association, v.115, March.

EAC (Environmental Advisory Council). 2007. *We Are All Downstream, We Are All Upstream, We Are All Part of a Watershed.* Charlottetown: Government of Prince Edward Island.

Ecojustice. 2012. *Legal Backgrounder: Bill C-45.* http://www.ecojustice.ca.

Environment Canada. 1993. *Flooding.* Ottawa: Environment Canada.

Environmental Defence. 2008. *11 Million Litres a Day: The Tar Sand's Leaking Legacy.* Toronto: Environmental Defence.

European Union. 2000. *Water Framework Directive.* http://ec.europa.eu/environment/water/water-framework/.

Evenden, Matthew D. 2004. *Fish versus Power: An Environmental History of the Fraser River.* Cambridge: Cambridge University Press. http://dx.doi.org/10.1017/CBO9780511512032.

Faucher, Philippe, and Johanne Bergeron. 1986. *Hydro Quebec: La Société de l'heure de point.* Montreal: Presses de l'université de Montréal.

Federal Environmental Assessment Review Office. 1992. *Oldman River Dam: Report of the Environmental Assessment Panel.* Hull: Government of Canada.

Fetter, C.W., Jr. 2004. "Hydrogeology: A Short History, Part 2." *Ground Water* 42 (6–7): 942–53.

Fortin, Pierre. 2005. "Clean Air, Renewable Energy and the Power of Water." Presentation to Ontario Waterpower Association, November 9. www.canadahydro.ca

Fortin, Pierre, and Gabrielle Collu. 2008. "Hydro Development in Canada: An Update." *Hydro Review* (November): 1–4.

Foucault, Michel. 1980. *Power/Knowledge: Selected Interviews and Other Writings, 1972–1977*, ed. Colin Gordon. Toronto: Random House.

Fradkin, Philip L. 1996. *A River No More: The Colorado and the West*. Berkeley: University of California Press.

Froshauer, Karl. 1997. *White Gold: Hydro-electric Power in Canada*. Vancouver: UBC Press.

Galloway, Gloria. 2013. "Industry Demands Guided Fisheries Act Changes." *Globe and Mail*, August 5.

Gaventa, John. 1980. *Power and Powerlessness*. Urbana: University of Illinois Press.

Geological Survey of Canada. 2003. *Canadian Framework for Collaboration on Groundwater*. Ottawa.

Glenn, Jack. 1999. *Once Upon an Oldman: Special Interest Politics and the Oldman River Dam*. Vancouver: UBC Press.

Great Bear Lake Working Group. 2005. *The Water Heart: A Management Plan for Great Bear Lake and Its Watershed*. Great Bear Lake Working Group.

Halliday, R., and Associates. 2009. "How Are We Living With the Red." Report to the Red River Board. Saskatoon: Halliday and Associates.

Hamilton, W.D. 1984. "Indian Lands in New Brunswick: The Case of the Little Southwest Reserve." *Acadiensis* 13 (2): 3–28.

Harris, Douglas C. 2001. *Fish, Law and Colonialism: The Legal Capture of Salmon in British Columbia*. Toronto: University of Toronto Press.

Hawley, Steven. 2011. *Recovering a Lost River: Removing Dams, Rewilding Salmon, Revitalizing Communities*. Boston: Beacon Press.

Hearne, Robert H. 2007. "Evolving Water Management Institutions in the Red River Basin." *Environmental Management* 40 (6): 842–52. http://dx.doi.org/10.1007/s00267-007-9026-x.

Heinmiller, B. Timothy. 2013. "Advocacy Coalitions and the Alberta Water Act." *Canadian Journal of Political Science* 46 (3): 525–47.

Hemmati, Minu. 2002. *Multi-Stakeholder Processes for Governance and Sustainability*. London: Earthscan.

Henstra, Dan, and Gordon McBean. 2005. "Canadian Disaster Management Policy: Moving toward a Paradigm Shift?" *Canadian Public Policy* 31 (3): 303–18. http://dx.doi.org/10.2307/3552443.

Hoberg, George, and Jeffrey Phillips. 2011. "Playing Defence: Early Responses to Conflict Expansion in the Oil Sands Policy Subsystem." *Canadian Journal of Political Science* 44 (03): 507–27. http://dx.doi.org/10.1017/S0008423911000473.

Hood, George. 1994. *Against the Flow: Rafferty-Alameda and the Politics of the Environment*. Saskatoon: Fifth House Publishers.

Horne, Matt. 2011. *Shale Gas in BC: Risks to BC's Water Resources*. Drayton Valley: Pembina Institute.

Hornig, James F. 1999. *Social and Environmental Impacts of the James Bay Hydroelectric Project*. Montreal: McGill-Queen's University Press.

Houck, Oliver A. 2006. "O Canada!: The Story of Rafferty, Oldman and the Great Whale." *Boston College International and Comparative Law Review* 29 (2): 175–243.

House of Commons. 2009. C-469. *An Act to Establish a Canadian Environmental Bill of Rights*. http://www.parl.gc.ca/LegisInfo/BillDetails.aspx?Bill=C469&Language=E&Mode=1&Parl=40&Ses=2.

Howard, Ross, and Michael Perley. 1980. *Acid Rain: The North American Forecast*. Toronto: Anansi.

Howell, James E. 1978. "The Portage Mountain Hydro-electric Project." In *Northern Transitions v.1: Northern Resource and Land Use Policy Study*, ed. Everett B. Peterson and Janet B. Wright, 21–64. Ottawa: Canadian Arctic Resources Committee.

IJC (International Joint Commission). 2000. *Living with the Red*. International Joint Commission.

IJC (International Joint Commission). 2001. Mandate to the International Red River Board. http://ijc.org/en_/irrb/Mandate.

Ingram, Helen M. 1969. *Patterns of Politics in Western Water Development*. Albuquerque: University of New Mexico Press.

Ingram, Helen M. 1990. *Water Politics: Continuity and Change*. Albuquerque: University of New Mexico Press.

International Hydropower Association. 2010. *Hydropower Sustainability Assessment Protocol*. London: International Hydropower Association.

IRN (International Rivers Network). 2003. "Twelve Reasons to Exclude Large Hydro from Renewable Initiatives." http://www.rivernet.org/general/hydropower/12reasons.pdf.

IRN (International Rivers Network). 2005. *From Commitment to Implementation: Report of the World Commission on Dams after Five Years*. Berkeley: International Rivers Network. http://www.irn.org.

Jackson, Robert B., Brooks Rainey Pearson, Stephen G. Osborn, Nathaniel R. Warner, and Avner Vengosh. 2011. *Research and Policy Recommendations for Hydraulic Fracturing and Shale-Gas Extraction*. Durham: Center on Climate Change, Duke University.

Johnson, Clare L., Sylvia M. Tunstall, and Edmund C. Penning-Rowsell. 2005. "Floods as Catalysts for Policy Change: Historical Lessons from England and Wales." *International Journal of Water Resources Development* 21 (4): 561–75. http://dx.doi.org/10.1080/07900620500258133.

Johnson, Steven. 2006. *The Ghost Map*. New York: Riverside Books.

Johnstone, Kenneth. 1977. *The Aquatic Explorers: A History of the Fisheries Research Board of Canada*. Toronto: University of Toronto Press.

Keenleyside, Miles H.A. 1959. "Effects of Spruce Budworm Control on Salmon and Other Fishes in New Brunswick." *Canadian Fish Culturist*. 24 (February).

Keepers of the Athabasca. 2008a. Pamphlet. http://www.keepersofthewater.ca/athabasca.

Keepers of the Athabasca. 2008b. *State of the Athabasca Watershed, 2008*. Compiled by the Canadian Parks and Wilderness Society (Northern Alberta), Edmonton. http://www.keepersofthewater.ca/athabasca.

Keepers of the Athabasca. 2011. *Annual Gathering and AGM*. Pembina.

Keepers of the Water. n.d. "Keeping the Arctic Ocean Basin." http://www.keepersofthewater.ca.

Kelly, E.N., D.W. Schindler, P.V. Hodson, J.W. Short, R. Radmanovich, and C.C. Nielsen. 2010. "Oil Sands Development Contributes Elements Toxic at Low Concentrations to the Athabasca River and Its Tributaries." *Proceedings of the National Academy of Sciences of the United States of America* 107 (37): 16178–83. http://dx.doi.org/10.1073/pnas.1008754107.

Kelly, E.N., J.W. Short, D.W. Schindler, P.V. Hodson, M. Ma, A.K. Kwan, and B.L. Fortin. 2009. "Oil Sands Development Contributes Polycyclic Aromatic Compounds to the Athabasca River and Its Tributaries." *Proceedings of the National Academy of Sciences of the United States of America* 106 (52): 22346–51. http://dx.doi.org/10.1073/pnas.0912050106.

Kendall, Matt. 2009. "National Groundwater Action Plan." Canberra: National Water Commission. http://archive.nwc.gov.au/__data/assets/pdf_file/0017/11708/Groundwater_Pp_to_WA_branch_of_AWA_25feb09.pdf.

KGS Group. 2001. *Flood Protection Studies for Winnipeg*. Winnipeg: K.G.S. Group.

King's College Program in Journalism. n.d. "Toxic Legacy: Original Documents." http://boatharbour.kingsjournalism.com/.

Krautwurst, Udo. 1998. "Water-Witching Modernist Epistemologies and Dowsing Rationality: Exporting Models of Non-Rationality through Colonial and Development Discourses." *PoLAR* 21 (2).

La Forest, G.V. 1960. "Riparian Rights in New Brunswick." *Canadian Bar Review* 3 (2): 135–43.

Land and Sea. 1988. "Boat Harbour." Canadian Broadcasting Corporation.

Leopold, Aldo. 1970. *A Sand County Almanac*. New York: Ballantyne Books.

Lower, A.R.M. 1938. *The North American Assault on the Canadian Forest*. Toronto: Ryerson Press.

Loxley, John. 1981. "The 'Great Northern' Plan." *Studies in Political Economy* 6: 151–82.

Lukes, Steven. 1974. *Power: A Radical View*. New York: Macmillan.

LWCB (Lake of the Woods Control Board). 2002. *Managing the Water Resources of the Winnipeg River Drainage Basin*. http://www.lwcb.ca.

Maass, Arnold. 1951. *Muddy Waters: The Army Engineers and the Nation's Rivers*. Cambridge, MA: Harvard University Press.

MacDonald, Doug. 1991. *The Politics of Pollution*. Toronto: McClelland and Stewart.

MacKay, Donald. 1978. *The Lumberjacks*. Toronto: McGraw-Hill Ryerson.

Mackenzie River Basin Board. 1997. *Agreement*. Yellowknife: Mackenzie River Basin Board.

Mackenzie River Basin Board. 2006. *Five Year Strategic Plan*. Yellowknife: Mackenzie River Basin Board. http://www.mrbb.ca/uploads/files/general/13//2006-strategic-plan-low-res.pdf.

Mackenzie Valley Land and Water Board. 2011. *Perspectives on Regulatory Improvement in the Mackenzie Valley*. Yellowknife: Mackenzie Valley Land and Water Board.

MacLaren Plansearch. 1983. *Hydrotechnical Study of the Antigonish Area Flood Plain*. Halifax: Canada-Nova Scotia Flood Damage Reduction Program.

MacLennan, Hugh. 1961. *Seven Rivers of Canada*, rev. ed. 1974. Toronto: Macmillan of Canada.

Manitoba. n.d. "Paleofloods in the Red River Basin." Government of Manitoba, Mineral Resources Division. http://www.manitoba.ca/iem/mrd/geo/pflood/index.html.

Marsh, John S., and Bruce W. Hodgins, eds. 1998. *Changing Parks: The History, Future and Cultural Context of Parks and Heritage Landscapes*. Toronto: Natural Heritage/Natural History Inc.

Martin, Thibault, and Steven M. Hoffman. 2008. *Power Struggles: Hydro Development and First Nations in Manitoba and Quebec*. Winnipeg: University of Manitoba Press.

Mascarene Treaty. 1725. http://www.cifas.us/page/treaty-1725-promises-lieutenant-governor-nova-scotia.

Massell, David. 2000. *Amassing Power: J.B. Duke and the Saguenay River, 1897–1927*. Montreal: McGill-Queen's University Press.

Mather, John. n.d. http://www.groundwateruk.org.

McCool, Daniel. 1994. *Command of the Waters: Iron Triangles, Federal Water Development and Indian Waters*. Tucson: University of Arizona Press.

McCrank, Neil. 2008. *Road to Improvement: The Review of Regulatory Systems across the North*. Ottawa: Indian Affairs and Northern Development.

McCully, Patrick. 1996. *Silenced Rivers: The Ecology and Politics of Large Dams*. London: Zed Books.

McGregor, Roy. 1989. *Chief: The Fearless Vision of Billy Diamond*. Toronto: Viking Press.

Miliband, Ralph. 1973. *The State in Capitalist Society: An Analysis of the Western System of Power*. London: Quartet Books.

Miramichi Salmon Association. n.d. http://www.miramichisalmon.ca.

Mitchell, Bruce, ed. 1975. *Institutional Arrangements for Water Management*. Department of Geography Publication No. 5. Waterloo: University of Waterloo.

Mitchell, Bruce, and Rob de Loe. 1997. *Reflections on Water: Canadian Water Resources Association, 1947–1997*. Cambridge, ON: CWRA.

Mitchell, Bruce, and James S. Gardiner, eds. 1983. *River Basin Management: Canadian Experiences*. Department of Geography Publication No. 20. Waterloo: University of Waterloo.

Mitchell, David J. 1983. *W.A.C. Bennett and the Rise of British Columbia*. Vancouver: Douglas and MacIntyre.

Mitchner, E. Alyn. 1967. "William Pearce and Federal Government Activity in the West, 1874–1904." *Canadian Public Administration* 10 (2): 235–43. http://dx.doi.org/10.1111/j.1754-7121.1967.tb00979.x.

Morse, Eric W. 1969. *Fur Trade Canoe Routes of Canada / Then and Now*. Toronto: University of Toronto Press.

MREAC (Miramichi River Environmental Assessment Committee) and ACAP (Atlantic Coastal Action Program). 2007. *State of the Environment Report for the Miramichi Watershed*. Miramichi City: Miramichi River Environmental Assessment Committee. http://www.mreac.org/Publications/SOERfinal_07.pdf.

Natural Resources Canada. 2007. "Study of the Impact of Nitrates on Groundwater Quality in Agricultural Areas." Factsheet. Ottawa: Natural Resources Canada.

Nedelsky, Jennifer. 1990. "From Private Property to Public Resource: The Emergence of Administrative Control of Water in Nova Scotia." In *Essays in the History of Canadian Law*, Vol. 3, ed. P. Girard and J. Phillips, 326–51. Toronto: University of Toronto Press.

Nelles, H.V. 1974. *The Politics of Development: Forests, Mines and Hydro-electric Power in Ontario, 1849–1941*. Toronto: Macmillan of Canada.

Netherton, Alexander. 2007. "The Political Economy of Canadian Hydro-Electricity: Between Old 'Provincial Hydros' and Neoliberal Regional Energy Regimes." *Canadian Political Science Review* 1 (June): 1.

New Brunswick Salmon Council. n.d. http://www.nbsalmoncouncil.com/.

Newell, Dianne. 1993. *Tangled Webs of History: Indians and the Law in Canada's Pacific Coast Fishery*. Toronto: University of Toronto Press.

Nikiforuk, Andrew. 2008. *Tar Sands: Dirty Oil and the Future of a Continent*. Vancouver: Greystone Books.

Norman, Emma S., Alice Cohen, and Karen Bakker. 2013. *Water without Borders? Canada, the United States and Shared Waters*. Toronto: University of Toronto Press.

Northwest Territories. 2010. *Northern Voices, Northern Waters: NWT Water Stewardship Strategy*. Yellowknife: Department of Environment and Natural Resources.

Northwest Territories. 2011. *NWT Water Stewardship: A Plan for Action, 2011–2015*. Yellowknife: Northwest Territories Department of Environment and Resource Protection.

Northwest Territories Legislative Assembly. 2007. *Right to Water Motion*. Motion 20–15(5).

Nova Scotia. 2002. *A Drinking Water Strategy for Nova Scotia*. Halifax: Department of Environment.

Nova Scotia Department of Transportation and Public Works. 2003. "Return of Boat Harbour to a Tidal Estuary—Project Description for Environmental Assessment." Halifax: Department of Transportation and Public Works.

Nova Scotia Salmon Association. n.d. http://www.nssalmon.ca/.

Nowlan, Linda. 2005. *Buried Treasure: Groundwater Permitting and Pricing in Canada*. Toronto: Walter and Duncan Gordon Foundation.

O'Connor, John. 2009. Testimony to House of Commons Standing Committee on Environment, June 11.

O'Connor, Justice Dennis R. 2002. *Report of the Walkerton Inquiry.* Parts 1 and 2. Toronto: Publications Ontario.

Oil Sands Advisory Panel. 2010. "A Foundation for the Future: Building an Environmental Monitoring System for the Oil Sands." A Report to the Federal Minister of the Environment. Ottawa.

Oil Sands Developers Group. 2012. *Oil Sands Project List.* http://www.oilsandsdevelopers.ca.

Oldman Watershed Council. 2010. *Oldman River: The State of the Watershed.* http://oldmanbasin.org/.

Oldman Watershed Council. 2011. *Priorities for the Oldman River Watershed: Promoting Action to Maintain and Improve Our Watershed.* Lethbridge: Oldman Watershed Council.

Ongley, Edwin D. 1996. *Control of Water Pollution from Agriculture.* Rome: Food and Agriculture Organization.

Osborn, Stephen G., Avner Vengosh, Nathaniel R. Warner, and Robert B. Jackson. 2011. "Methane Contamination of Drinking Water Accompanying Gas-Well Drilling and Hydraulic Fracturing." Proceedings of the National Academy of Sciences 108 (20): 8172–76. http://www.pnas.org/content/108/20/8172.full.

Page, Gillian A. 1980. "The Canadian Flood Damage Reduction Program." *Disasters* 4 (4): 411–21. http://dx.doi.org/10.1111/j.1467-7717.1980.tb00134.x.

Parenteau, Bill. 1998. "Care, Control and Supervision: Native People in the Canadian Atlantic Salmon Fishery, 1867–1900." *Canadian Historical Review* 79 (1): 1–35. http://dx.doi.org/10.3138/CHR.79.1.1.

Parenteau, Bill. 2004. 'A Very Determined Opposition to the Law': Conservation, Angling Leases, and Social Conflict in the Canadian Atlantic Salmon Fishery, 1867–1914." *Environmental History* 9 (3): 436–63. http://dx.doi.org/10.2307/3985768.

Parfitt, Ben. 2010. *Fracture Lines: Will Canada's Water Be Protected in the Rush to Develop Shale Gas?* Toronto: Munk School of Public Affairs. http://powi.ca/wp-content/uploads/2010/09/FINALFracture-Lines-Revised-Oct-6-no-embargo.pdf.

Parisien, Richard W. 1972. *The Fisheries Act: Origins of Federal Delegation of Administrative Jurisdiction to the Provinces.* Ottawa: Environment Canada.

Parlour, James W. 1981. "The Politics of Water Pollution Control: A Case Study of the Canadian Fisheries Act Amendments and the Pulp and Paper Effluent Regulations, 1970." *Journal of Environmental Management* 13: 127–40.

Pearse, Peter, F. Bertrand, and J.W. MacLaren. 1985. *Currents of Change: Final Report of the Inquiry on Federal Water Policy.* Ottawa: Environment Canada.

Pearse, Peter, and Frank Quinn. 1996. "Recent Developments in Federal Water Policy: One Step Forward, Two Steps Back." *Canadian Water Resources Journal* 21 (4): 329–40. http://dx.doi.org/10.4296/cwrj2104329.

Pearse, Peter H. 1988. *Rising to the Challenge: A New Policy for Canada's Freshwater Fisheries.* Ottawa: Canadian Wildlife Federation.

Peck, John C. 1980. "Kansas Groundwater Management Districts." *University of Kansas Law Review* 29 (1): 51–91.

Pembina Institute. 2012. *Solving the Puzzle: Lower Athabasca Regional Plan Performance Backgrounder.* Drayton Valley: Pembina Institute.

Pembina Institute. 2013. *Beneath the Surface: A Review of Key Facts in the Oil Sands Debate.* Drayton Valley: Pembina Institute.

Pembina Institute and World Wildlife Fund–Canada. 2008. *Under-Mining the Environment: Oil Sands Report Card.* Drayton Valley: Pembina Institute. http://www.pembina.org/pub/1571.

Pembina River Watershed Planning Authority. 2011. *Pembina River Integrated Watershed Management Plan.* Manitou: Pembina River Watershed Planning Authority.

Perkel, Colin N. 2002. *Well of Lies: The Walkerton Water Tragedy.* Toronto: McClelland and Stewart.

PFRA (Prairie Farm Rehabilitation Administration). 1980. *The Design and Construction of the Gardiner Dam.* Hull: Supply and Services Canada.

Phare, Merrell-Ann S. 2009. *Denying the Source: The Crisis of First Nations Water Rights.* Surrey: Rocky Mountain Books.

Pictou Landing First Nation. 2002. Information for Band Members on a Proposal for Improvements to and the Future of Boat Harbour. Pictou Landing: Pictou Landing First Nation.

Pictou Landing First Nation. 2010. *Notice of Action: Chief Aileen Francis et al. v. Attorney-General of Nova Scotia.* Supreme Court of Nova Scotia. September.

Pisani, Donald J. 1984. "Fish Culture and the Dawn of Concern over Water Pollution in the United States." *Environmental Review: ER* 8 (2).

Pisani, Donald J. 2006. "Water Planning in the Progressive Era: The Inland Waterways Commission Reconsidered." *Journal of Policy History* 18 (4): 389–418. http://dx.doi.org/10.1353/jph.2006.0014.

Postel, Sandra, and Brian Richter. 2003. *Rivers for Life: Managing Water for People and Nature.* Washington, DC: Island Press.

PPWB (Prairie Provinces Water Board). 1969. "Master Agreement on Apportionment," available at http://www.ppwb.ca/information/79/index.html .

Pratt, Larry. 1975. *The Tar Sands.* Edmonton: Hurtig Publishers.

Pratt, Larry, and Ian Urquhart. 1994. *The Last Great Forest: Japanese Multinationals and Alberta's Northern Forests.* Edmonton: NeWest Press.

Prince Edward Island. 2001. *Clear from the Ground to the Glass: Ten Points to Purity.* Charlottetown: Fisheries, Aquaculture and Environment.

Prince Edward Island. 2007. *A Guide to Watershed Planning on PEI.* Charlottetown: Department of Environment, Energy and Forestry.

Prince Edward Island. 2008. *Report of the Commission on Nitrates in Groundwater.* Charlottetown: Document Publishing Centre.

Prince Edward Island. 2011. *State of the Environment Report 2010.* Charlottetown: Department of Environment, Labour and Justice.

Prince Edward Island. 2012. *Report of the Action Committee for Sustainable Land Management.* Charlottetown.

Prince Edward Island. 2013. *Water Extraction Permitting Policy.* Charlottetown: Department of Environment, Labour and Justice.

Prince Edward Island. n.d. "Water Cycle on Prince Edward Island." *Science Curriculum Resource.*

Prins, Harald E.L. 1996. *The Mi'kmaq: Resistance, Accommodation and Cultural Survival.* Fort Worth: Harcourt Brace.

Pross, Paul. 1992. *Group Politics and Public Policy*, 2nd ed. Toronto: Oxford University Press.

Public Safety Canada. 2008. *Canada's National Disaster Mitigation Strategy.* http://www.publicsafety.gc.ca/cnt/mrgnc-mngmnt/dsstr-prvntn-mtgtn/ntnl-dsstr-mtgtn-strtg-eng.aspx.

Quebec. 1976. *The James Bay and Northern Quebec Agreement.* Quebec: Éditeur officiel du Québec.

Quebec. n.d. "Eastmain 1-A and Rupert River Diversion Hydropower Project." Quebec: Ministère du Dévelopment durable, de l'Environnement et des Parcs. http://www.mddep.gouv.qc.ca/evaluations/eastmain-rupert/rapport-comexen/project.htm.

Quebec and Grand Council of the Cree. 2002. *Agreement Respecting a New Relationship Between the Cree Nation and the Government of Quebec.* La Paix des Braves.

Raby, Stewart. 1964. "Alberta and the Prairie Provinces Water Board." *Canadian Geographer. Geographe Canadien* 8 (2): 85–91. http://dx.doi.org/10.1111/j.1541-0064.1964.tb00586.x.

Raby, Stewart. 1965. "Irrigation Development in Alberta." *Canadian Geographer. Geographe Canadien* 9 (1): 31–40. http://dx.doi.org/10.1111/j.1541-0064.1965.tb01331.x.

Raymond, Bruce. 2008. "Watershed Planning and Management: Implementaton on PEI." Presentation to the Atlantic Coastal Zone Information Steering Committee, Charlottetown, January.

Redekop, Bill. 2012. *Dams of Contention: The Rafferty-Alameda Story.* Winnipeg: Heartland Associates.

Red River Basin Commission. 2005. Red River Basin Natural Resources Framework Plan. http://www.redriverbasincommission.org/Services/the_plan.html.

Red River Basin Commission. 2011. *Long Term Flood Solutions for the Red River Basin.* Fargo and Winnipeg: Red River Basin Commission.

Red River Floodway Operation Review Committee. 1999. *A Review of the Red River Flood Operation Rules.* Winnipeg: Manitoba Water Stewardship.

Reisner, Marc. 1986. *Cadillac Desert: The American West and Its Disappearing Water.* New York: Penguin Books.

Reuss, Martin. 1985. "Andrew A. Humphreys and the Development of Hydraulic Engineering: Politics and Technology in the Army Corps of Engineers, 1850–1950." *Technology and Culture* 26 (1): 1–33. http://dx.doi.org/10.2307/3104527.

Rice-Snow, Scott. 2012. "The Geology of Prince Edward Island and Hydraulic Fracturing." Unpublished paper. http://dontfrackpei.com/web/wp-content/uploads/2013/01/Geology_and_Fracking.pdf.

Richardson, A.H. 1974. *Conservation by the People: A History of the Conservation Authority Movement to 1970.* Toronto: University of Toronto Press.

Richter, Brian D., and Gregory A. Thomas. 2007. "Restoring Environmental Flows by Modifying Dam Operations." *Ecology and Society* 12 (1).

Rivera, A., P. Crowe, A. Kohut, D. Rudolph, C. Baker, D. Pupek, N. Shaheen, M. Lewis, and K. Parks. 2003. *Canadian Framework for Collaboration on Groundwater.* Ottawa: Natural Resources Canada.

Robertson, Frank C. 1986. *Rawhide.* London: Collins.

Rojas, Alejandro, Lorenzo Magzul, Gregory P. Marchildon, and Bernardo Reyes. 2009. "The Oldman River Dam Conflict: Adaptation and Institutional Learning." *Prairie Forum* 34 (1) (Spring).

Rood, Stewart B., Glenda M. Samuelson, and Sarah G. Bigelow. 2005. "The Little Bow Gets Bigger: Alberta's Newest River Dam." *Wildlands Advocate* 13 (1): 14–17.

Rosenberg International Forum on Water Policy. 2009. *Report of the Rosenberg International Forum on Water Policy to the Government of the Northwest Territories.* Riverside: University of California.

Rosenberg International Forum on Water Policy. 2013. *The Mackenzie Basin.* Riverside: University of California.

Ross, Benjamin, and Stephen Amter. 2010. *The Polluters: The Making of Our Chemically Altered Environment.* New York: Oxford University Press.

Rothwell, Neil. 2006. "Canada's Watersheds: The Demographic Basis for an Urban-Rural Dialogue." *Rural and Small Town Canada Analysis Bulletin* 6 (6).

Sackville Rivers Association. n.d. http://sackvillerivers.ns.ca.

Salisbury, Richard F. 1986. *A Homeland for the Cree: Regional Development in James Bay, 1971–81.* Montreal: McGill-Queen's University Press.

Sandberg, Anders L., and Peter Clancy. 2001. *Against the Grain: Foresters and Politics in Nova Scotia.* Vancouver: UBC Press.

Sandberg, Anders L., and Peter Clancy. 2002. "Politics, Science and the Spruce Budworm in New Brunswick and Nova Scotia." *Journal of Canadian Studies. Revue d'Etudes Canadiennes* 37 (2): 164–91.

Sandford, Robert William. 2013a. *Cold Matters: The State and Fate of Canada's Freshwater.* Victoria: Rocky Mountain Books.

Sandford, Robert William. 2013b. *Saving Lake Winnipeg.* Surrey: Rocky Mountain Books.

Saskatchewan Nelson Basin Board. 1972. *Supply for the Saskatchewan-Nelson Basin: A Summary Report.* Edmonton: Saskatchewan Nelson Basin Board.

Saunders, J. Owen. 2006. "The Context for Freshwater Policy Initiatives in Canada." Powerpoint presentation to Freshwater for the Future Conference, May. http://www.law.ualberta.ca/centres/ccs/issues/waterlaw.php. Accessed October 2011.

Saunders, J. Owen, and Michael M. Wenig. 2007. "Whose Water? Canadian Water Management and the Challenges of Jurisdictional Fragmentation." In *Eau Canada: The Future of Canada's Water,* ed. Karen Bakker. Vancouver: UBC Press.

Saveela. n. d. *Save Canada's Experimental Lakes Area.* http://saveela.org.

Savoie, Donald J. 1999. *Governing from the Centre: The Concentration of Power in Canadian Politics.* Toronto: University of Toronto Press.

Schattschneider, E.E. 1960. *The Semi-Sovereign People.* New York: Holt, Rinehart and Winston.

Schattschneider, E.E. 1967. *Party Government.* New York: Holt, Rinehart and Winston.

Schindler, D.W. et al. 2012. Scientists Letter Regarding Bill C-38. http://www.theglobeandmail.com/migration_catalog/article542321.ece/BINARY/Scientists%27+letter+to+Prime+Minister+on+changes+to+Fisheries+Act.

Schindler, D.W., W.F. Donahue, and P. John Thompson. 2007. *Running Out of Steam? Oil Sands Development and Water Use in the Athabasca River Watershed: Science and Market-based Solutions.* Edmonton: Environmental Research and Study Centre, University of Alberta.

Scott, James C. 1990. *Domination and the Arts of Resistance: Hidden Transcripts.* New Haven: Yale University Press.

Shallat, Todd. 1994. *Structures in the Steam: Water, Science and the Rise of the U.S. Army Corps of Engineers.* Austin: University of Texas Press.

Sharma, Parmesh. 1998. *Aboriginal Fishing Rights: Laws, Courts, Politics.* Halifax: Fernwood.

Shiva, Vandana. 2002. *Water Wars.* Toronto: Between the Lines Press.

Shott, Alison K. 2012. "Ways But Not a Will: Addressing Nitrate Concentration on Prince Edward Island." *Public Policy and Governance Review* 3 (2): 48–62.

Shrubsole, Dan. 1992. "The Grand River Conservation Commission: History, Activities, and Implications for Water Management." *Canadian Geographer* 36 (3): 221–36. http://dx.doi.org/10.1111/j.1541-0064.1992.tb01136.x.

Shrubsole, Dan, G. Brooks, R. Halliday, E. Hague, A. Kumar, J. Lacroix, H. Rasid, J. Rousselle, and S.P. Simonovic. 2003. *An Assessment of Flood Risk in Canada.* London, ON: Institute for Catastrophic Loss Research.

Siddon, Thomas, John Fraser, Herb Dhaliwal, and David Anderson. 2012. "An Open Letter to Stephen Harper on Fisheries." *Globe and Mail,* June 6.

Simonovic, Slobodan P. 1999. "Decision Support System for Flood Management in the Red River Basin." *Canadian Water Resources Journal* 24 (3): 203–23. http://dx.doi.org/10.4296/cwrj2403203.

Sinclair, William F. 1990. *Controlling Pollution from Canadian Pulp and Paper Manufacturers: A Federal Perspective.* Ottawa: Queen's Printer.

Smith, Peter Andrey. 2013. "Troubled Waters." *The Walrus* (July–August).

Smith, Philip. 1975. *Brinco: The Story of Churchill Falls.* Toronto: McClelland and Stewart.

Smol, John. 2002. "Lessons Learned from the Acid Rain Debates: The Collision of Scientists, Industry and Policy Makers." Public Lecture, St. Francis Xavier University, November.

SMRID (St. Mary River Irrigation District). n.d. http://www.smrid.ab.ca.

Snider, Laureen. 2004. "Resisting Neo-liberalism: The Poisoned Water Disaster in Walkerton, Ontario." *Social & Legal Studies* 13 (2): 265–89. http://dx.doi.org/10.1177/0964663904042554.

Somers, George, M.M. Savard, and Y. Jiang. 2011. "Perspectives on Groundwater Management and Protection: Experiences with Nitrate Contamination in Groundwater in PEI." *Geo-Hydro.*

Sproule-Jones, Mark, Carolyn Johns, and B. Timothy Heinmiller. 2008. *Canadian Water Politics: Conflicts and Institutions.* Montreal: McGill-Queen's University Press.

Stanford, J.A., and J.V. Ward. 1992. "Management of Aquatic Resources in Large Catchments: Recognizing Interactions between Ecosystem Connectivity and Environmental Disturbance." In *Watershed Management: Balancing Sustainability and Environmental Change,* ed. Robert J. Naiman, 91–124. New York: Springer Verlag. http://dx.doi.org/10.1007/978-1-4612-4382-3_5.

Statistics Canada. 1992. *Electric Power Statistics.* Catalogue 57–2006. Ottawa: Statistics Canada.

Statistics Canada. 2009. *Human Activity and the Environment.* Ottawa: Statistics Canada.

Steinberg, Theodore. 1991. *Nature Incorporated: Industrialization and the Waters of New England.* New York: Cambridge University Press.

Steinberg, Theodore. 1996. "What Is a Natural Disaster?" *Literature and Medicine* 15 (1): 33–47. http://dx.doi.org/10.1353/lm.1996.0012.

Stolte, W.J., and M.H. Sadar. 1993. "The Rafferty-Alameda Project and Its Environmental Reviews: Structures, Objectives and History." *Canadian Water Resources Journal* 18 (1): 1–13. http://dx.doi.org/10.4296/cwrj1801001.

SWA (Saskatchewan Watershed Authority). 2006. *State of the Watershed Reporting Framework.* Regina: Saskatchewan Watershed Authority.

Taylor, Bill. 2013. "Leadership Begins at Home." *Telegraph-Journal,* June 29.

Taylor, Joseph E., III. 1998. "Making Salmon: The Political Economy of Fishery Science and the Road Not Taken." *Journal of the History of Biology* 31 (1): 33–59. http://dx.doi.org/10.1023/A:1004253405353.

Tingley, Donna. 1991. "Conflict and Coperation on the Environment." In *Canada: The State of the Federation, 1991,* ed. Douglas Brown, 131–58. Kingston: Institute of Intergovernmental Affairs.

Tolman, C.F. 1937. *Groundwater.* New York: McGraw Hill.

Topham, Harvey L. 1982. *History of Irrigation in Western Canada.* Ottawa: Prairie Farm Rehabilitation Administration.

Transport Canada. 2013. "Navigable Waters Protection Program—FAQ." http://www.tc.gc.ca/eng/marinesafety/oep-nwpp-faqs-202.htm.

Troyer, Warner. 1977. *No Safe Place*. Toronto: Clark Irwin.

Tuomi, A.L.W. 1985. *Transactions of the 1984 Canadian Sport Fisheries Conference*. Ottawa: Fisheries and Oceans.

United States. 2005. *Hydroelectric Power*. Washington, DC: Department of Interior, Bureau of Reclamation.

Upton, L.F.S. 1979. *Micmacs and Colonists: Indian-White Relations in the Maritimes, 1713–1867*. Vancouver: UBC Press.

Urquhart, Ian. 2006. "Scuttling the Mothership." Unpublished manuscript, Department of Political Science, University of Alberta.

Vannote, Robin L., G. Wayne Minshall, Kenneth W. Cummins, James R. Sedell, and Colbert E. Cushing. 1980. "The River Continuum Concept." *Canadian Journal of Fisheries and Aquatic Sciences* 37 (1): 130–7. http://dx.doi.org/10.1139/f80-017.

van Sittert, Lance. 2004. "The Supernatural State: Water-Divining and the Cape Underground Water Rush, 1891–1910." *Journal of Social History* 37 (4): 915–37. http://dx.doi.org/10.1353/jsh.2004.0067.

Vincent, Sylvie, and Garry Bowers, eds. 1988. *James Bay and Northern Quebec—Ten Years After*. Montreal: Recherches amérindiennes au Québec.

Vining, Adrian R. 1981. "Provincial Hydro Utilities." In *Public Corporations and Public Policy in Canada*, ed. Allan Tupper and G.B. Doern, 149–88. Montreal: Institute for Research on Public Policy.

Wahlberg, Meghan. 2013. "Draft NWT-Alta Bilateral Water Agreement Expected by Late Spring." *Northern Journal*, February 26.

Waldram, James B. 1988. *As Long as the Rivers Run: Hydroelectric Development and Native Communities in Western Canada*. Winnipeg: University of Manitoba Press.

Water Alliance of Prince Edward Island. 2013. *News*. July.

Waterkeeper Alliance. n.d. http://waterkeeper.org/.

Watt, W. Edgar. 1995. "The National Flood Damage Reduction Program: 1976–1995." *Canadian Water Resources Journal* 20 (4): 237–47. http://dx.doi.org/10.4296/cwrj2004237.

Weber, Max. 1947. *The Theory of Social and Economic Organization*. New York: Free Press.

Weeks, Edward. 1968. *Fresh Waters*. Boston: Little Brown.

White, Richard. 1995. *The Organic Machine: The Remaking of the Columbia River*. New York: Hill and Wang.

Wicken, William. 2002. *Mi'kmaq Treaties on Trial*. Toronto: University of Toronto Press.

Williams, Susan. 1993. *Hydro Quebec and the Great Whale Project*. Washington, DC: Investor Responsibility Research Center.

Wood, Chris. 2010. "The Last Great Water Fight." *The Walrus* (October).

Wood, June. 2013. *Home to the Nechako*. Victoria: Heritage Publishing.

World Commission on Dams. 2000. *Dams and Development: A New Framework for Decision-Making*. Overview.

World Commission on Environment and Development. 1987. *Our Common Future*. New York: Oxford University Press.

World Wildlife Fund–Canada. 2009. *Canada's Rivers at Risk: Environmental Flows and Canada's Freshwater Future*. Toronto: World Wildlife Fund–Canada. http://assets.wwf.ca/downloads/wwf_rivers_risk_2011.pdf.

Worster, Donald. 1992. *Rivers of Empire: Water, Aridity and the Growth of the American West*. New York: Oxford University Press.

Worster, Donald. 1993. "Thinking Like a River." In *The Wealth of Nature*. New York: Oxford University Press.

Index